A HISTORY OF THE AFRICAN AMERICAN CHURCH

CARTER G. WOODSON

This book is a publication of

Diasporic Africa Press, inc.
New York | www.dafricapress.com

The introduction originally appeared as Albert J. Raboteau et
al., "Retelling Carter Woodson's Story: Archival Sources for Afro-
American Church History," *The Journal of American History*
77, no. 1 (1990): 183-199. Copyright © 1990 Oxford University
Press. Reprinted by permission of Oxford University Press.

Carter G. Woodson's *The History of the Negro Church* was originally
published in 1920 by Associated Publishers of Washington, D.C.

2013 Diasporic Africa Press Edition
Library of Congress Control Number: 2013943681
ISBN-13 978-1-9373-0605-2 (pbk.: alk. paper)

Carter G. Woodson, like many who wrote before the 1960s, used the word "Negro" with a capital "N" as a statement of "race" pride and in opposition to terms as such "colored," which remained in lowercase. Readers will find that Woodson used both terms in precisely this way, though he did defend the use of "Negro" as opposed to "black" (spelled without a capital "B"). Today, the term "Negro" has been largely replaced by "Black," "Afro-American," "African American," without necessarily resolving the historic trend of imposed definitions from outside of the group for whom these terms exists.

CONTENTS

PREFACE

The importance of the church in the life of the Negro justifies the publication of this brief account of the development of the institution. For many years the various denominations have been writing treatises bearing on their own particular work, but hitherto there has been no effort to study the achievements of all of these groups as parts of the same institution and to show the evolution of it from the earliest period to the present time. This is the objective of this volume.

Whether or not the author has done this task well is a question which the public must decide. This work does not represent what he desired to make it. Many facts of the past could not be obtained for the reason that several denominations have failed to keep records and facts known to persons now active in the church could not be collected because of indifference or the failure to understand the motives of the author. Not a few church officers and ministers, however, gladly co-operated with the author in giving and seeking information concerning their denominations. Among these were Mr. Charles H. Wesley, Prof. J. A. Booker, and Dr. Walter H. Brooks. For their valuable assistance the author feels deeply grateful.

Carter G. Woodson
Washington, D.C., September, 1921

INTRODUCTION
RETELLING CARTER WOODSON'S STORY

Albert J. Raboteau et al.

For a survey history of the Afro-American churches in the United States, one will still not do better than Carter G. Woodson's *The History of the Negro Church (retitled, A History of the African American Church)*—a three hundred-page study first published more than ninety years ago.[1] Given the extraordinary increase during the last quarter century in scholarly attention to black religious life, it may seem surprising that there has not appeared a modern study capable of supplanting Woodson's classic but dated work. It is, however, in part the very increase in the scholarly literature on the black churches that has deterred would-be synthesizers from attempting a comprehensive survey. Where Woodson confronted his sources more or less unaided—and undetained—by a significant body of contemporary scholarship, the modern scholar faces a thickening array of articles, books, and dissertations.[2]

The contemporary student of Afro-American religious life also finds it far harder to focus his or her attention on the ecclesiastical history of black Christianity than Woodson did. *The History of the Negro Church* is not troubled by any deep concern with the possible African sources of Afro-American religious belief and practice. Neither does it inquire about the relationship between black religious life as it emerged on the North American mainland and the religious patterns evident among Caribbean slaves, nor worry very much about what was going on religiously among mainland blacks themselves before 1750. Instead, it moves briskly toward the history of black evangelicalism. Baptists and Methodists abound in Woodson's pages—and they are mostly male and usually clergy, and they are generally busy building institutions, conducting educational and social service enterprises, and fighting the good fight politically. One reads little there about the missionary societies of black women or the special performance styles of black preaching and worship. One also learns nothing from Woodson about the more or less continuous thread of Islam in Afro-American religious life. The concluding chapter, "New Temples for Strange Prophets," added for the 1945 edition, has only the most perfunctory discussion of the Holiness and Pentecostal churches, the Father Divine Peace Mission Movement, and the Nation of Islam. Of course, there is also nothing in Woodson's book about those African-based religious movements from the Caribbean that are such a fascinating part of the contemporary scene—Haitian vodun and Cuban santeria. Yet it is precisely an interest in all those things not found in *The History of the Negro*

Church that has animated much of the best recent work on Afro-American religion—and with good reason.

The study of the religious history of the United States has been for too long an examination of the institutional and intellectual development of American Protestantism—especially in the Northeast—and it is not the least contribution of much recent work in Afro-American religious history that it has helped break this mold. Students of American religious history generally are slowly—but, one hopes, surely—coming to see that Africans were as much a part of the earliest history of the Atlantic world as Europeans were, that the American story begins as much in the South as in New England or the Middle Colonies, and that throughout that history the encounter of blacks and whites has been as central a part of the American religious problematic as the heritage of Puritanism or the diversity of Euro-American religion.[3] Historians of religion in the United States have also come even more clearly to embrace a concern for popular as well as elite forms of religion, to make regular use of nonliterary as well as literary resources in their research and teaching, and to pay due attention to that part of the American religious spectrum that lies at the edge of or altogether beyond the Christian and Jewish traditions. Obviously, all these changes in the study of American religious history have occurred in relation to deep and pervasive changes, not only among historians and within the academy, but in the culture generally. Yet the study of Afro-American religious history has certainly been an integral part of these developments and has contributed importantly to them.

There may, however, be a certain irony in this, for it is possible that these changed directions in the study of American religion have helped keep the institutional (and intellectual) study of black American Christianity under a shadow of neglect. When many scholars who had previously considered themselves "church historians" abandoned that label in the 1960s to become "historians of American religion," they left behind library shelves well stocked with volumes devoted to the history of Euro-American Christianity in the United States, above all to the denominational history of Euro-American Protestantism. There existed no comparable body of modern scholarly literature on the black denominations. The ability of the black churches to generate histories from their own resources, though considerable in the nineteenth century, has seemingly diminished for most of the twentieth.[4] Meanwhile, outsiders attracted to the study of black religious life between World War I and the civil rights era seem more often to have been anthropologists interested in rural folkways or sociologists attracted by urban "sects and cults" than historians curious about the institutional history of the black churches. Important work that was done—especially work concerning the twentieth-century black churches—never made its way into print, it being a long-standing pattern, for example, that dissertations about Father Divine or the Black Muslims rapidly find a publisher while dissertations on major black urban congregations and pastors do not. In the last two decades increased attention to Afro-American religious history has produced significant advances, and the scholarly literature on the black churches is beginning to grow, especially for the nineteenth century. But in a time when church history generally and denominational history in particular are out of fashion, progress has been painfully slow. So Woodson's *The History of the Negro Church* remains the most adequate overall survey of its subject.

In our view the time has come for a major effort to retell the story of the black Christian churches in the United States. We do not put this goal ahead of the other major goals being pursued by scholars of Afro-American religious history, but we do put it alongside them. We think it is tremendously important, for example, to fill out the story of all those decades that Woodson so quickly glides over at the beginning of his work—or never really gets to at the end. But we also think it is equally important to retell the tale that *The History of the Negro Church* was mostly concerned to tell, the story of the emergence of the black churches, primarily out of the matrix of the eighteenth-century evangelical revivals, their development through the nineteenth century, and their changing experience in the twentieth. The story is one that includes both men and women, both eminent leaders and ordinary folk, both forceful assertions of black autonomy and doggedly determined efforts to make biracial collaboration work. The sources for this story are manifold and to a significant degree still untapped. But they are also widely dispersed, difficult of access, and often unrecognized or even unknown. What follows is a survey and assessment of some of the most important resources.

A major initial problem confronting scholars concerned to locate manuscript and archival sources for the history of the black churches is the lack of any current or comprehensive guide to such materials. Walter Schatz's *Directory of Afro-American Resources* remains a useful survey of a vast array of black history collections in cities and towns across the United States, and its index provides some help in identifying collections especially pertinent to black church history But it is now twenty years out-of-date. The more recent *Howard University Bibliography of African and Afro-American Religious Studies* is enormously useful for hard-to-find printed materials, but it has only a few pages on manuscripts. For current and continuously updated information on manuscript and archival sources for Afro-American religious history, researchers should therefore turn to the *Newsletter of the Afro-American Religious History Group*. Published semiannually at the W. E .B. Du Bois Institute for Afro-American Research, Harvard University, the newsletter has, since its beginning in 1976, regularly carried specialized bibliographies, reports by scholars and librarians about recently processed manuscripts, notes about finding aids, and research queries.[5]

An extremely valuable base line of data on the history and development of the black churches is to be found in the massive body of material gathered by the Historical Records Survey, under the auspices of the Works Projects Administration, in the years 1935-1942. Surveys of church records at the congregation level were conducted in each state, and the survey files for thirty-eight states and the District of Columbia survive. Those files make available in standardized form information about the founding and development of individual congregations and the availability of their minute books, membership registers, and other records. Some files also include news clippings and both unpublished and published historical sketches. A useful guide compiled by Loretta L. Hefner, *The WPA Historical Records Survey*, provides a state-by-state analysis of the location and scope of extant church records surveys.[6]

A second general resource, relevant to a wide range of topics in black church history is a group of clipping and vertical files that provide ready access to invaluable material in the black press. The black press, from its beginning in 1827, has published substantial information on churches, clergy, and denominational meetings at local, state, and national levels. Because complete texts of these papers often do not survive, they are sometimes accessible only through such clippings files.

Two collections stand out for the scope of their coverage. The first is the Clipping File of the Schomburg Center for Research in Black Culture, New York Public Library. Monumental in scope, with over ten thousand subject headings, it contains in addition to clippings, numerous broadsides, pamphlets, programs, book reviews, and ephemera. Information on religion is organized by individual congregation, geography, individual biography, and denomination, but relevant material will be found under other headings as well, such as bishops, race relations, spirituals, preaching, and religious education. The second is the Tuskegee Institute News Clipping File, which focuses on the period 1910-1966 and contains 352 linear feet of mounted clippings, plus a few unmounted clippings, reports, and letters. Categories to consult for information on the black church include biography, carnivals, church and religion, civil rights, education, "missions, foreign," temperance, "women's work," and "YMCA" and "YWCA."[7]

Two other clipping files deserve special mention. The Hampton University Newspaper Clipping File, assembled between 1900 and 1925, contains fifty-five thousand clippings from black and religious newspapers. A substantial number of files are biographical, while others focus on education, women, voluntary associations, and religion. The Gumby Collection of American Negro Scrapbooks, covering the years 1910-1950, is held by the Rare Book and Manuscript Library, Columbia University. Compiled by L. S. Alexander Gumby, individual scrapbooks deal with Catholics, Ethiopia,

Marcus Garvey, Harlem, "Jewish-Prophet-Others," the Negro in Africa, Negro religions, Protestantism, and Father Divine, among other topics.[8]

Research on the history of the major independent black churches is complicated by the wide dispersal of relevant material for each denomination. This is true for both the most recent and the earliest periods, but it holds in a special way for the late eighteenth and early nineteenth centuries. The written records, published and unpublished, of the rise and early history of the African churches (as they were originally designated) are in widely scattered locations. Consulting all the pertinent denominational archives cited below would not locate more than a fraction of the relevant materials. Some valuable items seem to have been lost. Some pamphlets, church minutes, and private diaries that were available to nineteenth-century black denominational historians have subsequently disappeared. The personal journal of Joseph Cox, influential African Methodist Episcopal (AME) preacher and brother of black Shaker visionary Rebecca Cox Jackson, was, for example, a century ago in the possession of AME historiographer Daniel A. Payne. Today it can no longer be located.[9] Happily, state archives and historical societies have preserved some manuscript minutes for a number of early and important local congregations, but scholars are more likely to find their way to some of these than to others. That the Historical Society of Pennsylvania's holdings include some records of the earliest African Baptist and African Presbyterian congregations in Philadelphia is not surprising, but researchers may easily miss the minutes of the Abyssinian Church of Portland in the Maine Historical Society, Portland. They may also overlook unexpected items in familiar places, such as the record book (1827-1848) of the Trenton, New Jersey, circuit of the AME church at the Library of Congress.[10] Similar examples could be given for the later stages of black church history. Research in the history of any of the denominational groupings of Afro-American Christians is then of necessity a multiarchival undertaking. It may well begin with whatever repositories are sponsored by the churches themselves but must also extend over a diverse range of public and private, familiar and unfamiliar archives.

For the black Baptist churches, there are no major archival centers associated with denominational schools, historical societies, or administrative headquarters that currently provide researchers with centralized access to the minutes, correspondence, and other records of major church bodies or the papers of notable church leaders. The National Baptist Convention, U.S.A., Inc., the largest of the black denominations throughout the twentieth century, has recently opened the Baptist World Center in Nashville, Tennessee. It holds important uncataloged materials, including the records of some denominational boards and agencies and the minutes of some state conventions and local associations. The best access to the records of the twentieth-century black Baptist denominations—and their nineteenth-century precursors—is provided by the microfilm collection of the Historical Commission of the Southern Baptist Convention (HCSBC), Nashville, Tennessee. The commission has filmed material from many repositories relevant to various Baptist denominations, both black and predominantly white. It has, for example, filmed minutes of the American Baptist Missionary Convention (1842-1872); the National Baptist Convention (1897-1915); the National Baptist Convention, U.S.A., Inc.; and the National Baptist Convention of America. It has also filmed National Baptist Publication Board materials, the *Mission Herald*, the *National Baptist Union-Review,* the *National Baptist Voice*, and the catalogs of Roger Williams University.[11]

The most complete collection of nineteenth-century materials dealing with black Baptist history is to be found at the American Baptist Historical Society (ABHS) in Rochester, New York. Included here is the single largest set of minutes and journals of black state conventions and local associations—some of it material not included in the HCSBC microfilm project. The ABHS also holds a virtually complete run of the *National Baptist Magazine* (1894-1901), the first denominational journal of the National Baptist Convention.[12] Broken runs of William Jefferson White's *Georgia Baptist,* the oldest black southern periodical in continuous publication (1880 to the present), are available at the ABHS and at the Atlanta University Center's Woodruff Library, Atlanta, Georgia.[13] Some of the records of the American Baptist Home Missionary Society are also to be found at the latter location, but for much of the critically important correspondence between this agency and black Baptist leaders, one must consult the holdings of the national headquarters of the American Baptist Churches in the U.S.A., in Valley Forge, Pennsylvania. Material relevant to the history of black Baptists, in a state especially important for both their early history and their eventual development into independent denominations, is also to be found in the Virginia State Archives and the Virginia Baptist Historical Society, both in Richmond.

Very substantial black Baptist material (though sometimes it is not identified as such) is also to be found in most of the major repositories familiar to students of Afro-American history. Especially notable here are the personal papers of some of the most influential Baptist leaders of the twentieth century. The Library of Congress, for example, holds the papers of Nannie H. Burroughs, longtime leader of the Woman's Convention of the National Baptist Convention, U.S.A., Inc., and nationally known political activist. Most of the papers of churchman and educator Benjamin Mays are now being cataloged at the Moorland-Spingarn Research Center of Howard University, Washington, D.C. His Morehouse College presidential papers, as yet entirely uncataloged, are held by the Woodruff Library of the Atlanta University Center. Most papers of Martin Luther King, Jr., for the years 1945-1962 are currently located at the Mugar Library of Boston University, while those for the period 1962-1968 are in the archives of the Martin Luther King, Jr., Center for Nonviolent Social Change in Atlanta.[14] Researchers should also be aware of significant manuscript collections for lesser-known but nonetheless important black Baptist figures, for example, the papers of Tennessee Reconstruction legislator David Foote Rivers at the Tennessee State Library and Archives, Nashville; those of twentieth-century Cleveland preacher Wade Hampton McKinney at the Western Reserve Historical Society, Cleveland, Ohio; and those of Nashville civil rights leader Kelly Miller Smith at the library of Vanderbilt University Divinity School in Nashville.

The major black Methodist bodies, whose histories reach much further back into the nineteenth century than any of the contemporary black Baptist denominations, have a slightly more established pattern of central archival collecting.[15] Wilberforce University in Wilberforce, Ohio, the oldest black church-related college in the United States, has long served as a major center for the collection of materials concerning the African Methodist Episcopal church (founded in 1816). Its holdings include the largest (but still quite incomplete) runs of general and annual conference minutes, an extensive collection of the published reports of church departments and organizations, a large but incomplete set of the denomination's quarterly, the *AME Church Review* (1884 to the present), and substantial manuscript materials relating to influential bishops Daniel A. Payne and Reverdy C. Ransom—as well as very substantial printed and manuscript materials related to the university and its faculty. These holdings are supplemented by the much smaller but parallel collections of nearby Payne Theological Seminary. The collections do not, however, include the records and papers of the denomination's major boards and agencies. The most important collection of these is held by the AME Financial Department in Washington, D.C. These holdings include not only the records of that department but also some material related to various other AME agencies. The records of the AME Department of Home and Foreign Missions for the years 1912 to 1960 have recently been acquired by the Schomburg Center. The Schomburg Center also holds an important collection of general conference minutes and a scattering of annual conference minutes for the late nineteenth and early twentieth centuries, and an extensive run of the *AME Church Review*, which is complete through the early 1920s and available on microfilm for the years 1884-1910. Significant though scattered holdings of annual conference minutes are also held by a number of state and local historical societies, such as the Library Company of Philadelphia and the Historical Society of Pennsylvania.[16]

The "Mother Church" of the denomination, Bethel AME in Philadelphia, has also played an important role in documenting African Methodist history from its earliest beginnings. In collaboration with the Historical Society of Pennsylvania, the congregation's Historical Commission has made available on microfilm both Bethel's own records from its founding until 1972 and its nearly complete run of the denomination's *Christian Recorder*, the oldest continuously published black newspaper in America, for the years 1854-1902. Another extensive collection of the *Christian Recorder*, from 1880 to 1917 and from 1941 to the present, housed at Drew University, Madison, New Jersey, nicely complements the microfilm run (1913-1936) produced by the American Theological Library Association.[17] Drew also holds a partial run of the *Southern Christian Recorder* for the years 1890, 1896-1897, and 1901-1904. Copies of the short-lived antebellum AME periodicals, the *African Methodist Episcopal Church Magazine* (1840-1848) and the *Repository of Religion and Literature, Science and Art* (1858-1864), are not available on film. Fisk University Library in Nashville, Tennessee, holds a complete set of the former, while runs of the latter may be found at the Indiana State Library, Indianapolis (1858-1861), and the Houghton Library, Harvard University (1862-1863), Cambridge, Massachusetts.

Collections—usually small—of the personal papers of important AME church leaders can be found in a wide variety of archives. The Moorland-Spingarn Research Center holds the 1856 and 1877-1878 journals of Daniel A. Payne and a collection of material on AME bishop and black nationalist leader Henry McNeal Turner. An intermittent series of personal diaries (1851-1869) and other papers belonging to AME theologian, editor, and bishop Benjamin Tucker Tanner are located at the Library of Congress. A very substantial collection of the diaries, correspondence, and other papers of another late nineteenth-century theologian, Theophilus Gould Steward, are held by the Schomburg Center, as are the papers of Bishop John Albert Johnson. Duke University in Durham, North Carolina, has the papers of Alabama presiding elder Winfield Henry Mixon, which consist primarily of an incomplete series of personal journals running from 1895 to 1915. The miscellaneous papers of Bishop Charles Spencer Smith (four linear feet) are available at the Bentley Historical Library at the University of Michigan, Ann Arbor, while a collection (five and a half linear feet) of the papers of pastor and presiding elder Charles Henry Boone are held by the Tennessee State Library and Archives. These two collections also contain, respectively, the papers of Christine Shoecraft Smith and Willie Boone, which bear in part on women's work in the AME church.

Livingstone College and Hood Theological Seminary in Salisbury, North Carolina, have the most important collections on the AME Zion church (founded in 1822).[18] They contain extensive though incomplete runs of general and annual conference minutes, as well as manuscript material of some of the denomination's bishops and other leaders, including Joseph Charles Price, John Bryan Small, and John Dancy, Sr. Records of the early history of Mother Zion Church in New York are located both at the historic John Street United Methodist Church and also in the New York Public Library. Various partial series of AME Zion conference minutes, together covering much of the nineteenth century, may be found at Boston University (Mugar Library), Wilberforce University, the John Carter Brown Library, and the Rhode Island Historical Society, the latter two in Providence. Of early denominational newspapers, only the *Star of Zion* is known to be extant. Drew University's holdings begin in 1884, and the microfilm run produced by the American Theological Library Association extends from 1896 to 1970. The papers (six linear feet) of Stephen Gill Spottswood, AME Zion bishop and longtime chairman of the national board of the National Association for the Advancement of Colored People (NAACP), are located at the Amistad Research Center at Tulane University in New Orleans.

The last organized (1870) of the major Afro-Methodist denominations, the Colored Methodist Episcopal (since 1954 the Christian Methodist Episcopal) church, has collected its church records, the papers of denominational leaders, and a long run of the *Christian Index*, a church weekly, at the CME Publishing House in Memphis, Tennessee. Drew University also holds a nearly complete set of the *Christian Index* from 1891 to the present. A sizable though as yet uncataloged collection of the papers of retired CME bishop Henry C. Bunton is to be found at the Schomburg Center.

Because the major independent black Methodist denominations emerged as secessions from the Methodist Episcopal Church and the Methodist Episcopal Church, South (the major predecessor bodies to the United Methodist church), the archival record of black Methodism is in many places bound up with archival records of Methodism generally in the United States. This is especially true for the late eighteenth and early nineteenth centuries, when early records of the Methodist Episcopal (ME) societies along the Atlantic seaboard vividly demonstrate an African presence. The United Methodist Historical Society at the Lovely Lane Museum in Baltimore contains class lists of that area's biracial Methodist societies for the period before a black secession created Baltimore's Bethel AME. Similar documentation is at the Maryland Hall of Records, Annapolis, for black Methodists in Annapolis and for their coreligionists in Richmond and Petersburg at the Virginia State Archives, Richmond.

Because many blacks, despite racial schisms, remained within the ME church throughout its history, the United Methodist church today has more Afro-American members than any other predominantly white Protestant denomination. The most important body of material on their history is held by the United Methodist archive at Drew University. It has collected minutes of the black annual conferences of the ME church and of the Central Jurisdiction of the Methodist church (1939-1968). It also holds the correspondence of the Freedmen's Aid Society of the ME church, which was crucially involved in black education in the post-Civil War South, and microfilm copies of the *Southwestern Christian Advocate* (1876-1929), the *Christian Advocate: Southwestern Edition* (1929-1940), and the *Central Christian Advocate* (1941-1968), which successively gave voice to the denomination's black constituency. Some papers (three linear feet) of Robert E. Jones, one of the first black Methodist Episcopal bishops elected to serve in the United States rather than in Africa, are at the Amistad Center.

Blacks have also held membership in many other predominantly white Protestant denominations in the United States besides those of the United Methodist tradition. Information concerning them is generally to be found at the major archival centers that most of those churches sponsor. The number of such groups is too large for us to discuss all of them.[19] We will comment, by way of illustration, on only one, the Episcopal church, which has a small but important black membership whose history reaches back into the prerevolutionary missionary efforts of the Church of England.

The starting point for research on black Episcopalians is the denominational archives. The Archives and Historical Collections of the Episcopal Church are located on the campus of the Episcopal Theological Seminary of the Southwest, in Austin, Texas. The extensive records of the Domestic and Foreign Missionary Society there include the especially important Liberian Records, 1822-1952, and the Haitian Records, 1855-1939. Indexes and collection descriptions are available. Among many other valuable collections are those of the American Church Institute for Negroes, organized in 1905 to secure funds for eleven Episcopal schools and hospitals for Afro-Americans throughout the South. For information about specific regions, parishes, or clergy, one must also consult the local diocesan archives. One such, the Maryland Diocesan Archives, located at the Maryland Historical Society in Baltimore, deserves special mention. Its more than sixty thousand items, chiefly manuscripts, include important materials dealing with slavery, emancipation, colonization, and the condition of blacks, as well as church work by them and on their behalf. Many items have been indexed by author and recipient, subject, and names of individuals mentioned in correspondence, which greatly facilitates their efficient and effective use.[20] Among seminary libraries, none is more important than that of General Theological Seminary in New York City. Its holdings include bound volumes of George F. Bragg's *Church Advocate* (1913?—1940) officially the parish monthly of Baltimore's St. James First African Episcopal Church. The paper also served for many years as the voice of the Conference of Church Workers among Colored People, a caucus of black Episcopal clergy organized in the late nineteenth century. The seminary also holds the papers of prominent Episcopal clergyman, Tollie L. Caution, Sr. Papers of individual priests are widely scattered. For example, the bulk of the papers of nineteenth-century intellectual Alexander Crummell are found at the Schomburg Center (though his papers as a whole are to be found in libraries on four continents), while the papers of Pauli Murray, the first female ordained in the Episcopal church and a major twentieth-century black religious activist, have recently been deposited at the Schlesinger Library, Radcliffe College, Cambridge, Massachusetts.

Until the 1930s, the number of black Roman Catholics was small. Steady growth in the last half century has, however, made black Catholics today the largest constituency of Afro-American Christians belonging to a predominantly white church.

Major resources for their history are contained in the archives of religious orders and organizations dedicated to a special mission to African Americans and in the archives of dioceses and archdioceses that have included significant numbers of black communicants. The Josephites, who began their work in the 1870s, have developed the most extensive archive of black Catholic history. Housed at the Josephite headquarters in Baltimore, it includes detailed records of numerous Josephite parishes scattered throughout the South; the letter books of Josephite superior John R. Slattery, an early advocate of the ordination of black priests; biographical files on black Catholic priests; runs of periodicals devoted to the "Negro Apostolate"; and a continuous clipping file of items concerning twentieth-century black Catholics. The archives of the Oblate Sisters of Providence, also located in Baltimore, contain the annual journals of the earliest community of black women religious, founded in 1829. The records of the Sisters of the Blessed Sacrament, founded by Katherine Drexel in 1891 to serve "Colored and Indian" missions, are available to researchers at the community's motherhouse in Philadelphia. They contain important information on Mother Katherine's extensive financial support (based on her inheritance of the Drexel fortune) of missions, parishes, and schools, including Xavier University in New Orleans, the only black Catholic university in the nation. The archives of the Archdiocese of Boston include papers dealing with the career of James A. Healy, the first Afro-American ordained to the priesthood. At the Archdiocese of Chicago archives, the development of black Catholic parishes and issues of black Catholic concern can be chronicled through chancery correspondence. The Msgr. Daniel Cantwell Papers at the Chicago Historical Society contain a wealth of information about the Catholic Interracial Council and other mid-twentieth-century Catholic efforts to improve race relations in that city. An incomplete run of the late nineteenth-century black Catholic newspaper, the *American Catholic Tribune*, edited by Dan Rudd, a layman who organized five black Catholic congresses between 1889 and 1894, is available on microfilm from the American Theological Library Association. The records of the Commission for Catholic Missions among the Colored People and the Indians, located at Marquette University, Milwaukee, Wisconsin, include reports (some detailing conditions) and requests for financial assistance from local parishes and missions from the 1920s.

Special problems arise concerning the rapidly growing Church of God in Christ (COGIC), reportedly now the second largest of all the black denominations and, indeed, for the other black Pentecostal — and the black Holiness —denominations as well. Charles Edwin Jones, *Black Holiness*, provides a useful orientation to the organizations, leadership, and literature of these increasingly prominent and influential churches, but it does not list manuscript holdings.[21] Efforts are underway at the Historical/Cultural Museum at COGIC headquarters in Memphis, Tennessee, to organize that denomination's archives. Some materials have already been assembled and cataloged, but a large body of minutes, records, and other material remains widely scattered and largely inaccessible, especially for the period before 1956. Difficult to locate too are the papers of major church leaders. The most readily accessible body of unpublished material on Charles H. Mason, the denomination's founder, may be the file assembled by the Federal Bureau of Investigation (FBI). A substantial run of the COGIC periodical *Whole Truth* (1907 to the present) was reportedly held by the late Pentecostal historian, James Tinney. Tinney's papers, currently in private hands, may represent the most significant new material on black Pentecostalism likely to become available for research in the 1990s. The most extensive collection of black Pentecostal and Holiness material currently available is that assembled by Sherry Sherrod DuPree at the Institute of Black Culture of the University of Florida in Gainesville. It contains more than eight thousand items, including minutes, yearbooks, pamphlets, clippings, and a small body of manuscripts. An important uncataloged collection of material on these churches, formerly held by the library of the Interdenominational Theological Center in Atlanta, is unfortunately now in storage at the Woodruff Library of the Atlanta University Center and therefore unavailable to researchers.

While a careful attention to denominational loyalties and structures is a necessary and important feature of the study of black church history generally, most scholars will not confine their interests to a single denomination or denominational family. They are likely instead to give their investigations a chronological or thematic definition. Myriad specific research possibilities and problems will naturally be suggested by the specific period or topic chosen. We can do no more here than hint at some of the resources pertinent to such work.

Scholars particularly interested in the mid-nineteenth century will find at the Amistad Center a critically important resource: the extensive correspondence and reports of the American Home Missionary Society and the

American Missionary Association, which together include some 550 linear feet of material. Especially important for the years surrounding the Civil War, these collections—like much else in the center's rich holdings—also illuminate black religious life in the twentieth century. For the Civil War and Reconstruction era, extensive if widely scattered materials are also to be found in the War Department records in the National Archives, particularly in the records of the Bureau of Refugees, Freedmen, and Abandoned Lands (Record Group 105). Especially rich are the records of the bureau's assistant commissioners for the different states, most of which are available on microfilm. The records of the Office of the Chief of Chaplains (Record Group 247) and of the Adjutant General's Office (Record Group 407) provide important information on the War Department's dealings with a range of black religious organizations over the first half of the twentieth century.[22] For the period from the 1920s until the early 1960s, researchers will find much of interest in the Claude A. Barnett Papers at the Chicago Historical Society. Founder and director of the Associated Negro Press (ANP), Barnett carried on a voluminous correspondence, thirteen boxes of which are directly cataloged under the heading "religion." Included as well are hundreds of ANP press releases, many concerning the black churches.[23] Important also for the mid-twentieth century are the holdings of the National Archives for Black Women's History and Mary McLeod Bethune Memorial Museum in Washington, D.C., which document the activities not only of Bethune (a Methodist activist) but also of many churchwomen's groups.[24]

For scholars taking a thematic more than a chronological or denominational approach to the study of the black church, one major focus has been—and is likely to remain—the churches' engagement in social reform movements and in electoral politics. The Black Abolitionist Papers project (in addition to publishing documents in what will be a five-volume edition) has microfilmed the correspondence and contributions to newspapers of three hundred Afro-Americans, and the minutes of religious and reform organizations connected with their careers. Since most of these persons were religiously active, this collection sheds important light on church- related participation in the abolitionist movement. The papers of white "carpetbagger" and social reformer Albion Tourgee, at the Chautauqua County Historical Museum, Westfield, New York, contain correspondence from important late nineteenth-century church-based black leaders such as Henry McNeal Turner and Joseph Charles Price.[25] The Amistad Center holds a small collection of the papers of Henry H. Proctor, an important black social gospeller. The Booker T. Washington Papers at the Library of Congress are rich in detailed information about the relation of the Tuskegee Machine to the black churches, while patronage-related correspondence involving politically active black clergy is to be found in the papers of every American president since Reconstruction. Certain to cast important new light on the role of the church in twentieth-century black politics, especially during the interwar period, are the papers of Washington's nephew and black Republican power broker Roscoe Conkling Simmons, recently acquired by the Harvard College Library. Consisting of twelve linear feet of correspondence, eight feet of speeches, twelve feet of newspapers, clippings, and political ephemera, and eight feet of photographs, this important new collection is currently being cataloged and should be open for use in 1991. Material pertinent to the activities of twentieth-century church-based reformers, both clerical and lay, is also to be found in the enormous body of archival resources documenting the struggle for civil rights from the founding of the NAACP and the Urban League to the present.[26]

As important as it is to track the churches' role in public life, it is equally important that scholars continue to explore the rich religious life that these institutions have sheltered and nourished for more than two centuries. The distinctive style of worship of black Christians, especially musical performance, has attracted the notice of observers since the eighteenth century. Historians, influenced by anthropologists and folklorists, have of late wisely begun to turn to religious performance, sermons, prayers, and hymns to get at the beliefs and attitudes of the "people in the pew," whose views might otherwise remain inaccessible. To document this crucial aspect of black church life, photographs, recordings, films, and videotapes are increasingly important resources.[27] The single most important collection providing photographic documentation of rural and urban black churches and religious services, though only for the depression era, is the Farm Security Administration Collection in the Prints and Photographs Division of the Library of Congress. Exceptionally rich visual documentation is also sometimes available for specific locations. The Center for Southern Folklore in Memphis, Tennessee, holds a collection of five hundred photographic prints and thirty thousand feet of raw film footage of black church life in and around Memphis from the 1920s through the 1950s.[28]

For the study of black religious music, as for black music generally, an important resource is the *Black Music Research Bulletin* (published semiannually by the Center for Black Music Research, Columbia College, Chicago), which carries information about research collections in its field. Another helpful publication is *Rejoice!* the gospel music magazine of the Center for Southern Culture at the University of Mississippi. John Michael Spencer, *As the Black School Sings*, provides a guide to the archival collections of ten historically black universities, which include printed, manuscript, recorded, and photographic materials important for the study of Afro-American religious music.[29] The Archive of Folk Music of the Library of Congress contains extensive field recordings of black religious music, some of them never issued. Beginning in the 1920s, recordings of black preachers and gospel singers were produced by many of the major record companies specifically for black audiences.[30] Over seventy of the sermons of the Reverend C. L. Franklin, a master of the art of chanted preaching (and the father of Aretha Franklin), were recorded, primarily under the Jewel and Chess labels.[31] A complete set may be found at the Music Library and Sound Recordings Archives of Bowling Green State University, Bowling Green, Ohio, which also holds an extensive collection of commercially released recordings of popular music, including black gospel music. The holdings of the Center for Popular Music at Middle Tennessee State University in Murfreesboro include a significant number of commercially released recordings of black gospel singers and some field recordings of the black sacred harp tradition. The DuPree collection on the Holiness and Pentecostal traditions includes some 650 audio and 50 video tapes of meetings, personal interviews, and worship services, mostly from Williams Temple (COGIC) in Gainesville, Florida.

Only when such sources as these are fully integrated with the more traditional sources detailed above will an adequate retelling of Carter Woodson's story be possible. And only with the retelling of Woodson's story will it be possible adequately to retell the religious history of the United States in its entirety.

CHAPTER I
THE EARLY MISSIONARIES AND THE NEGRO

ONE OF THE causes of the discovery of America was the translation into action of the desire of European zealots to extend the Catholic religion into other parts. Columbus, we are told, was decidedly missionary in his efforts and felt that he could not make a more significant contribution to the church than to open new fields for Christian endeavor. His final success in securing the equipment adequate to the adventure upon the high seas was to some extent determined by the Christian motives impelling the sovereigns of Spain to finance the expedition for the reason that it might afford an opportunity for promoting the cause of Christ. Some of the French who came to the new world to establish their claims by further discovery and exploration, moreover, were either actuated by similar motives or welcomed the cooperation of earnest workers thus interested.

The first persons proselyted by the Spanish and French missionaries were Indians. There was not any particular thought of the Negro. It may seem a little strange just now to think of persons having to be converted to faith in the possibility of the salvation of the Negro, but there were among the colonists thousands who had never considered the Negro as belonging to the pale of Christianity. Negroes had been generally designated as infidels; but, in the estimation of their self-styled superiors, they were not considered the most desirable of this class supposedly arrayed against Christianity. There were few Christians who did not look forward to the ultimate conversion of those infidels approaching the Caucasian type, but hardly any desired to make an effort in the direction of proselyting Negroes.

When, however, that portion of this Latin element primarily interested in the exploitation of the Western Hemisphere failed to find in the Indians the substantial labor supply necessary to their enterprises and at the suggestion of men like Bartolomé de las Casas imported Negroes for this purpose, the missionaries came face to face with the question as to whether this new sort of heathen should receive the same consideration as that given the Indians. Because of the unwritten law that a Christian could not be held a slave, the exploiting class opposed any such proselyting; for, should the slaves be liberated upon being converted, their plans for development would fail for lack of a labor supply subject to their orders as bondmen. The sovereigns of Europe, once inclined to adopt a sort of humanitarian policy toward the Negroes, at first objected to their importation into the new world; and when under the pressure of the interests of the various countries they yielded on this point, it was stipulated that such slaves should have first embraced Christianity. Later, when further concessions to the capitalists were necessary, it was provided in the royal decrees of Spain and of France that Africans enslaved in America should merely be early indoctrinated in the principles of the Christian religion.

These decrees, although having the force of law, soon fell into desuetude. There was not among these planters any sentiment in favor of such humanitarian treatment of the slaves. Unlike the missionaries, the planters were not interested in religion and they felt that too much enlightenment of the slaves might inspire them with the hope of attaining the status of freemen. The laws, therefore, were nominally accepted as just and the functionaries in the colonies in reporting to their home countries on the state of the plantations made it appear that they were generally complied with. As there was no such thing as an inspection of these commercial outposts, moreover, no one in Europe could easily determine exactly what attitude these men had toward carrying out the will of the home countries with respect to the Christianization of the bondmen. From time to time, therefore, the humanitarian world heard few protests like that of Alfonso Sandoval in Cuba and the two Capuchin monks who were imprisoned in Havana because of their inveighing against the failure on the part of the planters to provide for the religious instruction of the slaves. Being in the minority, these upright pioneers too often had their voices hushed in persecution, as it happened in the case of the two monks.

It appears, however, that efforts in behalf of Negroes elsewhere were not in vain; for the Negroes in Latin America were not only proselyted thereafter but were given recognition among the clergy. Such was the experience of Francisco Xavier de Luna Victoria, son of a freedman, a Panama charcoal burner, whose chief ambition was to educate this young man for the priesthood. He easily became a priest and after having served acceptably in this capacity a number of years was chosen Bishop of Panama in 1751 and administered this office eight years. He was later called to take charge of the See of Trujillo, Peru.

In what is now the United States the Spanish and French missionaries had very little contact with the Negroes during the early period, as they were found in large numbers along the Atlantic coast only. In the West Indies, however, the Latin policy decidedly dominated during the early colonial period, and when the unwritten law that a Christian could not be held a slave was by special statutes and royal decrees annulled, the planters eventually yielded in their objection to the religious instruction of the slaves and generally complied with the orders of the home country to this effect.

Maryland was the only Atlantic colony in which the Catholics had the opportunity to make an appeal to a large group of Negroes. After some opposition the people of that colony early met the test of preaching the gospel to all regardless of color. The first priests and missionaries operating in Maryland regarded it their duty to enlighten the slaves; and, as the instruction of the communicants of the church became more systematic to make their preparation adequate to the proper understanding of the church doctrine, some sort of instruction of the Negroes attached to these establishments was provided in keeping with the sentiment expressed in the first ordinances of the Spanish and French sovereigns and later in the Black Code governing the bondmen in. the colonies controlled by the Latins.

Although the attitude of the Catholic pioneers was not altogether encouraging to the movement for the evangelization of the Negroes, still less assistance came from the Protestants settling the English colonies. Few, if any, of the pioneers from Great Britain had the missionary spirit of some of the Latins. As the English were primarily interested in founding new homes in America, they thought of the Negroes not as objects of Christian philanthropy but rather as tools with which they might reach that end. It is not surprising then that with the introduction of slavery as an economic factor in the development of the English colonies little care was taken of their spiritual needs, and especially so when they were confronted with the unwritten law that a Christian could not be held a slave.

Owing to the more noble example set by the Latins, however, and the desirable results early obtained by their missionaries, the English planters permitted some sort of religious instruction of the bondmen, after providing by royal decrees and special statutes in the colonies that conversion to Christianity would not work manumission. Feeling, however, that the nearer the blacks were kept to the state of brutes that the more useful they would be as laborers, the masters generally neglected them.

The exceptions to this rule were the efforts of various clergymen in cooperation with the Society for the Propagation of the Gospel in Foreign Parts. This organization was established in London in 1701 to do missionary work among the heathen, especially the Indians and the Negroes. Its function was to prepare the objects of its philanthropy for a proper understanding of the church doctrine and the relation of man to God. This body operated through the branches of the established church, the ministrations of which were first limited to a few places in Virginia, New York, Maryland, and the cities of Boston and Philadelphia. From the very beginning this society felt that the conversion of the Negroes was as important as that of bringing the whites or the Indians into the church and such distinguished churchmen as Bishops Lowth, Fleetwood, Williams, Sanderson, Butler, and Wilson, persistently urged this duty upon their subordinates. In 1727 Bishop Gibson sent out two forceful pastoral letters outlining this duty of the missionaries, Bishop Secker preached a soul-stirring sermon thereupon in 1741, and in 1784 Bishop Porteus published an extensive plan for the more effectual conversion of the slaves, contending that "despicable as they are in the eyes of man they are, nevertheless, the creatures of God."

The first successful worker in this field was the Rev. Samuel Thomas of Goose Creek Parish in the colony of South Carolina. The records show that he was thus engaged as early as 1695 and that ten years later he reported 20 black communicants who, with several others, well understood the English language. By 1705 he had brought under his instruction as many as 1,000 slaves, "many of whom," said he, "could read the Bible distinctly and great numbers of them were engaged in learning the scriptures." When these blacks approached the communion table, however, some white persons seriously objected, inquiring whether it was possible that slaves should go to heaven anyway. But having the cooperation of a number of liberal slaveholders in that section and working in collaboration with Mrs. Haig, Mrs. Edwards, and the Rev. E. Taylor, who baptized a number of them, the missionaries in that colony prepared the way for the Christianization of the Negro slaves.

Becoming interested in the thorough indoctrination of these slaves, Mr. Taylor planned for their instruction, encouraging the slaveholders to teach the blacks at least to the extent of learning the Lord's Prayer. Manifesting such interest in these unfortunate blacks, their friends easily induced them to attend church in such large numbers that they could not be accommodated. "So far as the missionaries were permitted," says one, "they did all that was possible for their evangelization, and while so many professed Christians among the whites were lukewarm, it pleased God to raise to himself devout servants among the heathen, whose faithfulness was commended by the Masters themselves." In some of the congregations the Negroes constituted one-half of the communicants.

This interest in proselyting the Negroes was extended into other parts. In 1723, Rev. Mr. Guy of St. Andrew's Parish reported that he had baptized a Negro man and woman. About the same time Rev. Mr. Hunt, in charge of St. John's Parish, had among his communicants a slave, "a sensible Negro who can read and write and come to church, a catechumen under probation for baptism, which he desires."

A new stage in the progress of this movement was reached in 1743 when there was established at Charleston, South Carolina, a special school to train Negroes for participation in this missionary work. This school was opened by Commissary Garden and placed in charge of Harry and Andrew, two young men of color, who had been thoroughly instructed in the rudiments of education and in the doctrines of the church. It not only served as the training school for missionary workers, but directed its attention also to the special needs of adults who studied therein during the evenings. From this school there were sent out from year to year numbers of youths to undertake this work in various parts of the colony of South Carolina. After having accomplished so much good for about a generation, however, the school was, in 1763, closed for various reasons, one of them being that one of the instructors died and the other proved inefficient.

Farther upward in the colony of North Carolina, the same difficulties were encountered. There the motive was the fear that, should the slaves be converted, they would, according to the unwritten law of Christendom, become free. Some planters, however, were very soon thereafter persuaded to let these missionaries continue their work. "By much importunity," says an annalist, Mr. Ranford of Chowan, "in 1712 we prevailed upon Mr. Martin to let him baptize three of his Negroes, two women and a boy. All the arguments I could make use of," said he, "would scarce effect it till Bishop Fleetwood's sermon in 1711 turned ye scale." These workers then soon found it possible to instruct and baptize more than forty Negroes in one year, and not long thereafter some workers reported as many as 15 to 24 in one month, 40 to 50 in six months and 60 to 70 in a year. Rev. Mr. Newman, proclaiming the new day of the Gospel in that colony, reported in 1723 that he had baptized two Negroes who could say the Creed, the Lord's Prayer, the Ten Commandments and gave good sureties for their fuller information. According to the report of Rev. C. Hall, the number of conversions there among the Negroes for eight years was 355, including 112 adults; and "at Edenton the blacks generally were induced to attend service at all these stations where they behaved with great decorum."

In the middle colonies the work was given additional impetus by the mission of Dr. Thomas Bray. The Bishop of London sent this gentleman to the colony of Maryland for the purpose of devising plans to convert adult Negroes and educate their children. Having also the influential support of M. D'Alone, the private secretary of King William, who gave for its maintenance a fund, the proceeds of which were to be used to employ catechists, the Thomas Bray Mission decidedly encouraged these missionaries. The catechists appointed, however, failed; but the work was well extended throughout Maryland, into neighboring colonies, and even into the settlements of Georgia, through certain persons assuming the title of Dr. Bray's Associates. Traveling in North Carolina, Rev. Mr. Stewart, a missionary, found there a school maintained by Dr. Bray's Associates for the education of Indians and Negroes. They were supporting such a school in Georgia in 1751; but in 1766 the Rev. S. Frink, a missionary trying to secure a hearing in Augusta, found that he could neither convert the Indians nor the whites, who seemed to be as destitute of religion as the former; but he succeeded in converting some Negroes.

In Pennsylvania the missionary movement among the Negroes found apparently less obstacles. There are records showing the baptism of Negroes as early is 1712. One Mr. Yates, a worker at Chester, was commended by the Rev. G. Ross "for his endeavors to train up the Negroes in the knowledge of religion." Mr. Ross himself had on one occasion at Philadelphia baptized as many as twelve adult Negroes, who were examined before the congregation and answered to the admiration of all who heard them "The like sight had never been seen before in that church." Giving account of his efforts in Sussex County in 1723, Rev. Mr. Beckett said that many Negroes constantly attended his services, while Rev. Mr. Bartow about the same time baptized a Negro at West Chester. Rev. Richard Locke christened eight Negroes in one family at Lancaster in 1747 and another Negro there the following year. In 1774 the Rev. Mr. Jenney observed a great and daily increase of Negroes in this city, "who with joy attend upon the catechist for instruction." He had baptized several but was unable to add to his other duties.

The Society, ever ready to lend a helping hand to such an enterprise, appointed the Rev. W. Sturgeon as catechist for the Negroes in Philadelphia. At the same time the Rev. Mr. Neal of Dover was meeting with equally good results, having baptized as many as 162 Negroes within eight months. Now and then, however, as in the case of Rev. Mr. Pugh, a missionary at Appoquinimink, Pennsylvania, the missionaries received very few Negroes, because their masters here, as elsewhere, were prejudiced against their being Christians.

The Society did not operate extensively in the State of New Jersey. The Rev. Mr. Lindsay mentions his baptizing a Negro at Allerton in 1736. The missions of New Brunswick reported a large number of Negroes as having become attached to their churches, but this favorable situation was not the rule throughout the State. The missionary spirit was not wanting, however, and the accession of Negroes to the churches followed later in spite of local opposition and the general apathy as to the indoctrination of the blacks.

In those colonies further north where the Negroes were not found in large numbers, little opposition to their indoctrination was experienced; and their evangelization proceeded without interruption, whereas in most southern colonies the proselyting of the Negroes was largely restricted to what the ministers and missionaries could do during their spare time. There was in New York a special provision for the employment of 16 clergymen and 13 lay teachers for the conversion of free Indians and Negro slaves. Elias Neau, a worker in these ranks, established in New York City in 1704 a catechizing school for Negro slaves. After several years of imprisonment in France because of his Protestant faith he had come to New York as a trader. Upon witnessing, however, the neglected condition of the blacks, who, according to his words, "were without God in the world and of whose souls there was no manner of care taken," he proposed the appointment of a catechist to undertake their instruction. Finally being prevailed upon to accept the position himself, he obtained a license from the Governor, resigned his position as elder in the French church, and conformed to the established church of England. At first he served from house to house but very soon secured a regular place of instruction, after being commended by the Society to Mr. Vesey, as a constant communicant of the church and a most zealous and prudent servant of Christ in proselyting the Negroes and Indians to the Christian religion whereby he did great service to God and his church. There was a further expression of confidence in him in a bill to be offered to Parliament "for the more effectual conversion of the Negroes and other servants in the plantations, to compel owners of slaves to cause their children to be baptized within three months after their birth and to permit them, when come to years of discretion, to be instructed in the Christian religion on our Lord's Day by the missionaries under whose ministry they live." Neau's school suffered considerably in the Negro riot in that city in 1712, when it was closed by local authority and an investigation of his operations ordered. Upon learning, however, that the slaves primarily concerned in this rising were not connected with his school but had probably engaged in this enterprise because of their neglected condition, the city permitted him to continue his operations as a teacher, feeling that Christian knowledge would not necessarily be a means of more cunning and aptitude to wickedness. The Governor and the Council, the Mayor, the Recorder, and Chief Justice informed the Society that Neau had "performed his work to the great advancement of religion and particular benefit of the free Indians, Negro slaves and other heathen in these parts, with indefatigable zeal and application."

Neau died in 1722; but his work was continued by Huddlestone, Whitmore, Colgan, Auchmutty, and Charlton. The last mentioned had undertaken the instruction of the blacks while at New Windsor and found it practical and convenient to throw into one class his white and black catechumens. Mr. Auchmutty served from 1747 to 1764 and finally reported that there was among the Negroes an ever-increasing desire for instruction and not one single black "that had been admitted by him to the holy communion had turned out bad or been in any way a disgrace to our holy profession."

This good work done in the city of New York extended into other parts of the colony. We hear of Rev. Mr. Stoupe in 1737 baptizing four black children at New Rochelle. At New Windsor, Rev. Charles Taylor, a school-master, kept a night school for the instruction of the Negroes. Rev. J. Sayre, of Newburgh, promoted the education of the two races in four of the churches under his charge. In 1714 Rev. T. Barclay, an earnest worker among the slaves in Albany, reported a great forwardness among them to embrace Christianity and a readiness to receive instruction, although there was much opposition among some of the masters. Sixty years later Schenectady reported among its members eleven Negroes who were sober and serious communicants.

These missionaries met with some opposition in New England among the Puritans, who had no serious objection to seeing the Negroes saved but did not care to see them incorporated into the church, which then being connected with the state would grant them political as well as religious equality. There had been an academic interest in the conversion of the Negroes. John Eliot had no particular objection to slavery but regretted that it precluded the possibility of their instruction in the Christian doctrine and worked a loss of their souls. Cotton Mather, taking the task of evangelization seriously, drew up a set of rules by which masters should be governed in the instruction of their slaves. He had much fear of the prodigious wickedness of deriding, neglecting and opposing all due means of bringing the poor Negroes unto God. He did not believe that Almighty God made so many thousand reasonable creatures for nothing but "only to serve the lusts of epicures or the gains of mammonists." In the protest of Jonathan Sewell set forth in his *Selling of Joseph*, there was an attack on slavery because the servants differed from those of Abraham, who commanded his children and his household that they should keep the way of the Lord. In this they were standing upon the high ground taken by Richard Baxter, an authority among the Puritans, who, denouncing the use of the slaves as beasts for their mere commodity, said, that their masters who "betray or destroy or neglect their souls are fitter to be called incarnate devils than Christians though they be no Christian whom they so abuse."

The opposition there, however, was not apparent everywhere among the ministers of other sects. From Bristol, Rev. J. Usher of the Society for the Propagation of the Gospel in Foreign Parts, wrote in 1730 that several Negroes desired baptism and were able to "render a very good account of the hope that was in them," but he was forbidden by their masters to comply with the request. Yet he reported the same year that among others he had in his congregation "about 30 Negroes and Indians," most of whom joined "in the public service very decently." At Newton, where greater opposition was encountered, J. Beach seemed to have baptized by 1733 many Indians and a few Negroes. Dr. Cutler, a missionary at Boston wrote to the Society in 1737 that among those he had admitted to his church were four Negro slaves. Endeavoring to do more than to effect nominal conversions, Dr. Johnson, while at Stratford, gave catechetical lectures during the summer months of 1751, attended by "many Negroes and some Indians, as well as whites, about 70 or 80 in all." And said he: "As far as I can find, where the Dissenters have baptized two, if not three or four, Negroes or Indians, I have four or five communicants." Dr. Macsparran conducted at Narragansett a class of 70 Indians and Negroes whom he frequently catechized and instructed before the regular service. J. Honyman, of Newport, had in his congregation more than 100 Negroes who "constantly attended the Publick [*sic*] Worship."

The real interest in the evangelization of the Negroes in the English colonies, however, was manifested not by those in authority but by the Quakers, who, being friends of all humanity, would not neglect the Negroes. In accepting these persons of color on a basis of equality, however, the Quakers, in denouncing the nakedness of the religion of the other colonists at the same time, alienated their affections and easily brought down upon them the wrath of the public functionaries in these plantations. Believing that such influence would not be salutary in slaveholding communities, many of them, as they did in Virginia, prohibited the Quakers from taking the Negroes to their meetings. Such opposition was but natural when we find that their leader, George Fox, was advocating the instruction of Negroes in 1672 and boldly entreating his coworkers to instruct and teach the Indians and Negroes in 1679 how that "Christ by the grace of God tasted death for every man." When George Keith in 1693 began to promote the religious training of the slaves as preparation for emancipation and William Penn actually advocated the abolition of the system to commit the whole sect to a definite scheme to return the Negroes to Africa to Christianize that continent, such opposition easily developed wherever the Friends operated.

These people, however, would not be deterred from carrying out their purpose. The results which followed show that they were not frustrated in the execution of their plans. John Woolman, one of the fathers of the Quakers in America, always bore testimony against slavery and repeatedly urged that the blacks be given religious instruction. We hear later of their efforts in towns and in the colonies of Virginia and North Carolina to teach Negroes to read and write. Such Negroes as were accessible in the settlements of the North came under the influence of Quakers of the type of John Hepburn, William Burling, Elihu Coleman, Ralph Sandiford, and Anthony Benezet, who established a number of successful missions operating among the Negroes. As the Quakers were, because of their anti-slavery tendencies, the owners of few slaves and were denied access to those of others, what they did for the evangelization of the whole group was little when one considers the benighted darkness in which most Negro slaves in America lived. The faith of the Quakers, their religious procedure, and peculiar customs, moreover, could not be easily understood and appreciated by the Negroes in their undeveloped state.

Generally speaking, then, one should say that the Negroes were neglected. The few missionaries among them stood like shining lights after a great darkness. They, moreover, faced numerous handicaps, among which might be mentioned the conflicts of views, and especially that of the established church with the Catholics and later with the evangelical sects. There were also the difficulties resulting from dealing with a backward pioneering people, the scarcity of workers, and the lack of funds to sustain those who volunteered for this service.

Some difficulty resulted too from the differences of opinion as to what tenets of religion should be taught the Negro and how they should be pre-

sented. Should the Negroes be first instructed in the rudiments of education and then taught the doctrines of the church or should the missionaries
start with the Negro intellect as he found it on his arrival from Africa and
undertake to inculcate doctrines which only the European mind could
comprehend? There was, of course, in the interest of those devoted to exploitation, a tendency to make the religious instruction of the Negroes as
nearly nominal as possible only to remove the stigma attached to those
who neglected the religious life of their servants. Such limited instruction,
however, as the slaves received when given only a few moments on Sunday
proved to be tantamount to no instruction at all; for missionaries easily
observed in the end that Christianity was a rather difficult religion for an
undeveloped mind to grasp.

As long as these efforts were restricted to the Anglican clergy, moreover,
there could be little question among the British as to the advisability of
the procedure. When, however, upon the expansion of the territory of the
Catholics and other sects the Negroes came under the influence of different sorts of religion promoted by men of a new thought and new method,
some conflict necessarily arose. There was another handicap in that the Anglican clergymen in America during the seventeenth and eighteenth centuries were not of the highest order. Their establishments were maintained
by a tax on the colonists in keeping with the customs and laws of England,
so that their income was assured, whether or not they wielded an influence
for good among the people. The colonial clergy, therefore, too often became corrupt in this independent economic position. They spent much of
their time at games and various sports, tarried at the cup and looked upon
the wine when it was red, in fact, became so interested in the enjoyment of
the things inviting in this world that they had in some cases little time to
devote to the elevation of the whites, to say nothing about the elevation of
the Negroes. They did not feel disposed to undertake this work themselves
and in adhering to their rights as representatives of the established church
precluded the possibility of a more general evangelization of the Negroes
by the other sects. One might expect from a country, the religious affairs
of which were thus administered, a number of protests from those thus
served. There was such a general lack of culture among these backward
colonists, however, that no such complaint followed. Interest in religion
must come from the promoters of religion. If the clergymen themselves
did not manifest interest in this work, it was out of the question to expect
others to do so.

Another difficulty was the lack of workers. The colonies were not rapidly
becoming densely populated and it was not then an easy matter to induce
young clergymen to try their fortunes in the wilderness of the western
world for such remuneration as the colonists in their scattered and undeveloped economic state were able to give. As many of the white settlements,

therefore, were neglected, it would naturally follow that the Negroes suffered likewise. Some of these workers volunteering to toil in this field as missionaries were, of course, supported by funds raised for that purpose; but the difficulty in raising money for missions is still a problem of the church. At that time the people were generally more disinclined to contribute to such causes than they are today. That was the age of commercial expansion and available funds were drawn into that field, much at the expense of the higher things of life. The intelligent Christians, therefore, with a clear understanding of the Bible and the doctrines derived therefrom were not legion even among the whites prior to the American Revolution. The slaves with the handicap of bondage, of course, could not constitute exceptions to this rule.

CHAPTER II
THE DAWN OF THE NEW DAY

THE NEW THOUGHT at work in the minds of the American people during the second half of the eighteenth century, especially after the Seven Years' War, aroused further interest in the uplift of the groups far down. By this time the colonists had become more conscious of their unique position in America, more appreciative of their worth in the development of the new world, and more cognizant of the necessity to take care of themselves by development from within rather than addition from without. How to rehabilitate the weakened forces and how to minister to those who had been neglected became a matter of concern to all forward-looking men of that time.

The clergy thereafter considered the Negro more seriously even in those parts where slaves were found in large numbers. Among those directing attention to the spiritual needs of the race were Rev. Thomas Bacon and Rev. Jonathan Boucher of the Anglican Church. The former undertook to arouse his people through a series of sermons addressed to masters and slaves about the year 1750. He said: "We should make this reading and studying the Holy Scriptures and the reading and explaining of them to our children and servants or the catechizing and instructing them in the principles of the Christian religion a stated duty. If the grown up slaves from confirmed habits of vice are hard to be reclaimed, the children surely are in our power and may be trained up in the way they should go, with rational hopes that when they are old, they will not depart from it." In 1763 Jonathan Boucher boldly said: "It certainly is not a necessary circumstance essential to the condition of the slave that he be not indoctrinated; yet this is the general and almost universal lot of the slaves." He said, moreover: "You may unfetter them from the chains of ignorance, you may emancipate them from the bondage of sin, the worse slavery to which they could be subjected; and by thus setting at liberty those that are bruised though they still continue to be your slaves, they shall be delivered from the bondage of corruption into the glorious liberty of the children of God."

The accomplishment of the task of more thoroughly proselyting the Negroes, however, belongs to the record of other sects than the Anglican Church. Even if the Negroes had been given the invitation to take a part in the propagation of the gospel as promoted by the first sects in control, the organization of these bodies, the philosophical foundation of their doctrines, and the controversial atmosphere in which their protagonists lived in this conflict of creeds, made it impossible for persons of such limited mental development as the slaves were permitted to experience, to participate. The Latin ceremonies of the Catholic church and the ritualistic

conformity required by the Anglicans too often baffled the Negro's understanding, leaving him, even when he had made a profession of faith, in a
position of being compelled to accept the spiritual blessings largely on the
recommendation of the missionary proffering them. The simplicity of the
Quakers set forth as an attack on the forms and ceremonies of the more
aristocratic churches equally taxed the undeveloped intellect of certain Negroes who often wondered how matters so mysterious could be reduced to
such an ordinary formula.

During the latter part of the seventeenth century and throughout the
eighteenth, there were rising to power in the United States two sects, which,
because of their evangelical appeal to the untutored mind, made such inroads upon the Negro population as to take over in a few years thereafter
the direction of the spiritual development of most of the Negroes throughout the United States. These were the Methodists and Baptists. They, together with the Scotch-Irish Presbyterians, imbibed more freely than other
denominations the social-compact philosophy of John Locke and emphasized the doctrines of Coke, Milton, and Blackstone as a means to justify
the struggle for an enlargement of the domain of political liberty, primarily
for the purpose of securing religious freedom denied them by the adherents of the Anglican Church.

Neither the Baptists nor the Methodists, however, were at first especially
interested in the Negro. Whitefield in Georgia advocated the introduction
of slaves and rum for the economic improvement of the colony. He even
owned slaves himself, although Wesley, Coke, and Asbury opposed the
institution and advocated emancipation as a means to thorough evangelization. The work of the Methodists in behalf of the Negroes, moreover,
was still less directed toward their liberation in the West Indies than on the
continent, doubtless because of the fact that in that section there did not
develop the struggle for the rights of man as an attack upon the British
government as it happened in the colonies along the Atlantic. But it is
said that out of the 352,404 signatures to memorials sent by Dissenters to
Parliament praying for the abolition of slavery, 229,426 were the names of
Methodists.

The missionaries, however, seemed to be trying to steer between Scylla
and Charybdis. They were forbidden to hold slaves but they were required
to promote the moral and religious improvement of the slaves without
in the least degree, in public or private, interfering with their civil condition. One who served for twenty years in the West Indies said: "For half
a century from the commencement of Methodism the slaves never expected freedom, and the missionaries never taught them to expect it; and
when the agitation of later years unavoidably affected them more or less, as
they learned chiefly through the violent speeches of their own masters or
overseers what was going on in their favor in England; it was missionary

influence that moderated their passions, kept them in the steady course of duty, and prevented them from sinning against God by offending against the laws of man. Whatever outbreaks or insurrections at any time occurred, no Methodist slave was ever proved guilty of incendiarism or rebellion for more than seventy years, namely, from 1760 to 1833. An extensive examination of their correspondence throughout that lengthened period, and an acquaintance with their general character and history, enables me confidently to affirm that a more humble, laborious, zealous, and unoffending class of Christian missionaries were never employed by any section of the church than those sent out by the British conference to the West India Isles. They were eminently men of one business, unconnected with any political party, though often strongly suspected by the jealousies so rife in slaveholding communities. A curious instance of this jealousy occurred in regard to one who was firmly believed to be a correspondent of the Anti-Slavery Society in England. "I did not know," said Fowell Buxton, in the House of Commons, "that such a man was in existence, till I heard that he was to be hung for corresponding with me."

In what is now the United States, on the contrary, there developed among the Baptists and Methodists a number of traveling missionaries, seemingly like the apostles of old, who in preaching to blacks and whites alike won most Negroes by attacking all evils, among which was slavery. Freeborn Garretson, one of the earliest Methodist missionaries, said to his countrymen that it was revealed to him that "it is not right for you to keep your fellow creatures in bondage; you must let the oppressed go free." He said in 1776: "It was God, not man, that taught me the impropriety of holding slaves: and I shall never be able to praise him enough for it. My very heart has bled, since that, for slaveholders, especially those who make a profession of religion; for I believe it to be a crying sin."

Bishop Asbury recorded in his *Journal* in 1776: "I met the class and then the black people, some of whose unhappy masters forbid their coming for religious instruction. How will the sons of oppression answer for their conduct when the great proprietor of all shall call them to account?" In 1780 he records that he spoke to some select friends about slave keeping but they could not bear it. He said: "This I know. God will plead the cause of the oppressed though it gives offense to say so here. . . . I am grieved for slavery and the manner of keeping these poor people."

With these missionaries attacking slavery, the church as an organization had to take some position. In 1780 the church required traveling preachers to set their slaves free, declaring at the same time that slavery is contrary to the laws of God, man and nature, and hurtful to society; contrary to the dictates of conscience and pure religion, and doing that which we would not that others should do to us and ours. In 1784 the conference took steps for the abolition of slavery, viewing it as "contrary to the golden laws of God, on which hang all the law and the prophets; and the inalienable rights of mankind, as well as every principle of the Revolution, to hold in the deepest abasement in a more abject slavery, than is, perhaps, to be found in any part of the world, except America, so many souls that are all capable of the image of God." Every slaveholding member of their society was required to liberate his bondmen within twelve months. A record was to be kept of all slaves belonging to masters within the respective circuits and further records of their manumissions. Any person who would not comply with these regulations would have liberty quietly to withdraw from the society within twelve months, and, if he did not, he would be excluded at that time.[32]

Persons thus withdrawing should not partake of the Lord's Supper and those holding slaves would be excluded from this same privilege.

The Methodists who had taken this advanced position on slavery in 1784, however, soon found that they were ahead of the majority of the local members. Much agitation had been caused by this discussion in the State of Virginia and in 1785 there came several petitions asking for a suspension of the resolution passed in 1784 and it was so ordered in 1785 in the words: "It is recommended to all our brethren to suspend the execution of the minute on slavery *till the deliberations of a future conference*; and that an equal space of time be allowed to all our members for consideration when the minute shall be put in force." The conference declared, however, that it held in deepest abhorrence the practice of slavery and would not cease to seek its destruction by all wise and prudent means. These rules of 1784 were thereafter never put in effect but in 1796 the conference took the position of requiring the Methodists to be exceedingly cautious what persons they admitted to official stations in the church; "and in case of future admission to official stations, to require such security of those who hold slaves for the emancipation of them immediately, or gradually, as the laws of the States respectively and the circumstances of the case will admit." A traveling preacher becoming the owner of a slave forfeited his ministerial position. No slaveholder should be received in the society until the preacher who has oversight of the circuit had spoken to him freely and faithfully upon the subject of slavery. Every member who sold a slave should immediately after full proof be excluded from the society, and if any member purchased a slave, the quarterly meeting should determine the number of years in which the slave so purchased would work out the price of his purchase. The preachers and other members of the society were requested to consider the subject of Negro slavery with deep attention and to impart to the General Conference through the medium of yearly conferences, or otherwise, any important thought upon the subject. The annual conferences were directed to draw up addresses for the gradual emancipation of the slaves to the legislatures of those States in which no general laws had been passed for that purpose.

Locally the Baptists were winning more Negroes than the Methodists by their attack on slavery during these years, but because of the lack of organized effort the Baptists did not exert as much antislavery influence as the early Methodists. Through their conferences they often influenced the local churches to do more against slavery than they would have done for fear that they might lose their status among their brethren. As the Baptist church emphasized above all things local self government, each church being a law unto itself, it did not as a national body persistently attack slavery. The Baptists reached their most advanced position as an anti-slavery body in 1789 when they took action to the effect "that slavery is a violent depredation of the rights of nature and inconsistent with a republican government, and therefore, recommend it to our brethren, to make use of their local missions to extirpate this horrid evil from the land; and pray Almighty God that our honorable legislature may have it in their power to proclaim the great jubilee consistent with the principles of good policy."

From this position most Baptists gradually receded. Yet, although not working as an organized body, the Baptists in certain parts of the country were unusually outspoken and effective in waging war on slavery. As there were a number of disputes, owing to the fact that the denomination as a body was far from unanimity on this subject, some dissension in the ranks followed. Those who believed in the abolition of slavery by immediate means styled themselves the *Emancipating Baptists* or the *Emancipating Society* in contradistinction to the remaining Calvinistic Baptists who desired to be silent on the question.

The most outspoken of the former was David Barrow.[33] He was a native of Virginia, where he commenced his ministry in 1771, passing through the period of much insolence and persecution of the rude countrymen then denying the liberal sects religious freedom. He early became attached to the antislavery school and consequently emancipated his own slaves in Virginia without at first having so very much to say against the institution. After distinguishing himself in the State of Virginia for his unusual piety and great ability, he moved to Kentucky in 1798 and settled in Montgomery County. When the antislavery dispute became very ardent soon thereafter, he carried his opposition to the extent of alienating the support of his coworkers, who, sitting as an advisory council, expelled him from the ministry for preaching emancipation, and preferred similar charges against him that his local church at Mount Sterling might act accordingly. After having taken this drastic step, however, the Association at its next session voted to rescind this action; but Barrow had then joined with the emancipators and did not desire to return. Among those whom he found sufficiently companionable in the new work which he had undertaken were Rev. Donald Holmes, Carter Tarrant, Jacob Grigg, George Smith, and numerous other ministers, some of whom were native Americans and others native Europeans.

These emancipators began by inquiring: "Can any person whose practice is friendly to perpetual slavery be admitted a member of this meeting?" They thought not. They inquired, moreover: "Is there any case in which persons holding slaves may be admitted to membership into the church of Christ?" They said: "No, except in the case of holding young slaves with a view to their future emancipation when they reach the age of responsibility, in the case of persons who have purchased slaves in their ignorance and desire to leave it to the church to say when they may be free, in the case of women whose husbands are opposed to emancipation, in the case of a widow who has it not in her power to liberate them, and in the case when the slaves are idiots or too old to maintain themselves." Another query was: "Shall members in union with us be at liberty in any case to purchase slaves?" The answer was negative, except it was with a view to ransom them in such a way as the church might approve. These emancipators in Kentucky constituted themselves some years later an organized body and finally became known as the "Baptized Licking-Locust Association." In the course of time, however, feeling that that mode of association or the consolidation of churches was unscriptural and ought to be laid aside, they changed their organization to that of an abolition society.

It is interesting to note the attitude of the Presbyterians toward the amelioration of the condition of the Negroes. In 1774 when abolition was agitated in connection with the struggle for the rights of man, the Presbyterians were early requested to take action. A representation from Dr. Ezra Stiles and Rev. Samuel Hopkins respecting the sending of two natives of Africa on a mission to propagate Christianity in that land, brought before that body a discussion of all aspects of Negro slavery. In this debate a committee was requested to bring in a report on Negro slavery. The Assembly concurred in the proposal to send the missionaries to Africa, but deferred further consideration of slavery.

The first action taken on the subject came, after delay from year to year, in 1787. The committee on overtures brought in a report to the effect that the "Creator of the world having made of one flesh all the children of men, it becomes them as members of the same family, to consult and promote each other's happiness. It is more especially the duty of those who maintain the rights of humanity, and who acknowledge and teach the obligations of Christianity, to use such means as are in their power to extend the blessings of equal freedom to every part of the human race." Convinced of these truths, and sensible that the rights of human nature are too well understood to admit of debate, the Synod recommended in the warmest terms to every member of their body, and to all the churches and families under their care, to do everything in their power consistent with the rights of civil society, to promote the abolition of slavery, and the instruction of Negroes, whether bond or free.

After some consideration, however, the Synod reached the conclusion of expressing very much interest in the principles in favor of universal liberty that prevailed in America and also in that of the abolition of slavery. Yet inasmuch as it would be difficult to change slaves from a servile state to a participation in all the privileges of society without proper education and previous habits of industry, it recommended to all persons holding slaves to give them such education as might prepare them for the better enjoyment of freedom, and recommended further that in those cases in which the masters found the slaves disposed to make just improvement of the privilege they should give them "a peculium or sufficient time and sufficient means for procuring their liberty at a moderate rate."

There was some agitation of the question in 1793, when a memorial was addressed to the General Assembly by Warner Mifflin, a member of the Society of Friends; but no action of importance was taken again until 1795, when there arose the question as to whether the church should uphold communion with slaveholders. After due deliberation the General Assembly passed a resolution referring the memorialists to the action that the Assembly had already taken with reference to slavery in 1787 and 1793. As it seemed that the Presbytery of Transylvania was primarily concerned in this affair, Mr. Rice and Dr. Muir, ministers, and Mr. Robert Patterson, an elder, all of that section, were appointed a committee to draft the following pacifist letter to that Assembly, which determined for generations thereafter the policy of the Presbyterians with reference to slavery: "To our brethren, members of the Presbyterian Church, under the care of Transylvania Presbytery."

"Dear Friends and Brethren—The General Assembly of the Presbyterian Church hear with concern from your Commissioners, that differences of opinion with respect to holding Christian communion with those possessed of slaves, agitate the minds of some among you, and threaten divisions which may have the most ruinous tendency. The subject of slavery has repeatedly claimed the attention of the General Assembly, and the Commissioners from the Presbytery of Transylvania are furnished with attested copies of these decisions, to be read by the Presbytery when it shall appear to them proper, together with a copy of this letter, to the several Churches under their care."

"The General Assembly have taken every step which they deemed expedient or wise, to encourage emancipation, and to render the state of those who are in slavery as mild and tolerable as possible."

"Forbearance and peace are frequently inculcated and enjoined in the New Testament. 'Blessed are the peacemakers.' 'Let no one do anything through strife and vainglory.' 'Let such esteem others better than himself.'

The followers of Jesus ought conscientiously to walk worthy of their vocations, 'with all lowliness, and meekness, with long-suffering, forbearing one another, endeavoring to keep the unity of the Spirit in the bond of peace.' If every difference of opinion were to keep men at a distance, they could subsist in no state of society, either civil or religious. The General Assembly would impress this upon the minds of their brethren, and urge them to follow peace, and the things which make for peace."

"The General Assembly commend our dear friends and brethren to the grace of God, praying that the peace of God, which passeth all understanding may possess their hearts and minds."

CHAPTER III

THE NEW STAGE reached in the development of religious freedom in America in securing toleration for the evangelical denominations, meant the increasing importance of the Negro in the church. Given access to the people in all parts of the country by virtue of this new boon resulting from the struggle for the rights of man, the Methodists, Baptists and Presbyterians soon became imbued with the idea of an equality of the Negro in the church although they did not always militantly denounce slavery. Negroes were accepted in these congregations on this basis and when exhibiting the power of expounding the scriptures were sometimes heard with unusual interest. Such elevation of the blacks by these more liberal denominations, of course, incurred the displeasure and opposition of the aristocratic churchmen to the extent that these liberal denominations could not grant the Negroes as much freedom of participation in the church work as they were disposed to do.

In those cases in which Negroes were permitted to preach, they found themselves confronting not only the opposition of the more aristocratic sects but violating laws of long standing, prohibiting Negro ministers from exercising their gifts. When their ministrations were of a local order, and they did not seemingly stir up their fellow men to oppose the established order of things, not so much attention was paid to their operations. When, however, these Negroes of unusual power preached with such force as to excite not only the blacks but the whites, steps were generally taken to silence these speakers heralding the coming of a new day. This opposition on the part of the whites apparently grew more strenuous upon the attainment of independence. As British subjects, they had more feeling of toleration for the rise of the Negro in the church than they had after the colonies became independent. While struggling for liberty themselves, even for religious freedom, these Americans were not willing to grant others what they themselves desired. The attitude of most Americans then, unlike that of some of the British, seemed to be that the good things of this life were intended as special boons for a particular race.

The efforts to establish the early churches of South Carolina and Georgia are cases in evidence. The first Negro Baptist Church in America, according to Dr. W. H. Brooks, was founded by one Mr. Palmer at Silver Bluff across the river from Augusta, Georgia, in the colony of South Carolina, sometime between the years 1773 and 1775. This group was fortunate in having the kind master, George Galphin, who became a patron of this congregation. He permitted David George to be ordained for this special work after having formerly allowed George Liele to preach there during these early years. Upon the evacuation of Savannah by the Americans in 1778, the Silver Bluff Church was driven into exile. Called upon to decide whether they would support the American or British cause, friend separated from friend and sometimes master from slave. When Galphin, a patriot, abandoned his slaves in his flight for refuge from the British, David George and fifty of these slaves went over to the British in Savannah where they were freed. David George returned to South Carolina and resided for a time in Charleston, from which he went, in 1782, to Nova Scotia, where he abode for ten years, preaching to Baptist congregations at Shelburne, Birchtown, Ragged Island, and in St. John, New Brunswick. Because of the inhospitable climate, the Negro slaves who had escaped with their loyal masters crossing the Canadian border to these points in Nova Scotia, went in 1792 to Sierra Leone where they constituted themselves a colony, with David George the founder of their first Baptist Church. After peace was made in 1783, the Silver Bluff Church was revived under the direction of the Rev. Jesse Peter who, unlike George Liele in having departed with his master when the British evacuated Savannah in 1782, remained as a slave here in South Carolina to carry forward the work across the river from Augusta in South Carolina.

According to Dr. Walter H. Brooks, a portion of this Silver Bluff Church brought into Savannah, Georgia, at the time of the departure of certain Americans to join the British in 1778, took shape as an organized body under George Liele, who had been the servant of a British officer. It is highly probable that David George and Jesse Peter, who had served these people at Silver Bluff, did not have sufficient influence to secure a permit to preach to them in Savannah, although they did unite with the church there. Out of this effort of George Liele developed what Dr. Brooks considers the first Negro Baptist Church in the city of Savannah, which flourished during the British occupancy from 1779 to the year 1782. The oldest Negro Baptist Church in this country, however, was that of the Silver Bluff Church which, in another meeting place and under a new name, became established at Augusta, having existed from the year 1773 to 1793 before the time of Andrew Bryan's organizing efforts in Savannah.

The struggles of George Liele and Andrew Bryan throw additional light on these early efforts. George Liele was born in Virginia about the year 1750, but soon moved with his master, Henry Sharpe, to Burke County, Georgia, a few years before the Revolutionary War. As his master was a deacon of the Baptist church of which Matthew Moore was pastor, George, upon hearing this minister preach from time to time when accompanying his owner, became converted and soon thereafter was baptized by this clergyman. Not long thereafter upon discovering that he had unusual ministerial gifts, this church permitted him to preach upon the plantations along the Savannah river and sometimes to the congregation of the white church to which he belonged. As his master was much more liberal than most of his kind, Liele was permitted to extend his operations down the Savannah river as far as Brampton, Savannah, and Yamacraw, where he preached to the slaves.

His ministerial work became so important that his master finally liberated him that he might serve without interference; but his work was interrupted by the Revolutionary War, during which his master was killed. Upon the death of his master, moreover, some of the heirs to the estate, not being satisfied with the manumission of George Liele, had him thrown into prison, hoping to re-enslave him; but Colonel Kirkland, of the British Army, then in control of Savannah, came to his rescue by securing his release from prison. When the British evacuated that city, George Liele went with them to Jamaica, indenturing himself to Colonel Kirkland as a servant for the amount of money necessary to pay his transportation.[34] Before leaving Savannah, however, fortune brought it to pass that the vessel in which he embarked was detained for some weeks near Tybee Island, not far from the mouth of the Savannah River. While waiting there he came to the city of Savannah and baptized Andrew Bryan and his wife Hannah, Kate Hogg, and Hagar Simpson, who became the founders of the first African Baptist Church in Savannah.

When George Liele landed at Kingston he was, upon the recommendation of Colonel Kirkland to General Campbell, the Governor of Jamaica, employed to work out the money for which he had been indentured. Upon discharging the debt he obtained for himself and family a certificate of manumission and was free in 1784 to begin his work as a preacher. He preached first in a private home to a small congregation and then organized a church with four men who had emigrated from the American colonies. Delivering with power a message of such telling effect as the first dissenter to undertake the establishment of a liberal sect in the midst of communicants of the established church of England, he soon found his meetings interrupted and himself cruelly persecuted. Frequently memorialized for a grant of religious freedom, however, the Jamaica Assembly finally permitted George Liele to proceed with his work. Within a few years he had a following of about 500 communicants, and with the help of a number of inspired deacons and elders extended the work far into the rural districts. In addition to his ministerial work he administered the affairs of these various groups, taught a free school, and conducted a business at which he earned his living.

At first this work was largely inspirational, stirring up the people here and there; and many thought that it would be a movement of short duration: but becoming convinced that this was the real way of salvation and life, persons adhering to this new creed contributed sufficiently to its support to give it a standing in the community. Within a few years we hear of the purchase for a sum of nearly 155 pounds of about three acres of land at the east end of Kingston, on which they built a church. When success had crowned his efforts in Jamaica, he took steps toward the establishment of an edifice at Spanish Town, which was completed a few years later. The records show too that he interested in his cause some men of influence like Mr. Steven A. Cook, a member of the Jamaica Assembly, who solicited funds for him in England. Of him Mr. Cook bears this testimony: "He is a very industrious man, decent, humble in his manners, and, I think, a good man." Contemporaries speak of his family life as pleasant. He had a wife and four children, three boys and a girl. He was not a well educated man, but he found time to read some good literature.

The unusual tact of George Liele was the key to his success. He seemed to know how to handle men diplomatically, but some of his policy may be subject to criticism. Unlike so many Baptist and Methodist missionaries who came forward preaching freedom of body and mind and soul to all men and thereby stirring up the slaves in certain parts, George Liele would not receive any slaves who did not have permission of their owners, and instead of directing attention to their wrongs, conveyed to them the mere message of Christ. His influence among the masters and overseers became unusual, and the membership of his church rapidly increased. No literature was used and no instruction given until it had at first been shown to the members of the legislature, the magistrates, and the justices to secure their permission beforehand. One of the masters, speaking of the wholesome influence of Liele's preaching, said that he did not need to employ an assistant nor to make use of the whip whether he was at home or elsewhere, as his slaves were industrious and obedient, and lived together in unity, brotherly love, and peace.

The next pioneer preacher of worth among the Negroes was Andrew Bryan, George Liele's successor in Georgia. Andrew Bryan was born a slave in 1737 at Goose Creek, South Carolina, about sixteen miles from Charleston. He was later brought to Savannah, Georgia, where, as stated above, he came under the influence of the preaching of George Liele. He at first commenced by public exhortations and prayer meetings at Brampton. Nine months after the departure of George Liele, Bryan began to preach to congregations of black and white people at Savannah. Moved by his convincing message, his master and other whites encouraged him in his chosen field, inasmuch as the influence he had upon slaves was salutary. He was thereafter permitted to erect on the land of Mr. Edward Davis at Yamacraw a rough wooden building of which his group was soon artfully dispossessed. As his ministrations were opposed by others who did not like this simple faith, unusual persecution soon followed. Bryan's adherents were not permitted to hold frequent meetings, and in trying to evade this regulation by assembling in the swamps, they ran the risk of rigid discipline. With the aid of his brother Sampson, Andrew Bryan, however, gradually held this group together. At first it was small; but finally sufficiently large to receive the attention of the Rev. Thomas Burt in 1785, and that of the Rev. Abraham Marshall of Kioke in 1788. The latter then baptized forty-five additional members of this congregation, and on January 20, 1788, organized them as a church and ordained Andrew Bryan as a minister with full authority to preach the gospel and to administer the ordinances of the Baptist church.

This recognition of Bryan as a minister, however, did not solve all of his problems. The greater his influence among the slaves, the more the masters were inclined to believe that his work could result only in that of servile insurrection. It became more difficult, therefore, for slaves to attend his meetings; the patrols whipped them sometimes even when they had passes, and finally a large number of the members were arrested and severely punished. The culmination was that Andrew Bryan, their pastor himself, and his brother, Sampson Bryan, one of the first deacons, were "inhumanly cut and their backs were so lacerated that their blood ran down to the earth as they, with uplifted hands, cried unto the Lord; but Bryan, in the midst of his torture, declared that he rejoiced not only to be whipped but would freely suffer death for the cause of Jesus Christ." Accused of sinister plans, Andrew Bryan and his brother Sampson were, upon the complaint of their traducers, imprisoned and dispossessed of their meeting house. Lorenzo Dow, an eccentric itinerant preacher appearing in Savannah about this time, preached at Bryan's church to show not only his compassion for Bryan's waiting congregation, but his disapproval of the persecution to which this apostle was subjected.

Jonathan Bryan, the master of Andrew and Sampson, insisting that they were the victims of prejudice and wickedness, however, secured for them a hearing. They came before the Justices of the Inferior Court of Chatham County, Henry Osborne, James Haversham, and James Montague, who, finding no criminal intent in their efforts, ordered that they be released. They were then permitted by their master to resume worship in the barn on his plantation, but persecution followed them even there, where they were surrounded by spies and eavesdroppers. This continued until one of the eavesdroppers, upon listening to what was going on among these communicants at Andrew Bryan's private home, heard this man of God earnestly praying for the men who had so mercilessly used him. This enlisted so much sympathy among the people kindly disposed that the chief justice of the court, before whom they had been brought, granted them permission to continue their worship of God at any time between sunrise and sunset. They held meetings at Brampton about two years, during which they made a number of influential friends among the whites, who, along with the communicants of this group, assisted Bryan in raising funds to purchase a lot upon which to begin the erection of a church in 1794. The first African church stood for years on this lot on what is now known as Mill Street, running to Indian Street Lane in Savannah.

Andrew Bryan faced another crisis upon the death of Jonathan Bryan, his master. He succeeded, however, in emerging as a free man, the heirs of the estate having given him an opportunity to purchase his freedom for fifty pounds. Fortune prospered him thereafter to the extent that he soon bought in Yamacraw a lot on which he built a residence not far from the place of worship. Upon the final division of the Bryan estate it developed that the church building was still controlled by that family, but the worship of these communicants continued there under the supervision of the whites without serious interruption. The membership had then reached 700.

Bryan soon obtained a position of influence in spite of all of his difficulties, as is evidenced by his own testimony in addressing his coworker, Dr. Rippon, in 1800. He said: "With much pleasure inform you, dear sir, that I enjoy good health, and am strong in body, at the age of sixty-three years, and am blessed with a pious wife, whose freedom I have obtained, and an only daughter and child, who is married to a free man, though she, and consequently under our laws, her seven children, five sons and two daughters, are slaves. By a kind Providence I am well provided for, as to worldly comforts (though I have had very little given me as a minister), having a house and lot in this city, besides the land on which several buildings stand, for which I receive a small rent, and a fifty-acre tract of land, with all necessary buildings, four miles in the country, and eight slaves; for whose education and happiness I am enabled through mercy to provide."

As this congregation continued to increase, Andrew Bryan secured the services of his brother as an assistant pastor. He planned, moreover, to divide the church whenever the membership became too large for him to serve it efficiently. This was what led to the organization of the Second African Baptist Church of Savannah, with Henry Francis, a slave of Colonel Leroy Hamilton, as pastor. As the head of this congregation, Francis manifested power of remarkable leadership, and soon thereafter purchased his freedom to devote all of his time to his congregation. Bryan's church was further divided upon reaching the stage of having an unwieldy number, when there emerged from it the Third African Baptist Church. Bryan's church, moreover, became in the course of time the beacon light in the Negro religious life of Georgia. From this center went other workers into the inviting fields of that State, as to Augusta, where a flourishing Baptist church was established. This condition obtained until the Negro preacher became circumscribed during the thirties and forties by laws intended to prevent such disturbances as were caused by Nat Turner in Southampton County, Virginia. Andrew Bryan, however, did not live to see this. He passed away in 1812, respected by all who knew him and loved by his numerous followers. The position which he finally attained in the esteem and the respect of the community is well illustrated by the honor shown him by the following resolutions of the Savannah Baptist Association (white) on the occasion of his death: "The Association is sensibly affected by the death of the Rev. Andrew Bryan, a man of color, and pastor of the First Colored Church in Savannah. This son of Africa, after suffering inexpressible persecutions in the cause of his divine Master, was at length permitted to discharge the duties of the ministry among his colored friends in peace and quiet, hundreds of whom, through his instrumentality, were brought to a knowledge of the truth as 'it is in Jesus.' He closed his extensively useful and amazingly luminous course in the lively exercise of faith and in the joyful hope of a happy immortality."

In those parts of the South where the pro-slavery sentiment was not developed so early as in Georgia, the Baptists were able to give their Negro communicants more consideration. After this denomination had won toleration in Virginia, its leaders experienced much less difficulty in proselyting Negroes than in the case of other communicants. From 1770 to 1790 Negro preachers, thanks to the pioneer work of a man of color, Rev. Mr. Moses, were in charge of congregations in Charles City, Petersburg, Williamsburg, and Allen's Creek, in Lunenburg County. In 1801 Gowan Pamphlet of that State was the pastor of a progressive Baptist church in Williamsburg, some members of which could read, write and keep accounts. William Lemon was about this time chosen by a white congregation to serve at the Pettsworth or Gloucester church in that State.

In Portsmouth, Virginia, a Negro Baptist preacher attained unusual distinction. There the blacks and whites belonging to the same Baptist church experienced very little difficulty in their acceptance of each other on the basis of religious equality. They were constituted a church by the Association held in Isle of Wight County in 1789, and after the service of a number of pioneer ministers the church called one Thomas Armistead. The church fell into bad hands a few years thereafter and suffered a decline under one Frost, a Baptist preacher, who in the propagation of the doctrines of free will caused unusual excitement. This did not subside until he, according to the contemporaries, was stricken by the hand of God. While looking out for another pastor there came to this community, in 1795, from Northampton County, a black preacher whose name was Josiah Bishop. He preached with such fervor and with such success that the whites as well as the blacks hung, as it were, upon his words. He easily rallied the scattered forces of the church, revived their spirits, and lifted high the banner of the gospel. So impressed was the congregation with his work that the church gave Josiah Bishop the money with which to purchase his freedom and soon thereafter bought his wife and his eldest son.

It is said that his preaching was much admired by both saints and sinners wherever he went. "As a stranger," say Lemuel Burkett and Jesse Reed in their *Concise History of the Kehukee Baptist Association*, "few received equal degree of liberality with him." They were, therefore, advised, "that whereas the black brethren in the church seemed anxious for a vote in the conference that it would be best to consider the black people as a wing of the body, and Josiah Bishop to take over sight of them, as this church, at that time, fellowshipped a number of Negroes. The black people at first seemed pleased with the proposition, but soon repented and came and told the deacons they were afraid that matters might turn up disagreeable to them and dishonoring to God, and said that they would be subordinate to the white brethren, if they would let them continue as they were, which was consented to." Josiah Bishop, of course, could not long remain as the pastor of a mixed church in the slaveholding colony of Virginia. After toiling successfully for a short period in that city, he moved to Baltimore, where he helped to promote the cause of the rising Baptists in that city. When his work was well done there, he moved to the city of New York, where during 1810 and 1811 he served as the pastor of the Abyssinian Baptist Church.

Pioneering in this same field in 1792 was the famous "Uncle Jack," a full-blooded African, recognized by the whites as a forceful preacher of the gospel in the Baptist Church. For some years he preached from plantation to plantation, moving so many to repentance that the white citizens in appreciation of his worth had him licensed to preach and raised a fund with which they purchased his freedom. They bought him a small farm in Virginia, where for more than 40 years he continued his ministry as an instrument in the conversion of a large number of white people.

Contemporaneous with Uncle Jack was Henry Evans, a free Negro of Virginia. On his way to Charleston, South Carolina, to work at the trade of shoemaking, Evans happened to stop at Fayetteville, North Carolina. Having been licensed as a local preacher in the Methodist Church, he tarried there to work among the people, whose deplorable condition excited his sympathy. At first he worked at his trade and preached on Sunday. The town council, feeling that he was a public danger, ordered him to refrain from preaching. Whereupon he began to hold secret meetings. His preaching became so effective, however, and so many white persons attended his meetings, that the official opposition yielded sufficiently to have a regular Methodist Church organized there in 1790. The edifice was so constructed as to provide quarters for Evans, who remained there until his death in 1810, although a white minister was in actual charge of the church.

From the Methodists there emerged another such preacher, Black Harry, who, accompanying Mr. Asbury, learned from him to preach more forcefully than Asbury himself. According to a contemporary, Harry was "small, very black, keen-eyed, possessing great volubility of tongue; and, although illiterate so that he could not read," was one of the most popular preachers of that age. Upon hearing Harry preach, Dr. Benjamin Rush pronounced him the greatest orator in America. Desiring Harry to accompany him in 1782, Bishop Asbury made the request, saying that the way to have a very large congregation was to give out that Harry was to preach, as more would come to hear Harry than to hear Bishop Asbury. On one occasion in Wilmington, Delaware, where the cause of the Methodist was unpopular, a large number of persons came out of curiosity to hear Bishop Asbury. But, as the auditorium was already taxed to its fullest capacity, they could only hear from the outside. At the conclusion of the exercises, they said, without having seen the speaker: "If all Methodist preachers can preach like the Bishop, we should like to be constant hearers." Someone present replied: "That was not the Bishop, but the Bishop's servant that you heard." This, to be sure, had the desired effect, for these inquirers concluded: "If such be the servant, what must the master be?" "The truth was," says John Ledman in his *History of the rise of Methodism in America*, "that Harry was a more popular speaker than Mr. Asbury or almost anyone else in his day." In this same capacity Harry accompanied and preached with not only Mr. Asbury but with Garretson, Watcote, and Dr. Coke.

"After he had moved on the tide of popularity for a number of years," says John Ledman, "he fell by wine, one of the strong enemies of both ministers and people. And now, alas! this popular preacher was a drunken rag picker in the streets of Philadelphia. But we will not leave him here. One evening Harry started down the Neck, below Southwark, determined to remain there until his backslidings were healed. Under a tree he wrestled with God in prayer. Sometime that night God restored to him the joys of his salvation. From this time Harry continued faithful; though he could not stand before the people with that pleasing confidence as a public speaker that he had before his fall. About the year 1810 Harry finished his course; and, it is believed, made a good end. An unusually large number of people, both white and colored, followed his body to its last resting place, in a free burying ground in Kensington."

Among the pioneer Negro preachers one of the most interesting was John Stewart. He was born of free parents in Powhatan County, Virginia, where he received some religious training and attended a school during the winter, thus securing to him so much mental development by the time of reaching maturity that he could make a living much more easily than some of his fellows. This early training, however, did not seem to restrain him from certain temptations of this life; for, in going away from home to make his career, he fell a victim to bad habits, becoming a dissolute drunkard, drifting here and there. Finally he came to Marietta, Ohio, where under the influence of the gospel as it was preached among his lowly people in that center, he was converted and united with the Methodist Episcopal Church. He then became a man of very regular habits and devoted much of his time to meditation and prayer. On a certain occasion he said, "I heard a voice like a woman's singing and praising the Lord, while straight from the northern sky, which was filled with a great radiance, came a man's voice, saying, 'You must declare my counsel faithfully,' and I found myself standing on my feet speaking as to a congregation." He felt that this was a call to preach, but at first resisted the influence, hoping to escape therefrom. Having fallen sick not long thereafter, however, he looked upon this as a punishment and responded to the voices that he heard, overcoming his fears. Having his mind thoroughly made up, he set off then to preach the gospel, steering, as he said, "my course sometimes by the road, sometimes through the cities, until I came to Goshen, where I found the Delaware Indians."

He preached and sang among these people for a short period, and finally returned to Marietta. He was again summoned by the voices in the night impelling him to make another pilgrimage. This time he drifted into a settlement of whites, to whom he preached with much success, moving many of them to repentance and organizing them as a church. He then proceeded to Upper Sandusky, the home of the Wyandot Indians, who, having never received the gospel, although the Roman Catholics had unsuccessfully tried to evangelize them, had fallen back into a worse state of heathenism and especially drunkenness, resulting from the vices imported by traders. Here he had the opposition of William Walker, the government agent, who did not take well to his message, but on being converted very soon thereafter, Walker gave Stewart less trouble in reaching the Indians. Another great hindrance, however, was the coming of the other white traders, who prospered by the liquor traffic that they carried on with these Indians. At first they tried to show that Stewart was not properly authorized as a minister and should be denied the right to preach; but having then the support of William Walker, the zealous missionary succeeded in delivering his message. Some of the Indians, too, felt that the gospel which he preached was not intended for the Indians but for the white man, although Stewart endeavored to show that this boon was for all nations and for all people. He persisted in holding his position, and in the end success crowned his efforts in bringing about the conversion of all of the prominent chiefs of this group.

It is said that because of this success his enemies contrived to discourage him. They prepared for an unusually great celebration in accordance with the festive ideas of the Indians, trying to bring them back to their old habits. Becoming discouraged, John Stewart preached his farewell sermon and returned to Marietta. But he came back to Upper Sandusky after an absence of a few months and devoted the rest of his life to work among the Wyandot Indians. Fortunately be was then filled with enthusiasm and the word which he preached did not return void. As his mission was then a success, he appealed for help to the higher conference, then meeting at Urbana, in March, 1817. J. B. Finley was chosen to work in this field. Stewart had planned for a thorough elevation of these people, including industrial training, which centered around the erection of a sawmill and the purchase of a farm upon which he taught agriculture. A log structure was soon built for school purposes, and there soon followed Miss Harriet Stubbs, who volunteered to teach the Indians. Subsequent reports show that the work was in good condition in 1822. The religion of Jesus Christ was flourishing and everywhere the Indians were living upright lives. At this time, however, Stewart's health had failed him, as he had well run his course, having been exposed to all sorts of hardships. He passed away on the 17th of December, his hand in that of his wife. His last words, addressed to the sorrowing people about his bed, were: "Oh, be faithful."

Lemuel Haynes, another pioneer preacher, was born July 18, 1753, at West Hartford, Connecticut. His father was a man of unmingled African extraction and his mother a white woman of respectable New England ancestry. As he was a natural son, the mother abandoned him in infancy, but he fortunately found asylum at the home of one Haynes, whose name he took and with whom he lived until at the age of five months, when he was bound out to David Rose of Granville, Massachusetts, where Lemuel grew to manhood.

Lemuel was given the rudimentary training in the backwoods schools of the community, in which he learned to read and write. These meager advantages led him to seek an extension of his knowledge through the reading of good books. As these were scarce, he had to be content with the Bible, the Psalter, the writings of Watts and Doddridge, and Young's *Night Thoughts*. Before his education could be completed, however, Lemuel, having been prostrated with grief because of the loss of the wife of his kind master, entered the continental army, first as a minute man in 1774 and then as a regular soldier after the battle of Lexington.

Returning from the war, Lemuel engaged in agriculture; but he had early been given a pious trend and soon decided to study theology in anticipation of the designs of Providence concerning him. For some time he had been accustomed to read the Bible and sermons of others on the occasions of conducting family prayers in the home of David Rose. From this exercise he mustered sufficient courage to read one of his own sermons, and finally to preach before the local congregations, which marveled at the power of his words. To prepare himself thoroughly to preach, Haynes once planned to attend Dartmouth College, but shrank from it. After studying privately under Daniel Farrand of Canaan, Connecticut, and William Bradford of Wintonbury, Haynes spent a short period teaching a school for whites. He was licensed to preach in the Congregational Church in 1780 and was ordained soon thereafter, beginning his ministry at Middle Granville, where he labored five years. Here Bessie Babbit, a white woman of considerable education and piety, offered him her heart and they were married in 1783.

From this small charge Haynes was called to Torrington, Connecticut. A leading citizen was much displeased that the church should have a "nigger minister," and to show his lack of respect for the new incumbent this man went into the church and sat with his hat on. "He had not preached far," said the man, "when I thought I saw the whitest man I ever knew in that pulpit, and I tossed my hat under the pew." Haynes was then called to take charge of the Congregational Church in West Rutland. Here his usefulness was appreciated and his efforts were extended to other towns through his revivals, one of the most successful of which he conducted in Pittsfield. Having developed such power, he was employed, in 1804, by the Connecticut Missionary Society to labor in the destitute sections of Vermont. In 1809 he was appointed to a similar service by the Vermont Missionary Society. In 1814 he preached extensively in Connecticut, appearing before crowded houses, having in his audience on one occasion President Dwight of Yale.

With such standing in the church Haynes was expected to manifest interest in the great questions at issue in New England. One of these was the Stoddardian principle of admitting moral persons without credible evidences of grace, to the Lord's Supper, and the half-way covenant by which parents though not admitted to the Lord's Supper were encouraged to offer their children in baptism. In this debate Haynes, with his eloquence and logic, vanquished the famous Hosea Ballou by his powerful sermon based on the text *Ye shall not surely die*. There was also a difference of opinion with respect to the operations of the Holy Spirit, but Haynes stood with Edwards and Whitefield. Being thus active in dispelling clouds of doubt, he brought many back to a more righteous conduct.

Becoming involved in the partisan strife which characterized the rise of political parties after Washington's inauguration, Haynes alienated the affections of some of his communicants by his bold advocacy of the principle conducive to a strong national government as administered in the beginning by George Washington, whose policies Haynes admired. He then left West Rutland and preached a while in Manchester, Vermont, until 1822, when he accepted a call to Granville, New York. There he spent usefully the last eleven years of his life.

In spite of the fact that Lemuel Haynes was working altogether among white people, however, he was successful wherever he was stationed. His eloquence and Christian nobility won him much attention. "He always showed himself a man of a feeling heart, sensibly affected by human suffering," says Cooley, his biographer. "At home he was industrious, his family government was parental. He was the embodiment of piety and honesty." Churches and associations were strengthened by his labors. Their membership increased and the influence of the gospel was extended. So lived and died one of the noblest of the New England Congregational ministers of a century ago. Of illegitimate birth, and of no advantageous circumstances of family, rank or station, he became one of the choicest instruments of Christ. His face betrayed his race and blood, and his life revealed his Lord.

There served as a pioneer worker for the Presbyterians John Gloucester, who founded the first African Presbyterian Church in Philadelphia in 1807. According to Gillett's *History of the Presbyterian Church in the United States*, this church owed its existence, and for many years its continued support, largely to the "Evangelical Society of Philadelphia," organized upon the recommendation and influence of Dr. Alexander. "Its first pastor, although never installed," says Gillett, "was John Gloucester, a slave of Dr. Blackburn of Tennessee. He had attracted the attention of the latter, under whose preaching he was converted, by his piety and natural gifts, and by him was purchased, and encouraged to study with a view to the ministry. After having been licensed and ordained by the Union Presbytery, he was, in 1818, received from that body by the Philadelphia Presbytery, and, under the patronage of the 'Evangelical Society,' continued in charge of the African Church until his death in 1822. The house of worship, located on the corner of Shippen and Seventh Streets, was completed in 1811."

"Mr. Gloucester first commenced his missionary efforts by preaching in private houses," continues Gillett, "but these were soon found insufficient to accommodate his congregations. A schoolhouse was procured near the site of the future edifice; but in clear weather he preached in the open air. Possessed of a strong and musical voice, he would take his stand on the corner of Shippen and Seventh Streets, and while singing a hymn would gather around him many besides his regular hearers, and hold their attention till he was prepared to commence his exercises. Possessed of a stout, athletic frame, and characterized by prudence, forbearance, and a fervent piety, he labored with unremitting zeal, securing the confidence and respect of his brethren of the Presbytery, and building up the congregation which he had gathered. His freedom was granted him by Dr. Blackburn, and by his own application he secured the means in England and this country to purchase his family. He is said to have been a man of strong mind, mighty of prayer, and of such fervor and energy in wrestling supplication that persons sometimes fell under his power, convicted of sin."

To this class of Negro preachers in the South belongs John Chavis, mentioned in another connection below. Chavis was a full-blooded Negro of dark brown color, born probably near Oxford, Granville County, North Carolina, about 1763. From a youth he impressed the public as a man of unusual power and was, therefore, sent by his friends to Princeton to see if a Negro could take a collegiate education. Some have said that he was never a regularly enrolled student at Princeton. The records, however, show that he was under the direction of Dr. Witherspoon, who was soon convinced that the experiment "would issue favorably." In keeping with the course of study of that time, he was chiefly interested in the classics. In these fields he easily took rank as a good Latin and a fair Greek scholar. Exactly how much work he did in the field of theology is not known, but as the line drawn between theology and classical studies at that time was not very definite, he could easily lay a foundation for work in the ministry, and especially so if his instruction were under the direction of one man, who would shape his course of study in keeping with his practical needs rather than in conformity with the formal training of the school.

Whether Chavis was sent to Princeton to make a minister of him or not, however, he very soon bestirred himself in that direction. From Princeton he went to Lexington, Virginia, to preach. In the records of the Presbyterians for 1801, Chavis is referred to as "a black man of prudence and piety." "For his better direction in the discharge of duties which are attended with many circumstances of delicacy and difficulty" some prudential instructions were issued to him by the General Assembly, "governing himself by which the knowledge of religion among the Negroes might be made more and more to strengthen the order of the society." The annals of the year 1801 report him in the service of the Hanover Presbytery as a "riding missionary under the direction of the General Assembly." He was very soon stationed in Lexington as a recognized preacher of official status working among his own people. In 1805, however, he returned to his native State, where as a result of the close relations existing between the whites and blacks and his power as an expounder of the gospel, he preached to large congregations of both races.

Referring to his career, Paul C. Cameron, a son of Judge Duncan of North Carolina, said: "In my boyhood life at my father's home I often saw John Chavis, a venerable old Negro man, recognized as a freeman and as a preacher or clergyman of the Presbyterian Church. As such he was received by my father and treated with kindness and consideration, and respected as a man of education, good sense and most estimable character." Mr. George Wortham, a lawyer of Granville County, said: "I have heard him read and explain the Scriptures to my father's family repeatedly. His English was remarkably pure, containing no 'Negroisms'; his manner was impressive, his explanations clear and concise, and his views, as I then thought and still think, entirely orthodox. He was said to have been an acceptable preacher, his sermons abounding in strong common sense views and happy illustrations, without any effort at oratory or sensational appeals to the passions of his hearers."

In North Carolina the disastrous result of the reaction against the Negroes handicapped Chavis in his work. As a result of the fear of servile insurrection among the slaves after Nat Turner's uprising, the exercise of the gift of preaching was prohibited to Negroes in North Carolina. Chavis thereafter devoted himself to teaching, maintaining classical schools for white persons in Granville, Wake, and Chatham counties. He was patronized by the most aristocratic white people of that State. In the end he counted among his former students W. P. Mangum, afterward United States Senator; P. H. Mangum, his brother; Archibald and John Henderson, sons of Chief Justice Henderson; Charles Manly, later Governor of that commonwealth, and Dr. James L. Wortham of Oxford, North Carolina.

CHAPTER IV

THE INDEPENDENT CHURCH MOVEMENT

THE FACTS SET forth above easily lead to the conclusion that the rise of the Negroes in the church was impeded by connection with their self-styled superiors. At first the whites had seriously objected to the evangelization of the Negroes, feeling that they could not be saved and, when the latter had been convinced of this error, many of them were far from the position of conceding to the blacks equality in their church organizations. Negroes in certain parts, however, were at first accepted in the congregations with the whites and accorded equal privileges. During the American Revolution when there was a tendency to give more consideration to all persons suffering from restriction, this freedom was enlarged. After the reaction following the American Revolution when men ceased to think so much of individual or natural rights and thought more frequently of means and measures for centralized government, the Negroes, like most elements far down, were forgotten or ignored even by the church. In this atmosphere of superimposed religious instruction the Negro was called upon merely to heed the Word and live. Experience soon taught, however, that it is difficult for a people to maintain interest in a cause with the management of which they have nothing to do.

Having enjoyed for some time the boon of freedom in the church, moreover, the Negroes were loath to give up this liberty. The escape of a young Negro, a slave of Thomas Jones, in Baltimore County in 1793 is a case in evidence. Accounting for his flight his master said: "He was raised in a family of religious persons commonly called Methodists and has lived with some of them for years past on terms of perfect equality; the refusal to continue him on these terms gave him offense and he, therefore, absconded. He had been accustomed to instruct and exhort his fellow creatures of all colors in matters of religious duty." Another such Negro, named Jacob, ran away from Thomas Gibbs of that same State in 1800, hoping to enlarge his liberty as a Methodist minister; for his master said in advertising him as a runaway: "He professed to be a Methodist and has been in the practice of preaching [at] nights." Still another Negro preacher of this type, named Richard, ran away from Hugh Drummond in Anne, Arundel County, that same year, while another called Simboe escaped a little later from Henry Lockey of Newbern, North Carolina.

This was the beginning of something more significant. The free Negroes in the North began to assert themselves after the manumissions incident to the American Revolution, as they were not necessarily obligated to follow the fortunes of the white churches. Such self-assertion early culminated in the protest of Richard Allen, the founder of the African Methodist Episcopal Church. Richard Allen was the very sort of man to perform this great task. He was born a slave of Benjamin Chew of Philadelphia but very soon thereafter was sold with his whole family to a planter living near Dover, Delaware, where he grew to manhood. Coming under Christian influence, he was converted in 1777 and began his career as a minister three years later. Struck with the genuineness of his piety, his master permitted him to conduct prayers and to preach in his house, he himself being one of the first converts of this zealous messenger of God. Feeling after his conversion that slavery was wrong, Allen's master permitted his bondmen to obtain their freedom. Allen and his brother purchased themselves for $2,000 in the depreciated currency of the Revolutionary War.

Richard Allen then engaged himself at such menial labor as a Negro could then find, cutting wood and hauling, while preaching at his leisure. Recognizing his unusual talent, Richard Watcoat on the Baltimore circuit permitted Allen to travel with him, and Bishop Asbury frequently gave him assignments to preach. Coming to Philadelphia in 1786, Allen was invited to preach at the St. George Methodist Episcopal Church and at various other places in the city. His difficulties, however, had just begun. Yet he could not but succeed because he was a man of independent character, strict integrity, business tact, and thrifty habits. When he spoke a word, it was taken at its face value. His rule was never to break a promise or violate a contract.[35]

The special needs of his own people aroused him to action in their behalf. He said, "I soon saw a large field open in seeking and instructing my African brethren who have been a long forgotten people, and few of them attended public worship." Starting a prayer meeting in Philadelphia, he soon had 42 members. Encouraged thus, he proposed to establish a separate place of worship for the people of color, but was dissuaded therefrom by the protest of the whites and certain Negroes unto whom he ministered, only three of whom approved his plan. Preaching at this church, however, with such power as to move his own people in a way that they had never been affected before, he attracted them in such large numbers that the management proposed to segregate the Negroes. When, moreover, the management of the church undertook to carry out this plan so drastically even to the extent of disturbing Richard Allen, Absalom Jones, and William White by pulling them off their knees while they were in the attitude of prayer, the Negroes arose and withdrew from the church in a body.

This was the beginning of the independent Free African Society organized by Richard Allen and Absalom Jones. It appeared that Jones and Allen soon had differing plans; for the former finally organized the African Protestant Episcopal Church of St. Thomas, while the majority of the persons seceding from the St. George Methodist Episcopal Church followed the standard of Allen in effecting the independent organization known as

Bethel Church. Allen purchased an old building for the Bethel church and had it duly dedicated in 1794, when he organized a Sunday school and a day and night school, to which were sent regular ministers by the Methodist Conference. Richard Allen was ordained deacon by Bishop Asbury in 1799, and later attained the status of elder. Negroes of other cities followed this example, organizing what were known as African Methodist Episcopal churches in Baltimore; Wilmington; Attleboro, Pennsylvania; and Salem, New Jersey.

Having maintained themselves independently for some time, these African societies developed sufficient leaders to effect the organization of a national church. In Philadelphia there were in cooperation with Richard Allen such workers as Jacob Tapsico, Clayton Durham, James Champion, and Thomas Webster. In Baltimore there were Daniel Coker, Richard Williams, Henry Harding, Stephen Hall, Edward Williamson and Nicholson Gilliard; in Wilmington, Delaware, Peter Spencer, the popular leader of the Union Church of Africans, established in 1813; in Attleboro, Pennsylvania, Jacob Marsh, Edward Jackson and William Anderson; and in Salem, New Jersey, Peter Cuff. These met in Philadelphia on the 9th day of April, 1816, to establish the African Methodist Episcopal Church, the moving spirits being Richard Allen, Daniel Coker and Stephen Hall, an intelligent layman of Baltimore, Maryland. Equally interested in the same movement were Morris Brown, Henry Drayton, Charles Corr, Amos Cruickshanks, Marcus Brown, Smart Simpson, Henry Bull, John Matthews, James Eden, London Turpin and Alexander Harper of Charleston, who could not attend because of the restrictions there upon the travel of Negroes and the effort in the South to proscribe the independent church movement among persons of color.

The most important transaction of the Philadelphia meeting was the election of the bishop. Upon taking the vote the body declared Daniel Coker bishop-elect; but for several reasons he resigned the next day in favor of Richard Allen, who was elected on the 10th and consecrated the following day by regularly ordained ministers. The conference resolved, moreover, that the people of Philadelphia, Baltimore, and all other places, who might unite with them should become one body under the name of the African Methodist Episcopal Church. Hoping that this national church might have accessions from other ranks in which the Negroes were not welcome or at best tolerated, this conference passed a resolution to the effect that ministers coming from another evangelical church should be received in the same standing which they held in the connection from which they came. This body adopted a book of discipline with its articles of religion and general rules just as it had been drafted by the Wesleyans, following the general principles of government as had been in vogue among the Methodists already. The church then began its career with seven itinerants and Bishop Allen as the exponents of a new thought.

Much progress thereafter was noted. The Baltimore district under the direction of Daniel Coker reported 1,066 members in 1818, 1,388 in 1819, 1,760 in 1820, and 1,924 in 1822, while there were in Philadelphia about 4,000. With the establishment of the New York conference the limits of the connection extended eastward as far as New Bedford, westward to Pittsburgh and southward to Charleston, South Carolina. Thereafter, however, there was little hope of success in the South. The African Methodists had with some difficulty under the leadership of Rev. Morris Brown established in Charleston a church reporting 1,000 members in 1817, and increasing by 1822 to 3,000 in spite of the intolerant laws and the police regulations making it difficult for slaves and free persons of color to attend. In 1822, however, because of the spirit of insurrection among Negroes following the fortunes of Denmark Vesey, who devised well laid plans for killing off the masters of the slaves, the African Methodists were required to suspend operation. Their pastor, Morris Brown, was threatened and would have been dealt with foully, had it not been for the interference of General James Hamilton, who secreted Brown in his home until he could give him safe passage to the North, where he very soon reached a position of prominence, even that of bishop in the African Methodist Episcopal Church.

Another secession of the Methodists from the white connection was in progress in other parts. A number of Negroes, most of whom were members of the John Street Methodist Episcopal Church, in New York City, took the first step toward separation from that connection in 1796. They had not been disturbed in their worship to the extent experienced by Richard Allen and his coworkers in Philadelphia, but they had a "desire for the privilege of holding meetings of their own, where they might have an opportunity to exercise their spiritual gifts among themselves, and thereby be more useful to one another." Such permission was obtained from Bishop Francis Asbury by a group of intelligent Negro Methodists, chief among whom were Francis Jacobs, William Brown, Peter Williams, Abraham Thompson, June Scott, Samuel Pontier, Thomas Miller, William Miller, James Varick and William Hamilton. Three of these persons, Abraham Thompson, June Scott, and Thomas Miller, were at that time recognized preachers, and William Miller was an exhorter, all of them officiating in this capacity as opportunities presented themselves in their connection and under the supervision of the white Methodists.

These workers continued in this situation until the year 1799, when, with a further increase in the Negro membership of the Methodist Episcopal Church in New York City, they proposed to build a separate house of worship rather than merely hold separate meetings in the edifice belonging to the white Methodists. A meeting was held soon thereafter and arrangements were made for the purchase of a lot in Orange Street, between Cross and Chatham, on which after having paid the amount of $50, they found out that the title was involved and they thereafter purchased a site situated at the corner of Church and Leonard Streets and fronting on Church Street. Upon this site they erected a building in the year 1800, naming the edifice the African Methodist Episcopal Zion Church. Their white friends, seeing that they were determined to be a separate body, appointed as their adviser Rev. John McClaskey, who instructed them how to proceed in drawing up the articles of government. A charter was secured in 1801 and bears the signatures of Peter Williams and Francis Jacobs.

This church had not proceeded very far before there arose some dissension in the ranks. The first exhibition of this was the effort of two of the founders, Abraham Thompson and June Scott, who, "induced by the expectation of filthy lucre," tried to form a society separate from the Zion church. In this they were aided by a white man who desired to exercise his own spiritual gifts, the opportunity for which he could not secure among his own people who belonged to the *Society of Friends*, from which he had been expelled. This new organization was finally effected as the Union Society. Very soon thereafter Abraham Thompson repented of his action and abandoned the attempt, leaving June Scott to continue the work of the *Union Society* by himself. As he was unable to bear the expenses thereafter the society was consequently broken up and June Scott attached himself to another church.

Another obstacle appeared in 1813 when Thomas Simpkins, upon being expelled from the Zion Church, of which he had been a member and a trustee, undertook to establish a new society. He drew to himself William Miller, who had been ordained deacon in the Zion Church. Obtaining thereafter a site in Elizabeth Street, they succeeded in persuading a number of members of the Zion Church to unite with them to establish the Asbury Church. Unlike the unsuccessful attempt of Abraham Thompson and June Scott in forming the Union Society, the Asbury Church became permanently established. Desiring, however, to be regular in their operations, the members of the Asbury Church found themselves compelled to appeal to the same ecclesiastical authorities and to accept practically the same government as that already instituted for the Zion Church. This church was thereafter received in the Methodist Church. Although this was considered a very bad omen for the Zion Church, however, it continued to make progress in spite of expectations to the contrary. The members of the church decidedly increased and steps were taken for the construction of a house with a school room underneath on the site of the old meeting house. On the 25th of November there began the construction of a more suitable building which was completed by 1820.

Another disturbing factor appeared in the scheme of William Lambert. He had been a member of the Zion Church and seceded with those who formed the Asbury connection. Because the Zion Church refused to appoint him as a minister, and even Asbury refused to hear him preach, he returned from Philadelphia where he had been under the influence of Bishop Richard Allen, from whom he had obtained a license to preach, and endeavored to establish a church for Bishop Allen's denomination. He obtained a school house in Mott Street, and with the assistance of Rev. Mr. White, a member and an ordained deacon, it was fitted for a church. In the meantime Bishop Allen was in touch with some of the official brethren in New York City with a view to extending the jurisdiction of his own church. The supporters of Bishop Allen, moreover, appeared at the opportune moment when the Zionites were without a building and were also without the direction that it had formerly had from the white Methodists, inasmuch as the latter were disturbed by a schism resulting from differences as to church government.

Further disturbance was, therefore, caused when Henry Harden entered the city of New York in 1820 and commenced to form a society of African Methodists with the assistance of William Lambert and Rev. Mr. White. The Zionists bearing it rather grievously that Bishop Allen had thus tried to invade that field, decided that they would neither preach for the Allenites nor permit the Allenites to preach for them. In this resolution, William Miller, the minister of the Asbury Church, acquiesced and seemingly agreed thereby to connect himself closely with the Zionites. The church of Richard Allen's connection, however, did not displease all the persons concerned. According to the account of Christopher Rush, who himself became a bishop of the African Methodist Episcopal Zion Church, although Richard Allen arrived and sanctioned all that had been done by those men who were working for the progress of his denomination, "his presence seemed soon to alter the minds of the Zion preachers, for notwithstanding their resolution to discountenance the proceedings of the Bishop, yet some of them went to their meetings, some of them sat in their altar, and one of them, James Varick, opened meeting for the Bishop on the second or third Sunday night of the existence of that society."

During the first years of their separation the African Methodists in New York had the cooperation of the whites and the funds necessary for the construction of their building and the maintenance of their ministers came from that source. In the course of time, however, the funds contributed by the people of color themselves increased with this growing desire for independence. The schism in the white church, moreover, stimulated this desire for thorough separation from the white Methodists inasmuch as their so-called superiors were divided in their views as to questions of polity. These Methodists of color believed that they should avail themselves of the opportunity to control their own affairs. They had at first had for pastors white Methodist preachers with the local preachers of color serving under them. They thereupon notified the white Methodists that they no longer felt themselves obligated to look to them for supplying the pulpit and that they did not desire to have their property involved in the difficulties contemplated by the proposed act of incorporation which had led to the schism. The Zionites were in a state of indecision, however, for the reason that not having left the white Methodist Church in a snarl as did the followers of Richard Allen, the Zionites had no particular grievance to serve as a cohesive force. Many had thought either of returning to the white Methodists or joining the Allenites.

There soon came a time then when it was necessary for the Zionites to decide exactly what they would do. This being the case, an official meeting was held on August 11, 1820, for the purpose of considering the serious state of the church. Two important questions were propounded at this meeting, one being: "Shall we return to the white people?" The answer was negative. The next question was: "Shall we join Bishop Allen?" The answer was also negative. They, therefore, decided to take steps for establishing a firm church government of their own. Several efforts have since been made to unite the African Methodists but to no avail.

Being desirous, however, to proceed regularly rather than radically, these African Methodists sought ordination and consecration through some branch of the Christian Church. They sent a committee to make such a request of Bishop Hobart of the Episcopal Church, but he was unable to serve them. They then appealed to the bishop of the Methodist Church, but they were put off in one way or another, with excuses of the bishop having no power to act without the conference and with the request that they should defer action until the conference should have time to investigate. They thereafter appealed to the conference in session in Philadelphia and were encouraged by a favorable resolution to expect that such service would be rendered them. For some reason they appealed to the conference in New York, which finally refused to grant their request. The Zionites were then reduced to radical measures in that they had finally to follow in the footsteps of the Asbury Church in ordaining its own deacons and elder.

Becoming thus aggressive, the Zionites, like the Allenites, had taken the offensive. They extended their operations through missionaries into Flushing, New Haven, Long Island, and even into Philadelphia, where certain persons separating from the connection of Richard Allen, organized the Wesleyan Church and joined the Zionites. Under the leadership of such men as James Varick, George Collins, Charles Anderson, and Christopher Rush, they drew up the doctrines and discipline of the African Methodist Episcopal Church in America, elected a number of elders, and finally organized in 1821 a national body, of which James Varick became the first bishop in 1822.

Before the Negro Methodists perfected their organizations by which the influence of their churches might be permanently extended throughout the country, the Baptists had been locally trying to do the same thing. The Harrison Street Baptist Church was organized at Petersburg, Virginia, in 1776; another Negro Baptist Church at Williamsburg, Virginia, in 1785; the First African Baptist Church at Savannah in 1785, with a second Baptist Church in that city following fourteen years later; the African Baptist Church of Lexington, Kentucky, in 1790; and a mixed Baptist Church in the Mound Bayou, Mississippi district, in 1805, by Joseph Willis, a free Negro born in South Carolina in 1762.[36]

In the city of Philadelphia on May 14, 1809, thirteen colored members who had for some time felt that it would be more congenial for them to worship separately were dismissed to form the first African Baptist Church. On June 19, 1809, the use of the First Baptist Church (white) was given them for the meeting at which they were constituted an organized body. The main trouble with the First Baptist Church (white) seemed to be that it had suffered from having its anti-slavery ardor dampened during the reaction following the Revolutionary War. Whereas many of the Baptists in other parts had become radical emancipationists, the white Baptists of Philadelphia after having attacked the slave trade, tried to dodge the antislavery issue with the excuse that it was a political question with which the church had nothing to do. The anti-slavery sentiment was naturally suppressed during the pastorates of Holcombe, Brantly and Cuthbert, all southern men, partly in defense of their well-known sentiment and partly through the sentiment of the people themselves.

Complete separation of the Negro Baptists in this church was, therefore, deemed a necessity during the first quarter of the nineteenth century when there was an increasing prejudice against free persons of color because of the rapid migration of freedmen from the South to Pennsylvania.

When in 1809 the Negroes organized the African Baptist Church in Philadelphia, it was placed under the oversight of Rev. Henry Cunningham, and was directed for two years thereafter by John King. According to another record there was at this time in the South a slave named Burrows who felt that he was called to preach. Many encouraged him to come North to beg money to buy his freedom. Two of his friends, free persons of color, were so impressed with his worth and believed so implicitly in his word as his bond that they bound themselves in bondage for six months while he absented himself to solicit funds throughout the North. In a short time this man of such indomitable will and belief in himself and in the future, raised the required sum of money with which he effected his manumission and invited these loyal friends who had been instrumental in his liberation to come North to Philadelphia to assist him in establishing a Baptist church. This was the First African Baptist Church of Philadelphia, which, in 1809, became one of the substantial religious organizations of the city, having enjoyed the services of useful and influential preachers, four of whose long pastorates covered the whole period of one hundred years.

When the African Baptist Church of Philadelphia was being organized, the same movement was culminating likewise in Boston. Prior to 1809 the Baptists of color had worshiped along with their white brethren. The church record of November 1, 1772, says: "After divine service, Hannah Dunmore and Chloe, a Negro woman belonging to Mr. George Green, were received into the church." Speaking about this relation, this document says: "Our records have many notices of baptisms and marriages among the Negro people and until early in the present century there was a large group of them in this church." But the desire for independence and a more congenial atmosphere so obsessed them that they sought to form an organization of their own. This was finally effected in 1809 under the leadership of the Rev. Thomas Paul, a native of Exeter, New Hampshire, "where," according to the *Baptist Memorial*, "he was born of respectable parents on the third of September, 1773." He experienced faith in Jesus at an early age and was baptized in the year 1789 by the Rev. Mr. Locke; but, although impressed with the thought that his calling was the ministry, he was not ordained until 1804. Soon thereafter he well organized the African Baptist Church in Joy Street, in Boston, where he served this congregation for about twenty-five years. His labors, however, were not restricted to that city. He frequently made preaching excursions into different parts of the country where his "color excited considerable curiosity, and being a person of very pleasing and fervid address, he attracted crowds to hear him; at this period of his ministry his labors were greatly blessed with numerous conversions in several revivals of religion commenced in different towns under his ministration." It was while he was pastor of the Church in Boston, that in 1808 he organized in New York City the congregation now known as the Abyssinian Baptist Church and served it from June to September of that year, after which Josiah Bishop and others had charge of this very promising work.

The beginnings of this church are interesting. According to a contemporary, "About the year 1807, the colored brethren and sisters of the First Baptist Church, worshipping in Gold Street, for reasons unnecessary now to mention, respectfully proposed to the said church the expediency of a separation: seeing that the colored Methodists and Episcopalians had made similar propositions to their respective churches with success, they humbly desired the same. But they were unsuccessful until the year 1809. In the interim the Rev. Thomas Paul, of Boston, at their request, visited the city, and he was well received in the white churches, preaching to large congregations. Encouraged by such a state of things, they resolved on procuring a place of worship. The meeting-house in Anthony Street, the property of the Ebenezer Baptist Church, being for sale, was purchased by them, with the cooperation of their white brethren. The First Church, satisfied with the competency of brother Paul for the care and management of the petitioners, unanimously granted honorable letters of dismission to four brethren and twelve sisters, who, with three others, were constituted a gospel church on Wednesday, the 5th of July, 1809, under the name of the 'Abyssinian Baptist Church.' It is to be regretted that the order of exercises at the public recognition of this new interest cannot be found. Blest with the faithful labors of such a gifted man, crowded assemblies heard the word of the Lord, and many were added to the church on a profession of their faith in Christ."

Paul's interest in the Negro was not limited to those in this country. In 1823 he presented to the Baptist Missionary Society of Massachusetts a plan for improving the moral and religious condition of the Haitians, requesting that he be sent to these people as a missionary. His plan was received with considerable enthusiasm and he was appointed as a missionary and sent to that country for six months. President Boyer of the Republic of Haiti and other public functionaries kindly received this missionary, giving him permission to preach. There he soon met with some success in edifying a few pious people who seemed gratified beyond measure by his ministrations. Writing home, he frequently mentioned "the powerful precious soul reviving seasons" which he and the few disciples on the island enjoyed. Because of his lack of knowledge of the French language, however, he could not reach a large number of the inhabitants of that island. He was, therefore, compelled to leave Haiti with the regret that he could not do more for its general welfare and especially its deplorable moral condition.[37]

That the independent church movement among Negroes should be directed toward Methodism and Baptism requires some consideration. In those parts of the country in which most Negroes were found, the dominant communicants among the whites were at first Episcopalians, the successors to the rites and ceremonies of the Anglican Church. Among some of the best friends of the Negroes, moreover, were the Presbyterians, who often extended the blacks the same hand of welcome as did the Quakers. Whether this was due altogether to the emotional nature of the Negroes to which the Baptists and Methodists appealed, to chance, or to the wisdom of the leaders of the independent church movement among the Negroes, is a much mooted question. Discussing this matter, Bishop B. T. Tanner in his *Apology for African Methodism* (page 63), attributed the success of Methodism to the foresight of Richard Allen. The author of this work shows how Richard Allen at first cooperated with the Free African Society in Philadelphia until upon holding a meeting, November 15, 1788, they adopted a report of the committee providing for an organization of that society as a religious body, on a basis which, according to Allen's opinion, would have been a usage which prevented that freedom which the gospel permits. Feeling that the current of religious sentiment was not flowing in the desired direction, Allen refused further to cooperate with this group, which by a vote formally declared Allen's connection severed with that society, although Richard Allen retained the friendship of Rev. Absalom Jones, the first rector of the St. Thomas Church, which later developed from this organization.

Bishop Tanner contends that Allen appreciated the fact that, his people being undisciplined, a sound judgment educated with their emotional natures should not be forgotten and swallowed up in the cold intellectual ritual. As he believed that by blending together the emotional and intellectual, the minds of the Negroes could be better developed along religious lines, he refused the proffered rectorship of St. Thomas, saying that he could not be anything but a Methodist. He said, moreover: "I was confident that there was no religious sect or denomination which would suit the capacity of the colored people so well as the Methodist, for the plain, simple Gospel suits best for any people, for the unlearned can understand, and the learned are sure to understand; and the reason that the Methodists are so successful in the awakening and the conversion of the colored people, is the plain doctrine which they preach and having a good discipline."

The Episcopal Church, moreover, could hardly attract Negro churchmen of very much ambition, when it did not require very much reasoning to reach the conclusion that inasmuch as that church had too often neglected the poor whites, it would hardly be inclined to proselyte Negroes. Prior to the time that Absalom Jones was made priest, the St. Thomas Church, according to the Protestant Episcopal convention, was not entitled to send clergymen or deputies thereto nor to participate in the general government of the Episcopal Church. In the year 1795 they declared it was only for the present. The same position, however, was taken in 1843 and it was adhered to throughout the period of slavery; for the Episcopal Church persistently refused to make slavery a matter of discipline.

It is little wonder then that Episcopal churches among Negroes have much difficulty in their development, and only in a few large cities did we have churches even so successful as that of St. Thomas in Philadelphia. Among these may be mentioned the St. Phillips Church in New York. This prosperous church was organized in 1818 and incorporated in 1820. Peter Williams, the first Negro to be ordained as a priest in the Episcopal Church, served as its rector until 1849. He was a man of unusual beginnings. His father, Peter Williams, Sr., was for a number of years the sexton of the John Street Methodist Church, in which position he became distinguished among the white communicants for his fidelity and piety. He joined with other Negroes desirous of independent church action and established the Zion Church, out of which emerged the African Methodist Episcopal Zion Church. Peter Williams, the son, however, became an

Episcopalian, was educated for the ministry and served for years as the rector of St. Phillips Church. In this position he maintained himself as a man of usefulness and influence, touching the life of his people whenever the opportunity presented itself. Bishop Daniel A. Payne, who first came into contact with him in New York in 1835, considered him well educated, for his day, hospitable and generous. Bishop Payne said: "He loved to see talented young men educating themselves and substantially aided more than one in his efforts. Above all he valued an educated minister."

In this position of subjection to a church control in which he himself as a man of color did not largely figure, Peter Williams was handicapped and could not serve his race as he desired. At the time of the intense agitation during the great crisis when the Negroes were called upon to decide where they would stand on the questions of colonization and abolition, Peter Williams at first took an active part in pleading the cause of his people. Seeing, however, that this might bring the church to the position of having to declare itself on this important question, the bishops of the Episcopal Church, in keeping with the custom of that denomination, silenced Peter Williams with a decree that he should preach merely the gospel without interfering with the political affairs of the times. It does not appear that he had that moral stamina to impel him to renounce his connection with a church seeking to muzzle a man praying for the deliverance of his people. It may be, however, that, as he was too far advanced in years to make any radical change in his course, he followed the orders of his superiors.

In Baltimore the Episcopalians practically provided a separate church for Negroes known as the St. James. This was the first Negro church of this denomination established in slave territory. The Negroes were given a building of their own and one Levington was from time to time designated as rector for this special service. Although it appears, however, that for a time a Negro served in this capacity, this task was generally assigned to a rector of Caucasian blood, who fed the people from afar with a long-handled spoon, believing that haply they might be thereby fed. This church in Baltimore, therefore, did not figure so largely in the life of the Negroes as did the Negro Episcopal churches of Philadelphia and New York. In other places where Negroes of this faith were found they were dependent altogether on the ministers of whites. The records of the Protestant Church show here and there Negro rectors in remote parts as in the case of one in a small town in New York and another in Connecticut; but it is evident that they had no employment.

The Presbyterians, who welcomed the Negroes, moreover, were not much more successful in proselyting them. When one considers the liberality of this sect in that its theological seminaries, including even Princeton, opened its doors to Negroes and that the denomination too permitted persons of color to participate in the government of the church to the extent that they not only spoke and exercised the right to vote in their meetings but also served as moderators, this disinclination on the part of Negroes to attach themselves to the Presbyterian Church may require much explanation. Wherever the Presbyterians had the opportunity for proselyting the Negroes they usually embraced it. Yet there were hardly 20,000 Negroes in the Presbyterian Church prior to the Civil War. One of the important reasons is that the Methodists and Baptists were the first to reach the Negro. The Methodists, moreover, had an itinerant system serving like scouts to go out into the wilderness to find the people and bring them in. Then this disinclination was due also to the fact that the Presbyterian Church, somewhat like the more aristocratic churches, disregarded the "emotional character of experimental religion." Its appeal was too intellectual. As Bishop Tanner said: "It strove to lift up without coming down and while the good Presbyterian parson was writing his discourses, rounding off the sentences, the Methodist itinerant had traveled forty miles with his horse and saddle bags; while the parson was adjusting his spectacles to read his manuscript, the itinerant had given hell and damnation to his unrepentant hearers; while the disciple of Calvin was waiting to have his church completed, the disciple of Wesley took to the woods and made them re-echo with the voice of free grace, believing with Bryant, 'The groves were God's first temples.'"

This same appeal of the evangelical rather than the ritualistic explains also the slow progress of the Catholic work among Negroes. The Catholics were early concerned with the amelioration of the condition of the Negroes and were found among the first to bear testimony against slavery. This denomination opened schools to enlighten the children of the slaves, established missions to reclaim the wayward, and all but granted the despised bondmen in their circles the privileges of liberty and equality. The success of their workers among Negroes, however, was not phenomenal. The Catholics did not make much impression on the Negroes in the large cities of the North, where they were more accessible than in the South; but considerable good was accomplished by the promising beginnings in and around Baltimore, Washington, Mobile, and New Orleans. So well was the foundation laid that the reaction in favor of slavery did not altogether counteract this healthy influence in behalf of the enlightenment of the Negroes. Only a small percentage of the race thereby profited, however. The proportionately small number of Negroes now belonging to the Catholic Church have been proselyted largely since the Civil War.

The Congregationalists became interested in the uplift of the Negroes with whom they came into contact, although the number reached did not multiply. The leaders of this denomination sympathized with the slave, aided the fugitive, and preached to the unfortunate the principles of religion so dear to the hearts of their communicants. But so great was the hold of the more evangelical sects on the Negroes that the earliest successful effort to constitute a group of them as a working body in the Congregational Church was the establishment of the Dixwell Avenue Congregational Church in New Haven, Connecticut, in 1829. The records do not show any considerable accession of Negroes to these ranks until after the Civil War when the work of this denomination was popularized in various parts by that efficient worker and organizer, the late G. W. Moore.

CHAPTER V

EARLY DEVELOPMENT

THE NEGRO CHURCH continued to go forward. Eight years after the organization of the African Methodist Episcopal Church the membership easily reached 9,888, including 14 elders, 26 deacons, and 101 licentiates, itinerant and local. Its expansion had been so rapid that it was soon necessary to establish a western conference to administer the affairs of the many churches then rising in Ohio. Wishing further to extend its operations, the church ordained the Rev. Scipio Bean in 1827 to do mission work in the Island of Haiti. The church established there had as many as 72 members in 1828, and in 1830 it had extended its operations into the Spanish port of the Island and gained a foothold in the peninsula of Samana. That same year the Rev. R. Roberts was ordained a deacon and afterward an elder for missionary work in the same island, then under the successful administration of President Boyer. Although he met with some success in the beginning in answering this cry for help in a distant land, the work undertaken there was not finally successful.

There was an apparent falling off in the membership of certain conferences after 1830, but this did not indicate any step backward. Practically the whole membership in South Carolina was by the public opinion, custom, and laws of that commonwealth, cut off from the church. There was during this same period extensive progress in the west, especially in Cincinnati. Great efforts were made to put the church on a firm foundation. During the conferences of the thirties much attention was given to the preparation of the ministry through education, cleanliness in dress, high character, and loyalty to the church. The work suffered a loss, however, in that Bishop Allen, who had for years led this flock, passed away in 1831. Bishop Morris Brown, who had been ordained to the episcopacy in 1828, became then the sole bishop and continued so until 1836 when Edward Waters was ordained as his assistant.

Proceeding on a sound basis, the church could not but succeed. The membership rapidly grew, as is evidenced by the necessity for the organization of two other conferences in the year 1840. This was the conference of Canada, which was organized by Bishop Brown at Toronto, and then came the conference of Indianapolis as a culmination of the successful missionary labors of William Paul Quinn who was later honored as the fourth bishop of the African Methodist Episcopal Church. There was an improvement in church literature such as the *Book of Discipline* and the conference of the year 1836 decreed the publication of a quarterly magazine for the use and benefit of the connection, appointing George Hogarth of the city of Brooklyn as General Book Steward.

The denomination had much difficulty in maintaining the Book Concern. The problem of publication has always been a perplexing one and the experience of this church was no exception to that rule. The business seemed to follow the Book Steward from one city to another. In 1847 it was moved from Pittsburgh to New York. That same year it was decided to publish a weekly to be called *The Christian Herald*. The first copy of this publication was issued by the Rev. A. R. Green, in 1848, then in charge of the Book Concern. In 1852, however, the name of this publication was changed to *The Christian Recorder*. Its editor declared that it would be devoted to religion, morality, science, and literature. Some of the papers published therein show an intelligent insight into conditions, a deep interest in intellectual forces effective in the uplift of the people, and a general knowledge of the great factors which have made the history of the world.

The development of African Methodist Episcopal Zion Church was equally encouraging. After serving his people successfully for some time Bishop James Varick passed away in 1827. The following year the office was filled by the election of Christopher Rush, a man who had figured in the organization of the Zion Church in New York in 1796. Because of his good foundation in education, his equipoise, reliable judgment, and Christian piety, Christopher Rush made such a favorable impression upon those with whom he came in contact that he is often spoken of by the Zionites as the ablest preacher of his time. He lived throughout the crisis through which this church had to go, enabling it to extend its territory so as to compete favorably with the more extensive work then being accomplished by the African Methodist Episcopal Church. Rush served the connection from 1828 to 1840, a period during which the membership of the sect increased, new churches easily developed, and the denomination realized strength and influence. Associated with Bishop Rush in this effort were Elders Edward Johnson, Durham Stevens, George Stevenson, David Crosby, Jonathan Gibbs, Arthur Langford, Tower Hill, John Marshall, Richard Phillips, David Smith, Jacob Richardson, Samuel Johnson, Abraham Green, and David Stevens. In the New York conference at this time there were such men as Timothy Eato, Abraham Thompson, Charles Anderson, William Carmen, George Tredwell, William Miller, Levin Smith, Jacob Matthews, Peter Van Hass, and Jehiel Beaman.[38]

While the outstanding members of this group were those who became bishops of the Zionites, several others who did not attain the episcopacy, frequently showed exceptional power which materially aided the development of the church. Among these may be mentioned the Rev. S. T. Fray, a remarkable natural orator noted for his ability to rouse enthusiasm. He was a man of unusual acumen, easily triumphed in debate, and as a logician and parliamentarian could vanquish his opponent. There was also Rev. Henry Johnson who passed among his fellows as "Old Hickory" because of his strong force of character. Unusually great work for the church was accomplished by Rev. John A. Williams as a revivalist. Rev. Leonard Collins was one of the reliable pillars in the church for a number of years but lost his standing by yielding to the temptation of strong drink. Honorable mention may be given Basil McKall, Abraham Cole, and especially David Stevens for their forceful preaching which moved multitudes to come into the church.

It does not appear that some of the bishops left very much of an impression, although they were men of extraordinary following. Bishop Spywood, for example, was retired from his office because there were more bishops than were needed for that service in the church. Bishop Moore, who was an inspiring preacher, drawing large crowds and moving all classes to repentance, was not at ease as a bishop and he too was retired in 1860.

It was unfortunate, however, that in 1840 a very disturbing factor appeared so as to arrest the progress of this church. There arose in this connection an element desiring an assistant superintendent. It seemed that this desire came from the friends of Rev. William Miller, a man of changing tendencies. Although a preacher of unusual intellect and a man of general ability, he did not show much stability of character. When he was a deacon in the African Methodist Episcopal Church in 1813, it appeared that he used his position to do the Zion Church an injury. At a later period he, with the Asbury Church, joined the Zionites. Yet with this same church about 1820 he united with Bishop Allen so as to form the nucleus of the Bethel Church in New York City in 1830; but returned later to the Zion Church with a fragment of the Asbury congregation. In spite of this changing record, however, his friends felt that he should be made superintendent and it was finally done; but although an assistant superintendent, he never held a conference nor performed an ordination. It seemed that it was a position of honor rather than one of usefulness, but he was known as bishop until he died in 1846.

Two years later when Rev. George Galbreth was elected to this office, some dispute arose as to whether he should be a full bishop or a more assistant, but it was finally decided that he should be an assistant only. As this did not satisfy all concerned, the friends of Mr. Galbreth continued the fight and in the conference of 1852 they carried the point of placing all bishops on equality. Part of their program too was the retirement of Bishop Rush, who, being feeble and blind, could no longer serve efficiently. The conference thereupon proceeded to elect Galbreth, Bishop, and Spywood. Bishop Spywood was retired from this office in 1856 because there were too many bishops for the work to be accomplished in the field, and during the remainder of his life he was employed as an agent of the New England Mission Board in which he served successfully.

It happened that soon after the election of the three superintendents, that is, in 1853, Bishop Galbreth died, leaving two bishops in the field. How were these bishops then to stand? Was there such a thing as a senior bishop or were they on equality? Bishop insisted that he was the General Superintendent and above and beyond his coworker. As this did not satisfy both parties he was called to trial; but, insisting that he was right, he evaded the inquiry and caused a schism in the Zion Church. Those adhering to the suspended bishop held the territory north to Philadelphia, south to Charleston and west to Pittsburgh, and called themselves the Wesleyan Methodist Episcopal Church. The others held most of New York, New England, and Nova Scotia, and retained the original name of the body, the African Methodist Episcopal Zion Church. These two factions tended to drift in different directions. In the west there was a tendency toward Episcopalianism, whereas the east drifted toward Congregationalism. The question of the church property was finally taken into the courts, which decided in favor of those who remained with the denomination. Steps were thereafter taken to heal the breach which had been produced by the stubbornness of one man and the haste of a few others in dealing with him. In 1860 the schism was finally ended by an agreement of the two factions to bury their differences and unite for the good of the common church.

During these years some smaller movements were in progress. A division of the Union Church of Africans incorporated at Wilmington, Delaware, in 1807, resulted in the organization of the African Union Church and the Union American Methodist Episcopal Church in 1850. From the Methodist Protestant Church a sufficient number of Negroes finally withdrew to form, in 1860, the First Colored Methodist Protestant Church. These denominations, however, have not been able to compete in numbers and influence with the Allenites and Zionites.

These activities of the African Methodist denominations mentioned above would seem to indicate that the large majority of the Negroes became members of these new sects, leaving merely a few for the Baptists. As a matter of fact, however, the contrary was true. The Negro Methodists had national organization and in most cases intelligent men making a systematic effort to extend their work. The Baptists, on the other hand, had both the disadvantages and the advantages of local self-government. In their undeveloped state this unusual liberty sometimes proved to be a handicap to the Baptists in that the standard of the ministry and the moral tone of the churches were not so high as in the case of the Methodist bodies, whose conferences had power to make local churches do the right when they were not so inclined. This local self-government of the Baptists, on the other hand, made possible a more rapid increase in the number of churches established and the large influx of members in quest of the liberty wherewith they believed Christ had made them free.

What then was this peculiar feature of Baptist policy which explains the unusual growth? In the first place, the local Baptist Church is thoroughly independent of any other organization or church. It may become associated with other churches in bodies meeting periodically to devise plans for the common good of the denomination; but it is in no sense bound by the rules and regulations of such bodies. And should an association, moreover, exclude a church from its group, that church is still legally constituted a Baptist church and may join another association or form one of its own in cooperation with other churches similarly disposed. Any group of baptized believers of not less than four, moreover, may exercise the liberty of organizing a church under the direction of a regularly ordained minister of the denomination and ordination in the Baptist Church is not a difficulty. With the tendency of so many members to find fault, to disagree, to follow the advice of ill-designing persons seeking personal ends, it was a decidedly easy matter for Negro Baptist churches under these circumstances to split and thus multiply. While the Methodists might hesitate to establish an additional church so close to another as to hinder its growth, the Baptists in the heat of controversial excitement often established two or three churches where there were not at first enough people to sustain one; but in the course of time these churches, because of their unusual liberty in the evangelical effort, would attract so many more than the other liberal churches that they would all be filled. The Baptists finally aggregated about as many as all other Negro members of the various independent Negro churches. It soon happened in the South, moreover, that where the blacks were freely permitted to embrace religion the Negro Baptists outnumbered the whites in mixed churches two to one and sometimes three to one or four to one.

Detailed records of these achievements from a national point of view are lacking for the reason that the Negro Baptists prior to the organization of the National Baptist Convention had no national body of their own. During the antebellum period they belonged largely to the white churches in the South, occupying certain seats, the Negro pew, or meeting in the basement of the same edifice for worship at a special hour on the Sabbath day. In most cities in the North the independent movement among Negroes brought about the establishment of their own local churches; but, when associated, they generally belonged to the white bodies, used their literature, and followed their doctrines. As many of the white churches and organizations took little account of what these Negro communicants were doing but rather considered them as an undesirable but inevitable adjunct, no complete records of their achievements are extant. Here and there a writer of the history of the Baptists gave them honorable mention and now and then a Negro Baptist preacher in a locality had sufficient appreciation of the value of records to leave an account.

The location and the status of some of these Baptist churches will be interesting, especially in the South where their development was retarded by the restrictions of a slaveholding section living in dread of servile insurrection. During the thirties and forties a number of Negro Baptist churches were established in the District of Columbia, the first one being organized by Sampson White in 1839 and reaching its position of permanence some years later under William Williams, whose flock was the largest of this sect in the city. As it could not be associated with Negro churches in the South, then dominated by white men in the interest of slaveholders, it connected itself with the Philadelphia Baptist Association. The first Negro Baptist Church in Baltimore was organized in 1836 and was making unusual progress under the direction of M. C. Clayton, with a membership of 150 in 1846. A number of other Baptist churches in the city were soon organized thereafter, furnishing opportunity for development to its several useful Negro ministers, among whom was Rev. Noah Davis of the Saratoga Street Baptist Church.

These places in Maryland, however, were not strictly of the slaveholding attitude and so were parts of Virginia. An extensive account of the African Baptist Church of Richmond, established from the white church of that faith and placed in charge of Rev. Robert Ryland, a white man, serving at the same time as President of Richmond College, appears elsewhere. There had been for some years a Negro Baptist congregation in Portsmouth, mentioned above. There were elsewhere in the State other Baptist and Methodist churches and some of them almost entirely under the direction of Negroes. The first African Baptist Church in Petersburg had 664 communicants, the largest membership in the Middle District Baptist Association. The largest Baptist Church in Manchester (now South Richmond) in 1846 was the African Baptist Church with a membership of 487.

In South Carolina the Negroes were not permitted to separate from the whites, but they so decidedly outnumbered the latter that the churches had the aspect of Negro congregations. Of the 1,643 members belonging to the First Baptist Church in Charleston in 1846 all but 261 were persons of color. In the Second Baptist Church there were 200 white people and 312 Negroes; in the Georgetown Baptist Church 33 white persons and 298 Negroes. The Welsh Neck Church had 477 Negroes and only 83 whites. In the Association to which these churches belonged the blacks outnumbered the whites two to one. No distinction was made between the members of the two races in the minutes of the Association. The Bethel Association of this State, however, had for a number of years prior to 1838 reported the Negro members. It then had 1,502 whites and 637 blacks; but in 1843 the whites were 1,804 and the blacks 1,000.

The main interest in the Negro Baptists of Georgia during this period centered around the church established in Savannah by Andrew Bryan. For about two years after the death of the founder in 1812 the church remained without a pastor, having its pulpit supplied during this period by Rev. Evans Great. At the end of this interregnum the church set apart a Sabbath day to pray that the great head of the church would direct their choice to a worthy successor. Although Andrew Marshall had served as an assistant pastor under his uncle he had upon his death become largely engaged in business. The church, however, by a majority vote chose Andrew Marshall in preference to Evans Great, and the former entered upon the service with exercises auguring well for success. Being prosperous in his ministry as well as in his business, Andrew Marshall was respected not only by his own people but also by the most desirable whites.

His prosperity and his influence, however, led to a supposed violation of the laws. After having accumulated a goodly portion of money, he purchased from certain Negroes who had no permit to trade or sell, some bricks with which he constructed his two-story brick house. As this was a violation of the law, his traducers seized upon this opportunity to humiliate him, and, although his former master interceded in his behalf and enlisted the sympathy of the best white citizens, he was administered a whipping as a punishment for this so-called high crime. This crippled him in his ministry for a while, but he soon recovered therefrom, having the assistance of Henry Cunningham and Evans Great, who, in spite of the fact that the latter was defeated by Andrew Marshall for the pastorate of the church, served under him thereafter as an assistant pastor and cooperated with him loyally.

Andrew Marshall emerged from these trials but another of more consequence awaited him. He alienated the affection of the white people of this denomination by preaching what they considered false doctrines. Further trouble was caused when he permitted Alexander Campbell, then called the new light preacher, to speak in the African Baptist Church. The orthodox Baptist of the city disapproved of Marshall's admitting Dr. Campbell to his pulpit and disputes in the church immediately followed. The church became hopelessly divided and its strife was the topic of the town. Marshall withdrew from the building with one portion of the church, the other remaining under the leadership of Adam Johnson. As Andrew Marshall was much more powerful than any other man of his connection, he carried with him then out of this church a large majority.

The association to which this church belonged, however, took action in his case, recommending that Marshall be silenced indefinitely, that the African Church be dissolved, and that measures be taken to constitute a new body as a branch of the white Baptist church. The Negro members in the country, then members of the African Baptist Church in Savannah, were to take letters of dismission and either unite themselves with the neighboring churches of the Baptist faith or be constituted as separate churches. The association also gave its approval of the Christian deportment of the Second African Church. This, of course, made all of the Negro churches wards of the white and according to the law no Negro could exercise the gift of preaching in those churches unless he was endorsed by two or more white Baptist ministers. As the property of the First African Church was under the trusteeship of the association, its will had to be respected. There is no evidence, however, that these orders of the association were ever carried out. As most of the members of the churches lived in the country rather than in the city of Savannah, moreover, the dispute was one in which the minority rather than the majority of the members were concerned.

Marshall, however, solved his own problems with the assistance of certain influential white men who enabled him to purchase the old building of the white Baptists, out of which they moved into a new church edifice on Chippewa Square. As this was a much larger building than the old meeting house constructed by Andrew Bryan and Marshall could preach with more power than any other minister in that vicinity, he had little difficulty in attracting a larger following, although most of the official class of the First African Baptist Church deserted him.

Upon the withdrawal of Andrew Marshall and his supporters from the edifice of the First African Baptist Church and their taking over of a new edifice, there arose a serious question which even today has not been really settled. This question was whether or not Marshall and his followers continued the church established by Andrew Bryan or abandoned it to the control of those who remained and were later accepted in the Sunbury Association of Georgia as the Third African Baptist Church, still later known as the First Bryan Baptist Church. The officers in the control of this church contended that they rather than the followers of Marshall represented the church as it was established by Bryan. They insist that, although in being received in the Sunbury Association they were designated as the Third African Baptist Church, they, nevertheless, represented the church as it was originally established by Andrew Bryan. All of the actual officers of the original church and all of the persons who had represented the church as it originally was in the Sunbury Association remained to carry on the work as it had been theretofore without any special organization of a new church and succeeded at the same time to the possession of this property. They emphasized also the fact that Andrew Marshall had never represented the church in this association and that he himself was a member of the Second African Church rather than of the church of which he was pastor.

This Third African Church, later the First Bryan Baptist Church, then extended a call to Thomas Anderson, who served them until 1835, when the congregation secured the services of Steven McQueen. In 1841 the church was again without a regular pastor but accepted the services of John Devous, a former deacon of the Second African Church. Soon thereafter we hear of the resignation of Mr. Devous and the installation of Isaac Roberts, also a member of the Second African Church. Mr. Roberts proved to be the most energetic of all pastors in the city after the rise of Andrew Marshall. He improved the building, inspired the members, and edified their souls. But upon the death of Thomas Anderson, the pastor of the Second African Church, Mr. Roberts resigned to accept that pastorate, in 1849. The church then extended a call to Bristol Lawton of Beaufort, South Carolina, who preached for just one year and was succeeded by Garrison Frazer, a Baptist from the State of Virginia. Mr. Frazer was a man of high church principles and was a good worker in the ranks. About the time of the outbreak of the Civil War, he resigned and the church then had ordained for its leadership Rev. Ulysses L. Houston, who developed much power as a preacher. In this position he extended the influence of the church and made himself a great factor even among the white Baptists of the community. He served in this capacity for some years, laboring through the war into freedom. Andrew Marshall continued in charge of his church, maintaining himself with the same prestige and retaining a large following until he passed away in 1856, when he was succeeded by Rev. William J. Campbell. Andrew Marshall was mourned by thousands unto whom he had ministered and by tens of thousands who had observed his good work in delivering the poor that cry and in directing the wanderer in the right way.

Alabama also had a large number of Negro Baptists although there did not develop as many independent churches as there were in Georgia. The Negro membership in the mixed churches was a little more than one-half of the number. In the city of Montgomery the Negroes were almost three to one. Probably the most flourishing center was the African Baptist Church at Mobile. This congregation had once been a part of the First Baptist Church (white), but in 1839 the congregation was dissolved to form two. That year the Negro church was admitted to the Bethel Association. The Negroes had a fine house of worship built by themselves and had developed among them some intelligent local preachers, among whom were certain gentlemen known as Heard, Hunton, Hale, Stowe, Collins, Schroebel, and Grant.

The center of interest among the Negro Baptists in Florida was Jacksonville. There the First Bethel Baptist Church was organized in 1838 with four whites and two Negroes as charter members. These were Rev. J. Jaudan and wife, Deacon James McDonald and wife and two slaves belonging to Jaudan. They held their first meetings in the Government Block House near the County Court House but later purchased on Church Street, between Hogan and Julia Streets, a lot on which was built the first edifice. When later the whites decided to separate from the Negroes and undertook to dispossess them altogether the court decided that the property belonged to the Negroes in as much as they were in the majority. Later, however, the Bethel Baptist Church sold out this property to the whites and purchased property on the corner of Main and Union Streets. In our day we have seen the Bethel Baptist Church incorporated by the State as an institutional church which figures as an important factor in the life of the Negroes of Jacksonville.

In the western slave States, where the Negroes were few, they were, nevertheless, found in considerable numbers in the Baptist Church. One-fourth of the Baptists in Tennessee were Negroes. The membership in Kentucky was of a much larger proportion. The African Baptist Church of Lexington was founded by a thrifty Negro who, in spite of the law, was permitted to remain in the State as a worthy free Negro and as such not only preached but as early as the thirties had accumulated a fortune valued at $20,000. In 1846 this church under the leadership of L. Terrell was the largest in the Elkhorn Association and was considered "orderly and flourishing." During these years the First African Baptist Church of Louisville had been developing along the same line and was the largest in its association, having 644 members. Under the pastorate of Rev. Henry Adams, a man of considerable education and ability to lead, it attained a position of much usefulness. The Negro Baptist Church of St. Louis, founded in 1827, was, in 1848, the largest in its connection and with the impetus given the work by its pastor, J. B. Meacham, it became still more influential.

In the North the development of the Negro Baptists did not proceed so smoothly. In the first place, neither the majority of the Negroes nor a large percentage of the whites in that section belonged to the Baptist Church. The northern Negroes, moreover, had something to conjure with. Methodism among them was a radical independent movement offering liberty in a sphere in which the Negro had never freely moved. Many Negroes, therefore, heeded the call of the African Methodists to "come ye out from among them and work out your own salvation with fear and trembling." Independent Methodists in the South, however, were more of an exception to the rule than was the case of the Baptists in the North, for the Negro Baptists had every opportunity so to worship God in the North, if they desired, whereas the independent Negro Methodists were actually prohibited from invading most of the South.

As a matter of fact the Baptist churches were among the first separate organizations established in the North for Negroes, and as the free Negroes and fugitives were in the course of time driven out of the South by the intolerable conditions obtaining there during the reactionary period, the northern Negro Baptist churches multiplied and their membership increased. Practically all large urban communities of the North had some Negro Baptists. Philadelphia was especially well supplied. There was the First African Church founded by Negroes in 1809, with a membership of 257, under Richard Vaughn in 1846. The Union Colored Church, with a membership of 200, was in charge of Daniel Scott. J. Henderson was the pastor of the Third African Baptist Church, with a membership of only

61, and William Jackson ministered to a similar number in the so-called African Church.

Farther north the Baptists were also making progress. The Abyssinian Baptist Church of New York City was, in 1846, doing well under the direction of Rev. Sampson White, with a membership of 424. In Boston the African Baptist Church had held its own, but in New England, where the abolition sentiment was developing and there resulted a more healthy sentiment in behalf of fairness for the Negro, the independent movement among Negro Methodists and Baptists was not generally considered necessary. Negroes were accepted in white churches and heard preached and saw practiced the principles of the brotherhood of man and the fatherhood of God. Only in centers of large Negro population then, as in Boston, Providence, Newport, New Haven and Hartford, did the Negroes tend largely to separate from the whites.

To the west, however, where came Negroes fleeing from the persecution of the southern whites, independent churches flourished much better. Pittsburgh, Buffalo, Cleveland, Columbus, Cincinnati, Detroit, and Chicago soon found Baptist as well as Methodist churches common. Some of the pioneers in the group of Baptists were Richard DeBaptiste of Detroit and later of Chicago, and James Poindexter of Columbus. These in the course of time so rapidly increased that the Negro Baptists finally established an independent connection, the Providence Baptist Association the first Negro body of the kind in the United States, organized in Ohio in 1836. Such was the case in Illinois where the Baptist churches of St. Clair and Madison counties, of Shawneetown, Vandalia, Jacksonville, Springfield, Galena, and Chicago, representing about twelve churches, organized in 1838 the Wood River Baptist Association. Feeling that there was a need for a still larger body, the churches of these parts organized in 1853 the Western Colored Baptist Convention.

The progress of these independent churches in the west suffered no interruption until the passage of the Fugitive Slave Law of 1850, when many Negroes who had escaped from the South and settled in these cities had to flee to Canada for safety. In Canada West, the various settlements saw the influence of the Baptists and Methodists extended, but for a long time there had been a Baptist church in Toronto which under Rev. W. Christian was flourishing in 1846, and the Methodists soon made there a more systematic effort.

CHAPTER VI
THE SCHISM AND THE SUBSEQUENT SITUATION

AN IMPORTANT FACTOR in the growth of the Negro Church was that the Negroes found the white churches of their choice less friendly and finally saw them withdrawn from the churches in the North to perpetuate slavery. In the South, the slaves and free Negroes had to accept whatever religious privileges were allowed them; but when the national bodies grew lukewarm on abolition, receded from the advanced position which they had taken in the defense of the Negro, and persistently compromised on the question to placate their southern adherents to maintain intact their national organizations, Negroes forgot the stigma attached to their radical religious bodies and united freely with their brethren who during the first years of their independence found it difficult to secure a following.

In 1808 the general conference of the Methodists provided that the annual conferences should form their own regulations relative to buying and selling slaves, thus making it possible for the body of preachers to act efficiently in one direction against slavery, even should the general conference choose wholly to refrain. This rule was abrogated in 1820, however, and the only important changes made thereafter with reference to the Negroes were some rules adopted in 1824, one of which provided that all preachers should prudently "enforce upon their members," the necessity of teaching their slaves to read the word of God, and to allow them time to attend upon the public worship of God on our regular days of divine service. Another rule provided that Negro preachers and official members should have all the privileges which are usual to others in the district and quarterly conferences, where the usages of the country did not forbid it, and that the presiding elder might hold for them a separate district conference, when the number of Negro local preachers would justify it. The annual conferences might employ Negro preachers to travel and preach, where their services were judged necessary, provided that no one should be so employed without having been recommended according to the form of discipline.

The Presbyterians had tried to evade the Negro question but it was again brought up in view of the cruelty practiced in the traffic of slaves during the first decade of the nineteenth century. The General Assembly was forced to take some action again in 1815. It then referred to its previous resolutions on the subject and expressed regret that slavery of Africans existed, hoping too that such measures might be taken as would secure religious education at least to the rising generation of slaves as a preparation for their emancipation at some time in the future. As to the transfer of slaves necessary in the economy of the slave States the General Assembly regarded this as unavoidable; but it denounced the buying and selling of slaves by way of traffic and all undue cruelty among them as inconsistent with the spirit of the Gospel, recommending it to the presbyteries and sessions in their care to make use of all measures to prevent such shameful conduct. In 1818 there came before this General Assembly a resolution to the effect that a person who should sell as a slave a member of the church, who should be at the time in good standing in the church and unwilling to be sold, acted inconsistently with the spirit of Christianity and ought to be debarred from the communion of the church.

After considerable discussion, the subject was submitted to a committee to prepare a report for the adoption of the General Assembly, embracing the object of the above resolution and also expressing the opinion of the Assembly as to slavery. This report, unanimously adopted, carried, among other things, a declaration that the voluntary enslaving of one portion of the human race by another is a gross violation of the most precious rights of human nature, utterly inconsistent with the law of God which requires us to love our neighbors as ourselves, and totally irreconcilable with the spirit and principles of the gospel of Christ, which enjoins that all things whatsoever ye would that men should do to you, do ye even unto them.[39]

In another part of this report, however, the Assembly seemed to undo what it had done; for it exhorted others to forbear harsh censures, and uncharitable reflections on their brethren, who unhappily live among slaves whom they cannot immediately set free, but who, at the same time, are really using all their influence, and all their endeavors, to bring them into a state of freedom, as soon as a door for it can be safely opened. It also encouraged the members of the Society to patronize the American Colonization Society with a view to sending the Negroes to Africa and thus deliver themselves and their country from the calamity of slavery. The General Assembly recommended the encouragement of religious instruction of the slaves in the principles of the Christian religion, granting them liberty to attend on the preaching of the gospel, when they have opportunity, by favoring the instruction of them in the Sabbath schools wherever those schools should be formed and by giving them all other proper advantages for acquiring the knowledge of their duty both to God and man. The General Assembly further recommended that it was incumbent on all Christians to communicate religious instruction to those who are under their authority, so that the doing of this "in the case before us so far from operating as some have apprehended that it might, as an incitement to insurrection, would, on the contrary, operate as a most powerful means for the prevention of those evils."

In this straddling position these churches tried to discountenance as far as possible all cruelty of whatever kind in the treatment of slaves, especially the cruelty of separating husband and wife, parents and children, and that which consisted in selling slaves to those who would either themselves deprive these unhappy people of the blessings of the gospel or who would transfer them to places where the gospel was not proclaimed, or where it was forbidden to slaves to attend upon its instruction. During the thirties most of these churches were taking the position of evading the question, but the abolition members therein kept the problem before them. Postponement of the discussion thereafter became the order of the day. One decade later many took the position assumed by the Presbyterian Church in 1845 when, as a result of various memorials on slavery, the Assembly, deploring the division of the church on slavery, passed a resolution that the church could not legislate where Christ has not legislated, that as Christ and the Apostles admitted slaveholders as members of the church, they could not be expected to do otherwise. Some disclaimed, however, any desire to deny that slavery is an evil, or to countenance the idea that masters may regard their slaves as real property and not as human beings. They merely intended to say that since Christ and his Apostles did not make the holding of slaves a bar to communion, the church organizations as the court of Christ had no authority to do so. The apostles of Christ sought to ameliorate the condition of the slaves, not by denouncing and excommunicating their masters but by teaching both masters and slaves the glorious doctrines of the gospel and enjoining upon each a discharge of their relative duties. These sects rejoiced rather that the ministers and churches of the slaveholding States were awakening to a deeper sense of their obligations to extend to the slave population generally the means of grace, for many slaveholders not professedly religious favored this object. They deplored the agitation which tended to separate the northern from the southern portion of the church, "a result which every good citizen must deplore as tending to the disunion of our beloved country and which every enlightened Christian will oppose as bringing about a ruinous and unnecessary schism between brethren who maintain a common faith."

The schism, however, was impending; for the southern members of the churches boldly defended slavery as justified by the scriptures, while many northerners differed from them. Ministers and laymen wrote works setting forth these doctrines while pseudo-scientists and philosophers undertook to justify the enslavement of the Negroes on the ground of racial inferiority. Southerners who would not go to the extent of justifying the institution on these untenable grounds merely deprecated it as an evil for which they were not responsible and of which they could not rid themselves. Richard Fuller, a southern Baptist of unusual influence in shaping the policy of that sect in his section, expressed this thought in the words: "I am willing to appear in any controversy which can even by implication place me in a false light and odious attitude representing me as a eulogist and abettor of slavery, and not as simply the apologist of an institution transmitted to us by former generations—the existence of which I lament—for the commencement of which I am not at all responsible—for the extinction of which I am willing to make greater sacrifices than any abolitionist has made or would make, if the cause of true humanity would be thus advanced."

The outbreaks soon followed, however, in spite of efforts to heal the breach. There came from the Alabama State Baptist Convention a memorial with respect to the discrimination of the Foreign Mission Board against slaveholders in making its appointments. The reply of the Board was conciliatory but was to the effect that a slaveholder could not be consistently appointed as a missionary for the reason that such action would involve an approval of slavery. This and other Baptist conventions thereafter severed their connection with the national body, and in 1845 organized the Southern Baptist Convention. That same year occurred the secession of the Southern Methodists. That denomination had for years struggled with this question and had undertaken to maintain the position that slavery is an evil to be deplored and that ministers and bishops at least should abstain therefrom. When, in 1845, the Methodists undertook to discipline one of its bishops, James O. Andrew, charging him with holding slaves, the southern delegates stood by him and withdrew to organize the Methodist Episcopal Church, South. In 1857, the Presbyterians who had all but compromised sufficiently to hold their national body intact gave an expression of opinion on the Fugitive Slave Law which so offended its southern members that they withdrew and formed the nucleus around which the Southern Presbyterian Church was established in 1861.

In spite of the reactionary tendencies of the white churches, however, no such thing as the independence of the Negro had ever been possible in the South and could not be so after the radical aspect which this movement assumed in the North. In slave States, the majority of Negroes became a decidedly neglected mass during the reaction, although many of them were nominally members of churches. When because of the insurrectionary movement led by certain blacks like Gabriel Prosser, Denmark Vesey and Nat Turner, it became unpopular to teach Negroes to read and the educated white persons were not willing to supply this lack of religious workers among the blacks, there was no longer hope for ordinary religious instruction. This reaction was unusually disastrous to the Negro preacher when it was noised abroad that Nat Turner was a minister. The rumor attached to Negro ministers throughout the South the stigma of using preaching as a means to incite their race to servile insurrection.

Some of the legislation enacted by the States after this great upheaval will indicate the extent to which this fear controlled the minds of the southern people. In 1832 Virginia passed a law to silence Negro preachers, making it impossible for them thus to function except in compliance with very rigid regulations and in the presence of certain discreet white men. In 1833, Alabama made it unlawful for slaves or free Negroes to preach unless before five respectable slaveholders and when authorized by some neighboring religious society. Georgia enacted a law in 1834 providing that neither free Negroes nor slaves might preach or exhort an assembly of more than seven unless licensed by justices on the certificate of three ordained ministers. Other Southern States soon followed the example of these, passing more drastic laws prohibiting the assembly of Negroes after the early hours of the night, and providing for the expulsion of all free Negroes from such commonwealths, so as to reduce the danger of mischief from the spread of information by this more enlightened class.

Thus circumscribed, the Negroes in the South had to follow their masters in religious matters. They continued to join the Methodist and Baptist churches, but constituted a part of a mixed membership worshiping under the same roof. The masters had long since learned that coincidence of religious belief on the part of the slave and the owner was a necessity in the economy of the slaveholding States. No master would look with favor upon seeing his slave proselyted or influenced by a minister whom he would not tolerate as his own spiritual adviser. Later there was not much commingling of the two races in the same meetings. White ministers preached to the Negroes in their special meetings or provided some Negro exhorter of power to supply that need, but only when such Negro minister's character had been thoroughly investigated and approved in accordance with the law and public opinion. Where there were not so very many Negroes in the churches, they were segregated in the gallery or certain pews, which they entered by a side door, as provided in the Court of the Gentiles in the Temple of Jehovah; but if there were many Negroes and very few whites in these congregations, they usually provided separate buildings or used the same edifices at different hours. The argument in favor of this segregation was that God in making the races different intended that they should be kept separate and distinct.

Where there was allowed much liberty in seating, very often grave problems arose. Such was the case in Charleston, South Carolina, in the Bethel Church in 1833 on an occasion when Dr. Capers was to preach. As more whites came than could be seated and the Negroes refused to vacate their customary seats, a number of uncouth young white men forcibly ejected them therefrom. Because one of the preachers a few days thereafter sharply criticized this action of the uncouth element they became unusually indignant, registering a protest against such censure. An effort was made to settle the matter by reconciliation, but when that failed, nine of the young men were expelled only to be followed by 150 others to form a new organization, which established connection with the Methodist Protestant Church.

This sort of segregation was common to all of the denominations alike. The Presbytery of Charleston, finding the church in that city unusually crowded in 1850, built a structure for the worship of the Negro member-ship, costing $7,700. The edifice was of the shape of a "T" to provide seats for the whites in the transepts. It had connected with it all of the facili-ties for religious instruction in the other churches with the exception that teaching was oral. The Episcopalians in that city, however, found it more difficult to carry out such a policy in relieving the congestion of the Negro pews in St. Michael's and St. Phillip's. These communicants decided to build what was to be called the Calvary Church for the accommodation of the blacks who were then occupying temporary quarters in Temperance Hall. Because of certain radical action of the burial societies among the Negro communicants, however, the owner of Temperance Hall refused further to accommodate the Negroes and the Calvary Church was demol-ished while it was in the process of construction.

The Negroes seemed to have retained several separate places of worship in the State of Virginia, as in the case of Georgia. Among the churches established for Negroes at a very early period was that of Williamsburg, Virginia, organized exclusively for Negroes in 1776 and admitted as such to the Dover Baptist Association in 1791. Upon petitioning the state leg-islature in 1823, however, the Negroes were refused the permit to build a Baptist church in Richmond, although the one used by the whites was not sufficiently spacious to permit their attendance. In 1841, however, when the Baptist church was finally compelled to build a new structure to ac-commodate its increasing membership, they turned over to the Negroes for their special place of worship the old building in which they organized what is known as the first African Baptist Church under the pastorate of the Rev. Robert Ryland, a white man, who served during the same period as president of Richmond College. When this became unusually crowded the Ebenezer Baptist Church was organized by the overflow membership in 1855 and was controlled very much in the same way. There were flourish-ing Negro Methodist and Baptist churches in other parts during the forties, fifties, and sixties, conducted very much on the order of the First African Baptist Church in Richmond, or like the Anthony Street Church in Mo-bile, Alabama, in charge of the Rev. Keidor Hawthorne. In other centers in Virginia, however, the Negroes were proceeding almost independently. There was then a representative Baptist congregation in Portsmouth un-der the direction of the noted builder and organizer, E. G. Corpew. Rev. Mr. Morris, another pioneer in the work, was at this time leading forward the Court Street Baptist Church in Lynchburg. In 1837 and 1838 Sampson White was reported as a successful minister in charge of the Gillfield Bap-tist Church of Petersburg, which as early as 1803 undertook to erect its first structure. Sampson White then went to Norfolk for a short stay in this in-viting field, and in 1839 came to Washington and organized the Nineteenth Street Baptist Church.

In the District of Columbia, where, as in Maryland, the restrictions on Negroes were not so rigid as in some other parts of the South, the Negroes had numerous churches of the Baptist and Methodist faith, and under the leadership of John F. Cooke established, in 1843, the Fifteenth Street Presbyterian Church.

Baltimore was no exception to this rule. As the slave and free membership freely mingled in that city they had, as early as 1835, ten congregations, and by 1847 thirteen, ten of which were Methodist. The work of the Baptists had been largely promoted by M. C. Clayton, the preacher of versatile genius, who founded the First African Church in that city in 1836, and by Noah Davis, a leader and organizer of much ability.

This favorable condition, however, obtained in the South only in those communities where the authorities winked at the violation of the law by free Negroes and where slaves enjoyed unusual privileges because their masters were a law unto themselves. In 1828 the Alabama Baptist Association conditionally purchased a slave named Caesar at the cost of $625 and sent him to preach the gospel and live among his people. He was then made the companion of the famous white evangelist, James McLemore, of much note in Alabama. Caesar was respected alike for piety and his ability as a preacher. Not infrequently he addressed audiences composed entirely of whites. Another slave of Alabama, Doc Phillips, was a Baptist preacher of a commanding influence among his people. The Tuskegee Association of that State undertook to purchase him that he might be appointed a missionary, but he declined to be severed from his master, who allowed him whatever time he might desire for preaching. So was this true of George Bentley of Giles County, Tennessee, a slave of unusual note, having attained distinction as a preacher of power, well versed in polemic theology. Out of a debate on baptism lasting more than four days he emerged victor over a white minister in that county challenging him to a discussion of the principles of baptism. He numbered among his communicants the best white people of the community, who paid him a salary of more than $600. He, like Doc Phillips, refused to have his congregation purchase his freedom, as he did not care to be separated from his kind master.

Here and there in the South, however, there developed certain Negro preachers better known to fame. A striking example of this class was Lott Cary, who was born a slave in Virginia. When quite young he was hired out and thereby came under the influences which caused him to be a man given to profane and intemperate habits, although his parents were of the higher class of slaves. In 1807, however, he was awakened by hearing a sermon from the third chapter of John on the interview of Nicodemus, from the words: "Notwithstanding what I say unto you, you must be born again." So powerful was the preaching and so telling was the effect on the mind of this slave that he immediately secured a copy of the New Testament and almost miraculously learned to read by studying that chapter. Upon developing into a strong spiritual man, he was made superintendent of all the laborers in the tobacco warehouse in which he was working in Richmond. Not long thereafter he received permission to serve as an exhorter in the First African Baptist Church of that city, the membership of which, then being about 2,000, required the services of a number of assistant pastors.

Lott Cary reached a new stage in his development in the fall of 1813, when Luther Rice, who had just returned from the East, appeared in that city preaching rousing sermons urging the Baptists to enter upon and to support the work of missions in foreign fields. In November of that year the Richmond Foreign Missionary Society was organized and delegates were sent to Philadelphia the following spring to participate in the organization of the Baptist Triennial Convention. As this new body had for one of its objects mission work in foreign fields, the national interest aroused therein excited also a deep interest among the Negro members of the churches in Richmond. Two years later, therefore, the Richmond African Baptist Missionary Society, with Lott Carey as the moving spirit, was formed with the sole object of sending the gospel into Africa. This society was composed of the Negro members of the First African Baptist Church and of other churches throughout the city. It held annual meetings and with their small donations accumulated as much as $700 during the first four years.

As no one volunteered to go abroad to extend this mission work, Lott Cary himself determined to go to Africa, accompanied by Collin Teague. They were, therefore, duly appointed by the Board of the Baptist Triennial Convention as missionaries to Liberia. In 1821 Cary and Teague with many others sailed from Norfolk for the land of their fathers beyond the Atlantic. Before leaving Richmond, Cary and wife, Teague and wife with their son Hillary, who later became editor of the *Liberian Herald*, and Joseph Sanford and his wife, formed what is called the First Baptist Church of Monrovia. This congregation was later designated as the mother of the Providence Baptist Association in Liberia.

Upon arriving in Liberia, Lott Cary addressed himself with much energy to the task of reconstruction and organization in this foreign field. He easily became a leader among the communicants of that denomination and preached for years among them as a man representative of the power of the gospel unto the salvation of the heathen. Wielding such influence in the religious field, he easily convinced others of the necessity for availing themselves of his services in another line. He was, therefore, made vice-agent of the whole colony of Liberia. After administering the affairs of this country a short period he fell a victim to an explosion which swept way several others who gave their lives as a sacrifice in that foreign land.

His fate, too, was not unlike that of Harrison Ellis of Alabama. In that rapidly developing slaveholding commonwealth where men gave little attention to things spiritual, even for the whites themselves, Harrison Ellis rose to great eminence as a power in the church. Born a slave, he was, of course, denied the opportunities for mental development. He was, however, a man of such strong character and so efficient in his work as a blacksmith, a trade in which he excelled, that it was possible for him to secure privileges denied so many others of his race. He soon mastered the rudiments of education, and building upon this foundation, began to acquire knowledge of Latin. Having a deep impression as to the worth of Christianity and the influence of the gospel as a factor in the uplift of his people, he thought of preparing himself for the ministry. The study of Latin then was to some extent neglected for a more thorough study of Greek with a view to reading the New Testament. Some attention was thereafter given to Hebrew to get a better grasp of the linguistic setting of the Old Testament. He thereafter took up the principles of theology.

A man of such unusual attainments in spite of the various difficulties with which he had to struggle in earning a livelihood and securing instruction, Ellis naturally impressed the people of his community. Coming under the influence of the Presbyterians, he was encouraged by them to make an effort for the exercise of his gifts as a minister. As a man of such a well developed mind could not find in this country adequate opportunity for service in this field, he was urged to go to Liberia. The Presbyterian synod of Alabama, therefore, examined him with a view to testing his efficiency. In this examination he proved himself a good Latin and Hebrew scholar and showed still greater proficiency in Greek. His attainments in theology were highly satisfactory. Giving an account of the rise of this prodigy the *Eufala Shield*, an organ of that State, referred to him as a man "courteous in manners, polite in conversation and missionary in demeanor." Impressed with his usefulness, the Presbyterians of Alabama finally purchased him and his family, in 1847, at a cost of $2,500, that they might go to Liberia and work among their own people.

In Liberia, Harrison Ellis took up his post under very favorable auspices. He quickly impressed those with whom he came in contact, attracted to him a sufficient number of persons to constitute a respectable following, easily held his own among other intelligent Negroes, and finally became one of the most influential men in the colony. Soon thereafter, however, like so many others, who in that land of their fathers gave their lives as a sacrifice for their many persecuted brethren in the western world, he finally proved inadequate to the demands of that climate and passed away, admired by those who knew and mourned by his coworkers and friends.

These few Negro ministers, however, could not reach the masses of their race. In their undeveloped state the rural Negroes depended upon the crumbs that fell from the white ministers' tables. The religious experience of such Negroes, therefore, was more nominal than rational. Many of them obtained their first religious impressions in some camp meeting during a special effort in behalf of the lost. These meetings were looked forward to with a great deal of anticipation and persons, knowing of the good supposedly derived therefrom, came from afar and remained about the place, thus giving to such convocations the well-known name of camp meetings. As these assemblages were social as well as religious and sometimes partook of a festive nature, the Negroes easily became attracted to this more liberal method of promoting the cause of Christ.

The Negroes in these meetings appealed especially to the white ministers because of their quick response to the appeal to come out of darkness into light. While an Episcopal clergyman with his ritual and prayer book had difficulty in interesting the Negroes, they flocked in large numbers to the spontaneous exercises of the Methodists and Baptists, who, being decidedly evangelical in their preaching, had a sort of hypnotizing effect upon the Negroes, causing them to be seized with certain emotional jerks and outward expressions of an inward movement of the spirit which made them lose control of themselves. The program of the day was a delivery of sermons at intervals, interspersed here and there by appeals to sinners to come forward to be prayed for at the anxious seat, while various members, having unusual influence over the unconverted and in touch with God, whispered in their ears the way to find salvation and life.

Among the Baptists, the soul-stirring reunion was known as a protracted meeting, which differed very little from that of the Methodist camp meeting. The preacher came forward, declaring the dawn of a new day and the shower of blessings that everyone could receive. The burden of his message was that he had come to set forth those things which had been hitherto kept from the wise and prudent but lately revealed unto fools. Seeing that they were made a special object of the philanthropy of these new workers, the Negroes became seized with hysteria because of this new boon; and the interest in the work passing from one to another, spread almost like a contagion, moving communities to seek salvation. Persons passing as sinners were made to feel that they were wretches in the sight of God and that direful punishments awaited them as the lot of the wicked. Their state was awful to behold, and their opportunities were swiftly passing away. That moment was the accepted time; for their delay would mean damnation. Persons fell helpless before the altar of the church and had to be carried out to be ministered unto, and when they emerged from their semi-conscious state they came forward singing the song of the redeemed who had been washed white in the blood of the Lamb.

Statistics show, however, that such a conversion of people who were given no opportunity for mental development amounted to very little in the edification of their souls. Not long after these exciting camp meetings and protracted efforts had passed over many of these persons, who had been most vociferous in their praise of God for cleansing them of their many sins, readily fell thereafter by the wayside in engaging in what is known as pleasurable evils. Baptists and Methodists during this period insisted that dancing was an evil, but how could the plantation Negro resist the temptation when he heard the clapping of the hands and the tune of the banjo? It became fashionable, therefore, for a person to be converted several seasons, sometimes once every four or five consecutive summers before his feet could be completely taken out of the mire and the clay and placed upon the solid rook where the wind might blow and the storm might rise, but none should frighten them from the shore.

Because this wild religious excitement meant very little in the uplift of the slaves, there were throughout the South members of other than Methodist and Baptist churches who still adhered to the idea of the literary instruction of the blacks. Although there were soon laws on the statute books to the contrary in practically all of the Southern States, the wives and children of ministers taught their few slaves to read the Bible, and when this was unpopular or prohibited, they made use of the catechism in requiring the Negroes to memorize the principles of religion and to learn formal prayers. There were some masters who went to the extent of opening private schools for their slaves.

The more the Negroes were instructed by these rather intellectual denominations, however, the less they, as a group, seemed inclined to join their fortunes with those persons who were disposed to lay a foundation for an intensive spiritual development. When the Methodists and Baptists had had a chance to proselyte the Negroes, the Episcopalians and the like were almost relieved of the necessity for any effort among them. From the report of Alston's Parish in South Carolina, in which there were 13,000 slaves, for example, 3,200 were Methodists and 1,500 Baptists, while only 300 belonged to the Episcopal Church. In St. Peter's Parish of that State the Methodists had 1,335 of 6,600 in 1845. In the Parish of St. Helena the Baptists reported 2,132 communicants, the Methodists 314, and the Episcopalians only 52. The Episcopalians discounted the religious benefit derived by attendance upon the Methodist and Baptist evangelical meetings, feeling that because of their social and festive nature the Negroes lost more in worldly pleasures thereby than they gained in spiritual uplift. Many of them believed that it would have been much better for the slaves, had their masters kept them at home. They did not think very well of the influence of the Negro preachers, contending that they often did harm. Where there was an improvement in Negro character many insisted that it was due to the religious and moral training given by their masters, and still more largely by their mistresses. For this reason it was strongly urged upon masters to manifest more interest in the morals of their bondmen, as it would not only make them better men spiritually but would increase their economic efficiency.

From the Negroes' point of view, however, religious experience did not result from instruction in books. Persons known to be illiterate had strange visions and prophesied with such success as to move multitudes. Slaves prohibited from attending meetings violated the law and braved the dangerous network of the patrols enforcing the police regulations. When converted they made no secret of their new experience and boldly shouted before their masters, praising the Lord. That they should, contrary to instructions, frequent the places of these emotional upheavals was considered crime enough, but to appear before their owners themselves, telling them about what the Lord had done for their souls and at the same time warning these aristocratic "Christians" to repent of their sins and flee from the wrath to come, was more than the ruling class could endure. These Negro converts were cruelly told to hush up because they "were getting above themselves," and if they refused to obey, many of them were whipped until they stood in puddles of blood drawn by the lashes inflicted upon their bodies, while others, stricken down with heavy blows or subjected to mortal torture, went to their death rather than cease to bear witness for Jesus.

CHAPTER VII
RELIGIOUS INSTRUCTION REVIVED

BECAUSE SUCH RELIGIOUS instruction as the Negroes received after the enactment and the enforcement of the reactionary legislation of the South failed to secure to them that mental development necessary to understand the Christian doctrine and to connect it with the practical problems of life, northern friends of the Negroes forced a change in their religious instruction by exposing the unchristian policy of preventing a people from learning of God through the only source of revelation, the Bible. Abolitionists like William Jay and many northern ministers who did not consider themselves anti-slavery, fearlessly branded as Sinners the so-called southern Christians who were thus preventing the coming of the kingdom of God. Southerners eloquently retorted on the defensive, of course, but believed in their hearts that the deplorable situation should be remedied. Much effort was made thereafter to render more thorough the oral instruction of slaves, but without very much success. Nearer the middle of the nineteenth century, however, there appeared among the clergy and sympathetic whites in the South some inclination to disregard the custom and laws of that section that the necessary foundation for the instruction of the Negroes in the Christian doctrine might be given.

In this work the evangelical denominations participated more freely than others. From the Episcopal Church to which most of the richest slaveholders belonged, not very much help came because that church never considered slavery a sin and never made it a matter of discipline. That the bodies of the Negroes were made miserable in this world and that their souls might be damned were of little concern to some persons, who were not especially interested in monopolizing heaven even for poor whites. The gospel, moreover, as some saw it, had little to do with the settlement of differences between the races in this world, since it was rather concerned with the adjustment of affairs in the kingdom to come.

There were among the Episcopalians, however, some striking exceptions to this rule. Among these should be mentioned Bishop Polk of Louisiana. In 1854, he informed Frederick L. Olmsted, who was then traveling through that country, that he had confirmed thirty black persons near the station assigned to the Legree estate, where the conditions set forth in *Uncle Tom's Cabin*, he contended, did not obtain. Bishop Polk owned 400 slaves himself but endeavored to bring them up in a religious manner, baptizing all of their children and teaching them the catechism. "All without exception," says Olmsted, "attend the church service, and the chanting is creditably performed by them in the opinion of their owner. Ninety of them are communicants, marriages are celebrated according to the church ritual, and the state of morals is satisfactory. Twenty infants had been baptized by the Bishop just before his departure from home, and he had left his whole estate, his keys and the like, in the sole charge of one of his slaves, without the slightest apprehension of loss or damage." Referring further to the slaveholding of this minister of the gospel, Olmsted remarked that "in considering the position of this Christian prelate as a slaveholder, the English reader must bear in mind that by the laws of Louisiana emancipation had been rendered all but impracticable, and that if practicable it would not necessarily be in all cases an act of mercy or of justice."

Taking up again the religious instruction of the slaves, Olmsted found "that there were widely different practices in that State." He observed that there were some other slaveholders who, like Bishop Polk, encouraged and even obliged their slaves to engage in religious exercises. Yet among the wealthier slave owners, and especially in that section of the country where the blacks outnumbered the whites, there was generally a visible and often an avowed distrust of the effect of religious exercises upon slaves and even the preaching of white clergymen to them was permitted by many only with reluctance. The prevailing impression among northern people with regard to the important influence of slavery in promoting the spread of religion among the blacks, he contended, was erroneous. Northern clergymen supposed as a general thing that there was a regular daily instruction of the slaves in the truths of Christianity. "So far as this is from being the case," said Olmsted, "although family prayers were held in several of the fifty planters' houses in Mississippi and Alabama in which I passed a night, I never in a single instance saw a field hand attend or join in the devotions of the family."

There should be mentioned also in this connection the services of Bishop Meade of the Protestant Episcopal Church of Virginia. Early in his career he addressed himself to the neglected condition of the Negroes, preaching rousing sermons, telling them their duty toward their own group. He was interested in the colonization movement and hoped to secure the release of certain recaptured Africans to encourage the manumission of others who might be given a chance to establish a nation for their race in Africa. Although thereafter he did not emphasize the emancipation of the slaves very much because of the reactionary influences at work in the country, he did advocate the thorough education of those slaves who were to be colonized abroad. As an impetus in this direction he republished the sermons of the Rev. Thomas Bacon, who answered every argument presented against the religious instruction of Negroes. He especially besought the ministers of the gospel to take into serious consideration a matter of which "they also will have to give an account." "Did not Christ," said he, "die for these poor creatures as well as for any others, and has he not given charge to the minister to gather his sheep into the fold?"

The Presbyterians, much more liberal in their attitude toward the blacks than the Episcopalians, manifested an unfailing interest in the condition of these people far down. Although the church as a national body receded from its early position of attacking slavery and thereafter compromised with the institution, there was among these people in the various parts of the country a continuous effort to promote the religious instruction of the Negroes. Early manifesting interest in the preparation of Negroes for colonization in Africa, the Presbyterians planned to bring out of the South Negroes liberated for expatriation that they might be first trained in a school for this purpose established at Parsippanny, New Jersey. As this failed, this church finally established for this purpose, in 1854, Ashmun Institute, now Lincoln University.

In the very heart of the South, however, the Presbyterians did not fail to aid the instruction of Negroes wherever public opinion permitted it, although they had to confine themselves largely to verbal instruction. In the mountains of Virginia, North Carolina, and Kentucky, where the Scotch-Irish element dominated, there was no diminution of ardor in the religious instruction of the Negroes. Expressions of interest came also from the Presbyterian synods of Georgia and Alabama, while those in the mountains openly advocated literary instruction as a preparation for thorough indoctrination. In the States of Maryland, Tennessee, and Kentucky, they were not handicapped by laws prohibiting the education of the Negroes. They, therefore, spoke out more boldly for the establishment of schools, and especially Sabbath schools, which paid as much attention to the teaching of reading as it did to the actual instruction in the Bible.

Among the Presbyterians in the South the most efficient worker was the Rev. C. C. Jones, who toiled among the Negroes in Georgia. Taking the situation as it was rather than complaining because it was not different, Jones addressed himself to the task of trying to convince the slave owners as to the advisability of religious instruction. He believed that if the circumstances of the Negroes were changed, they would equal if not excel the rest of the human family in religion, intellect, purity of morals and ardor of piety. He feared that white men would cherish a contempt for the Negroes which would cause them to sink lower in the scale of morality and religion. He, therefore, advocated the attendance of both races upon the same services that they might learn by contact from their masters. The independent church organization for which the Negroes contended, he believed, would rather give them an opportunity to deteriorate.

By a logical array of facts, moreover, he tried to prove that Negroes who had been instructed in the doctrines of Christianity had less tendency toward servile insurrection than those who had been left in heathenism. Even the Southampton insurrection started by Nat Turner, he believed, was due to the fact that, being unable to understand the real scheme of things, he had misguided the slaves by his false prophecy. Those Negroes who had been well instructed in the principles of Christianity had never been found guilty of any such crimes.

In this effort Jones had a very difficult task; for the tendency during that day was rather toward segregation in the church. Most southern men had no idea of elevating the Negroes to the status of white men, not even in matters of religion. The whites believed that the domestic element of the system of slavery itself afforded adequate means for their improvement and the natural safe and effective means of their elevation. In other words, their instruction must be decidedly different from that of white men, in regard to whom the term education had widely different significations. The best the Negro could hope for would be an imitation of the white man to call into action that peculiar capacity for copying the mental and moral habits of the superior race.

Jones's work did not differ materially from that of the Rev. Josiah Law of Georgia, who was almost as successful in grappling with the same problem. These workers, however, soon found that there was a strenuous objection even to the verbal instruction of Negroes for fear that the oral exercise would inspire a desire for literary training, which was out of harmony with the status of the Negro in a slaveholding commonwealth. Thinking that it might lead to such a state of affairs, most masters in some parts of the South opposed all instruction of Negroes during the thirties and forties.

Thereafter appeared occasional evidences of further interest in the religious instruction and the evangelization of the slaves and free people of color, however, in spite of this opposition. Much interest was manifested in this work by the Presbyterians of Charleston; Union, Georgia; Concord, South Alabama; and Mississippi. In 1825 the General Assembly went on record to the effect that "no more honored name could be conferred on a minister of Jesus than that of Apostle to the American slaves, and no service can be more pleasing to the God of Heaven, or more useful to our beloved country, than that which this title designates."

The minutes quoted from the report of the Presbytery of Georgia in 1839 said: "We are happy to say, in regard to the religious instruction of the Negroes, that this important part of our service has received a new impulse during the last year. This business receives considerable attention in many parts of our bounds. Plantations are open to all our ministers and fields presented among this people which it is impossible for them to occupy. Sabbath schools, for their exclusive benefit, exist in some of our churches, and we are happy to believe that there is an increasing interest felt on this subject. Within our bounds there is one minister whose whole ministry is devoted exclusively to this people, and most, if not all, the several pastors and stated supplies preach as often as once a week to this class of our population. In Liberty County there is at this time very considerable attention to religion among the blacks, not less than fifty being under serious impressions. A beloved brother in Augusta and another in the vicinity of Natchez are following the noble example by devoting their whole time to this interesting work."

The Presbytery of Georgia remarked in referring to one of their number who devoted his whole time to this work: "During the year he has been blessed with a revival in one part of his field of labor. Fourteen professed conversion, and were added to the church. Another brother, in another part of our bounds, reports the conversion and reception into the church to which he ministers, of eight colored persons." And the Presbytery of Hopewell spoke of their churches generally as cheerfully yielding the half of their pastor's services to this department of labor. It also expressed a belief that several churches "will soon be erected for the exclusive accommodation of the Negroes, and that the field will be occupied as missionary ground by at least one who is deeply interested in the work."

The Presbytery of South Alabama said in 1847: "Perhaps without a solitary exception our ministers are devoting a considerable part of their labors to the benefit of the colored population. It is a field which we all hope to cultivate; and to some the great Head of the Church is intimating an abundant harvest." "Most of our pastors," said the Presbytery of Charleston, "devote a part of the time to the exclusive service of the blacks and in some instances with the most pleasing success. A scheme is now in agitation for the full consent of the Presbytery for establishing an African Church in the city of Charleston."

In 1854 the report of the General Assembly on the instruction of the Negroes in the slave States said that instead of abating, the interest in the religious welfare of the Negroes was increasing. In their houses of worship provision at once special and liberal was made for the accommodation of the people of color so that they might enjoy the privileges of the sanctuary in common with the whites. "Besides this, nearly all of our ministers hold a service in the afternoon of the Sabbath, in which all exercises are particularly adapted to their capacities and wants. In some instances ministers are engaged in their exclusive service . . . not ministers of inferior ability, but such as would be an ornament and a blessing to the intelligent, cultivated congregations of the land. In a still larger number of instances the pastor of a church composed of the two classes, inasmuch as the blacks formed the more numerous portion, devotes to them the greater share of his labors, and finds among them the most pleasing tokens of God's smiles upon his work. Besides the preaching of the word to which they have free access, in many cases a regular system of catechetical instruction for their benefit is pursued, either on the Sabbath at the house of worship or during the week on the plantations where they reside. . . . The position taken by our Church with reference to the much agitated subject of slavery secures to us the unlimited opportunities of access to master and slave, and lays us under heavy responsibilities before God and the world not to neglect our duty to either."

Among the Methodists who directed their attentions to mission work among Negroes no one was more prominent than Bishop William Capers of South Carolina. He had no idea of preparing Negroes for manumission, but looked to the edification of their souls as a preparation for the life to come, justifying the relation of slave and the master by the Bible in keeping with most ministers of his time. He emphasized, on the other hand, the necessity of the masters' being kind to their bondmen and especially in providing for their spiritual needs. After preaching a number of sermons to this effect, he devised a scheme for adapting the teachings of the Christian truth to the mental condition of the slaves. He planned to have the old Negroes instructed by preachers and the children through catechists by the memory method, while their minds were in a plastic state, always remembering, however, that any minister who did not believe in the southern religion of the relation of master and slave as sanctioned by his sort of Christianity should not enter upon this work. With the support of a number of leading men in that commonwealth Bishop Capers established two missions in 1829 and two additional ones in 1833. Thereafter one or two others were added every year until 1847, when there were seventeen engaging the attention of twenty-five preachers. When Bishop Capers died in 1855 he saw his work, according to his plan, very well done. The Methodists then had 26 missions manned by 32 preachers, having in their churches 11,546 communicants. The cost of this religious instruction had, during the Bishop's time, increased from $300 to $25,000 a year.

The work of the Baptists here and there was almost as effective, but because of their lack of a national body to concentrate the effort of the various local churches, such good results did not always follow. In certain communities, however, especially in the State of Virginia, there were obtained unusually desirable results. This was the case in the cities of Portsmouth, Norfolk, and Petersburg; and still better success was achieved in Richmond through the well organized work of the First African Baptist Church, which, under the direction of the Rev. Robert Ryland, President of Richmond College, served not only to benefit the Negroes of that community, but also to inspire other white churches to make similar provisions for the instruction of the blacks.

Lott Cary himself speaks of religious instruction in this church at an early period. He said: "I was, during the years 1815, 1816, 1817 and 1818, engaged for the benefit of the leading colored members of the church" (referring to the First Baptist Church) "in a gratuitous school at the old Baptist meeting house . . . at first in connection with Rev. David Roper . . . and subsequently with Rev. John Bryce, co-pastor of the church."

The work of this church, however, was largely in the hands of the whites. The local government was changed from the democratic to something more Presbyterial than Congregational, because of the belief that the Negroes were not prepared for democracy. The government was vested in the pastor and thirty deacons exercising general supervision over the church and constituting the source of authority in the church. The instruction, of course, was at first confined to the catechism and to the memorizing of hymns and special passages of the Bible. Ryland himself compiled a catechism for the colored people and hoped to add to it such books as *Pilgrim's Progress, The African Preacher, The Life of Samuel Pierce* and *The Church Member's Guide.*

Ryland did not share the distrust of the Negroes who might learn to read. Unlike most of the ministers after this reactionary period, he advocated the thorough instruction of the slaves. He said: "They will make more useful servants, if in a state of bondage, and more safe and reliable residents, if free, by having their minds imbued with rational views of Christianity. How can we expect them to develop the great principles of the gospel in a well ordered life while they are dependent on desultory oral instruction for their entire knowledge? I am fully aware that some will think that I am approaching delicate ground, and yet with the most considerate feelings and with the admission that grave abuses might follow, I am constrained to believe, nevertheless, that greater benefit will accrue both to themselves and to society by increasing their facilities to understand the gospel whose maxim is 'On earth peace, good will toward man.' I am a Southern man by birth, education and habits. I deplore the ultraism and recklessness of the North on this subject and in the least on account of *increased restrictions* which have been thus occasioned to the colored people. But I would respectfully ask Southern Christians if they are not in danger of neglecting *known, imperative duty*, because others are not disposed to mind their own business. Let us not be led from the path of *real benevolence* either by the abolitionists of the North or by the morbid sensitiveness of the South."

Exactly how much Ryland accomplished at the First African Baptist Church is not known. Referring to his communicants, Ryland recorded that their general appearance was that of serious, intelligent worship. It is certain that many Negroes, who became impressed with Christianity and endeavored to embrace it, looked upon it as an opportunity and a privilege to belong to this church, and inasmuch as he emphasized consistent Christian conduct, it certainly forced a number of them to live more righteously than they would have, if these rules had not been rigidly enforced. The attitude here might be criticized in that the church was accepting merely those who were known to be persons of good conduct and did not seemingly go out to stir up and reform those who made no pretense to be Christians. When a person made a profession of faith and wanted to join this church he was required to present a certificate of good conduct.[40]

In this work Ryland had the cooperation of Joseph Abrams, a Negro who had been licensed to preach and ordained but had been prohibited from the exercise of his gifts by the hostile legislation proscribing Negro preachers after Nat Turner's insurrection. During the days prior to this reaction Abrams had been a preacher of much success among the Negroes of the First Baptist Church. Afterward he could take no more conspicuous part in the Sunday exercises than to pray a long prayer, into which he sometimes worked a short sermon. "As he enjoyed, however, the confidence of the citizens," says a writer in the *American Baptist Memorial* of 1853, "he was tolerated in preaching funerals at private houses, and was sparingly invited to close the worship in the church by words of exhortation." "He was heard with far more interest than I was," said Ryland, "and on this account I should have often requested him to speak but for the fear of involving him and the church in legal trouble." Abrams died in 1854. From the same pulpit which he had once occupied, his former pastor, John Bryce, delivered to a large crowd of grieving persons within and as many more without one of the most eloquent eulogies in keeping with the life of the man. A long procession of hundreds of persons followed him to his grave, over which the people erected a beautiful monument in the form of an imposing obelisk.

So emphatically was duty of religious instruction urged in certain parts of the South, that not only sympathetic clergymen and their children but men high in official positions championed the cause of literary instruction for the Negroes that they might learn the principles of religion. One important case in evidence is that of J. B. O'Neal of South Carolina. Discussing this matter in detail, O'Neal observed that the extension of the instruction of the Negroes to the extent of learning to read the Bible would hardly do any harm. He did not believe that the Christianization of the Negroes in a slave commonwealth would tend to lift them above their masters and destroy the "legitimate distinction" in the community. General Coxe of Fluvanna County, Virginia, had all of his slaves taught to read the Bible in spite of the law and public opinion to the contrary, and so did a farmer whom Frederick Law Olmsted visited in Mississippi. Other instances here and there may be mentioned. Exactly how many other persons of the aristocratic folk of the South had the same attitude is difficult to determine; for the white people of that day, like those of the present time, often conceded privately that the Negroes should enjoy their rights, but were unwilling to suffer the stigma of being called the champions of their cause.

With this new impetus given religious instruction in many parts, however, it was very difficult to overcome the desire for the more thorough evangelization of the Negroes. There was not only a manifestation of interest here and there in the South; but during the forties and fifties there followed considerable improvement, especially through such local organizations as those in Liberty and MacIntosh counties in Georgia and in the Presbyterian synods of Kentucky, Alabama, North Carolina, and Tennessee. A few Negroes, who prior to the reaction had learned to read and write and had a rudimentary knowledge of the Bible, were sometimes employed in the more liberal portions of the South to teach the aged and the young to say prayers, repeat a little of the catechism, and to memorize hymns. Here their instruction depended entirely upon the memory. What could not be thus done for them was neglected. Literature especially adapted to this end prepared by churchmen safeguarding the interests of the slaveholding South was preferably used. Some of these works were Dr. Capers' *Short Catechism for the Use of Colored Members on Trial in the Methodist Episcopal Church in South Carolina*, *A Catechism to be Used by Teachers in the Religious Instruction of Persons of Color in the Episcopal Church of South Carolina*, John Mines' *Catechism*, Dr. C. C. Jones' *Catechism of Scripture, Doctrine and Practice Designed for the Original Instruction of Colored People*, Dr. Robert Ryland's *The Scripture Catechism for Colored People*, and E. T. Winkler's *Notes and Questions for the Oral Instruction of Colored People with Appropriate Texts and Hymns*.

CHAPTER VIII
PREACHERS OF VERSATILE GENIUS

THE SITUATION IN the North was then more encouraging, though far from being ideal. During the critical period through which the Negroes were passing between 1830 and the Civil War the Negro minister had to divide his attention so as to take care of all of the varying interests of an oppressed race. Among the poor it has never been considered exceptional for a minister to work at some occupation to increase the meager income which he receives from his parishioners. We have already observed above that Andrew Bryan made himself independent as a planter, that Richard Allen at first earned his living as a teamster, and that Andrew Marshall with much business acumen maintained himself in a local express business. During the critical period from 1830 to 1860, however, the Negro minister was not only compelled sometimes thus to support himself, but often had to devote part of his time to the problems of education, abolition, colonization and the Underground Railroad.

Education for the Negro was both a test and a challenge. Few persons believed that the Negro was capable of the mental development known to the white man. The challenge to them, then, was: Show that your race has possibilities in the intellectual world, bring forth proof to uproot the argument that your race is the inferior of the other peoples. To make the challenge more concrete, can a Negro master the grammar, language, and literature of Latin, Greek, and Hebrew? Can he learn to think? Can he understand the significant things of life as expounded by mathematicians, scientists, and philosophers? A few Negroes had demonstrated here and there unusual ability in these fields; but they were not generally known or their achievements were accounted for by their racial connection with the white race in this country or with some Arabic stock of Africa, known to be Caucasian rather than Negroid.

The greater impetus to education among Negro ministers, however, came not so much from the desire to meet this requirement as from the need of it in promoting the work of the church. It is true that the whites were subjecting the blacks to a mental test, but it required very little logic to show that the contention as to Negro inferiority was a case of making desire father to the thought. The independent church movement had to depend on education; and the Negroes themselves, as they made progress, required of their ministry the service of instructors to bring the people to a higher 169 standard of thought. Acquiring an education then was not always an easy task. Negroes had no advanced schools of their own and they were generally refused in most of those of the North. Until the rise of the Union Literary Institute in Indiana, Oberlin and Wilberforce in Ohio,

Ashmun Institute in Pennsylvania, and Oneida Institute in New York, the Negro had to break his way into whatever institution of learning he entered. Negroes who were ignorant themselves could not always appreciate what the struggle for educational opportunities actually meant.

The Negro ministers, moreover, were at the same time in the midst of a life and death struggle. During the thirties and forties the questions involving the Negroes engaged the attention of almost everybody. The Negro ministers, the then best developed leaders among their people, could not be silent. Inasmuch as men had to be won to the support of the cause, these apostles to the lowly had to appear before the other race in the North as spokesmen of an oppressed people. Preaching was important enough, but there could be no preaching without the liberty to preach. Except in a few such cases as that of William Douglass, the rector of St. Thomas Church, Philadelphia, and that of Peter Williams, the rector of St. Phillips in New York City, where the proslavery church hierarchy hushed the Negro ministers loyally speaking for their people, the Negro 170 clergyman spoke out fearlessly for the emancipation of his race and its elevation to citizenship.

As the American Colonization Society went only half way in carrying out this program in that it advocated the emancipation of the Negroes for deportation to Africa, merely to rid the country of freemen belonging to another than the Caucasian race, the Negro ministers were generally opposed to that organization. They fearlessly attacked the promoters of the cause, saying, "Here we were born, here we fought for the independence of this country, and here we intend to die and be buried in the soil hallowed by the blood of our fathers shed in defense of this country." When, however, the increasing intelligence of the Negroes made their humiliation in this country less and less durable, the Negro ministers became divided among themselves on this important question; for a few of the leaders of that day began to advocate colonization in some other country than Africa.

In the meantime, moreover, almost every Negro minister was otherwise engaged in spiriting away fugitives from the slaveholding States through the North into Canada. They were in touch with men in other centers, found out what was going on, learned what was the trend of things, and planned to act accordingly. And well might they be so engaged; for not a few of these ministers were fugitives themselves, and whether or not their freedom had such origin, all Negroes in the North were, after the passage of that unconstitutional drastic Fugitive Slave Law of 1850, in danger of being apprehended and enslaved without what civilized countries regard as due process of law. Some of the ministers themselves had to move for safety into Canada during this crisis, carrying in some cases practically all of their congregations with them.

The Negro minister easily learned also the power of the press. Much time which they would have under other circumstances devoted to the edification of their flocks they had to spend in raising funds to purchase printing plants and in editing the publications issuing therefrom. They could deliver their message to their congregations, they could occasionally address thus groups of the other race; but their message needed a wider circulation in a more enduring form. There were, therefore, during this crisis few Negro ministers of literary attainments who did not either undertake to edit a newspaper or to contribute thereto. If they had a message worthwhile, the abolition papers would generally delight in publishing it. If they refused and the message was a burning one, the Negroes would establish an organ of their own.

To bring out this idea of the minister of divided interests serving his people in many ways, no career is more illuminating than that of Bishop Daniel A. Payne. Having been much better trained than most of his co-workers, he emphasized education as a necessary foundation for thorough work in the ministry. Taking this position, he made himself at first more of a teacher than a preacher, devoting most of his time to actual classroom instruction, hoping to raise the standard of the ministry in the African Methodist Episcopal Church, with which he finally cast his lot after being graduated at the Lutheran Seminary at Gettysburg. Taking this position, he had arrayed against him all the enemies of culture. One writer charged him with branding the ministry with infamy and with reckless slander on the general character of his own denomination. There was great fear that there might follow discord and dissolution between the ignorant and the intelligent portion of the church. Preaching to his congregation, the ignorant minister would often boast of having not rubbed his head against the college walls, whereupon the congregation would respond: "Amen." Sometimes one would say: "I did not write out my sermon." With equal fervor the audience would cry out: "Praise ye the Lord." Working zealously, however, Bishop Payne committed the denomination to the policy of thorough education for the ministry, a position from which the African Methodist Episcopal Church has never departed, and to which it owes not a few of the advantages that it now enjoys in having so many intelligent men in its ministry.

While Bishop Payne as a churchman did not become altogether involved in the anti-slavery movement, so many distinguished men in the church did. John N. Marrs of the African Methodist Episcopal Zion Church was more of an anti-slavery lecturer than a preacher. Thomas James of the same denomination was equally as effective as an anti-slavery lecturer. He was much readier to fight than to preach when he thought of the enormities of slavery. Another Zionite, Dempsey Kennedy, a pioneer preacher of remarkable skill in stirring up audiences, rendered as much service as an abolitionist as he did as a minister.

One of the best examples of this type is Charles Bennett Ray, born in

Falmouth, Massachusetts, December 28, 1807. He was educated at the Wesleyan Academy of Wilbraham, Massachusetts, and later at Wesleyan University, Middletown, Connecticut. After studying theology he became a Congregational minister. For twenty years he was the pastor of the Bethesda Church in New York City, where many learned to wait upon his ministry. He is better known to fame, however, by the work which he did outside of his chosen field in connection with the anti-slavery movement, the Underground Railroad, and *The Colored American*, which he creditably edited from 1839 to 1843.

Ray aided the cause of liberty by lending practical aid which men in high places often had neither the time nor the patience to give, using his home as a Mecca for the meetings of such men as Lewis Tappan, Simeon S. Josselyn, Gerit Smith, the land philanthropist, and James Sturge, the celebrated English philanthropist, interested in the abolition of slavery. In cooperation with wealthy abolitionists he assisted many a slave to the light of freedom, especially through the aid of Henry Ward Beecher of the Plymouth Church in Brooklyn. Ray found himself cooperating also with the group of radical free people of color meeting in Philadelphia and in other cities of the North from 1830 until the Civil War. When one reads of his participation in this work with James Forten, a business man, and Charles B. Purvis, another layman, he is inclined to forget that Charles B. Ray was a minister, as his name appears in the records of practically all of these conventions of the free people of color and his work stands out as an important factor contributing to the success with which these aggressive Negroes kept their case before the world and gradually hastened the dawn of their freedom. In all of his various employments, however, Ray did not lose interest in and did not necessarily neglect his mission to promote the moral uplift of his fellows. A contemporary, William Wells Brown, paying him a tribute as a terse, vigorous writer and an able and eloquent speaker, well informed upon all subjects of the day, says also that he was "blameless in his family relations, guided by the highest moral rectitude, a true friend of everything that tends to better the moral, social, religious and political condition of man."

In the class with Ray should be mentioned Henry Highland Garnett, another minister of the Presbyterian Church, devoting most of his time to the many movements which attracted the attention of his co-laborers. Having escaped from Maryland to the North in 1822, Garnett experienced sufficient mental development to ask for admission to the Canaan Academy, where he, along with Alexander Crummell and others, caused the school to be broken up by a mob arraying itself against the idea of permitting persons of color to enjoy such privileges in that community. Proceeding, however, to the Oneida Institute in New York, he succeeded in laying a foundation for his work under the noble-hearted friend of man,

Beriah Green. Here Garnett attained the reputation of an accomplished man, an able and eloquent debater and a good writer. He soon developed into a preacher of power of the evangelical type, whose discourses showed much thought and careful study. He had complete command of his voice and used it with skill, never failing to fill the largest hall. Soon there was a demand for him as a preacher. He was sent as a missionary to the Island of Jamaica. He later spent some time in Washington as the pastor of the Presbyterian Church and served at another time at the Shiloh Church in New York City.

Garnett, however, was soon more than a preacher. From the time he made his first public appearance in New York City in 1837 he secured for himself a standing among first-class orators. In 1843 he delivered before the National Convention of Colored Americans at Buffalo, New York, one of the most remarkable addresses ever uttered by man. His contemporary says: "None but those who heard that speech have the slightest idea of the tremendous influence which he exercised over the assembly." For forty years thereafter he was an advocate of the rights of his race, a forcible and daring speaker wherever he had an opportunity to present his cause. Visiting England in 1850, he was well received as an orator. Garnett, moreover, served much of his time as an educator, having been President of Avery College, where he passed as a man of learning.

In this group of enterprising clergymen of this period should be mentioned Alexander Crummell, although his more important service to the race belongs to the two generations following the Civil War. Crummell was a native of New York, but a descendant of a Timanee chief in West Africa. Early in his career he attended a Quaker school with Thomas S. Sidney and Henry Highland Garnett in New York, and later experienced with the latter, as mentioned above, the humiliation of seeing the Academy of Canaan, New Hampshire, broken up because of the admission of Negroes. Crummell then studied three years under Beriah Green at the Oneida Institute. Having then the aspiration to enter the ministry of the Episcopal Church, he applied for admission to the General Theological Seminary of the Protestant Episcopal Church of New York, which, in keeping with its hostile attitude toward the Negro, refused to accept him.

Thus barred from entering upon his life's work, Crummell could not then influence the public to the same extent as Negro leaders laboring in the more inviting fields. Presenting his case to the clergy in Boston in 1842, he was ordained deacon by Bishop Griswold. After studying two years under Dr. A. H. Vinton of Providence, Rhode Island, Crummell was ordained priest by Bishop Lee of Delaware at St. Paul's Church in Philadelphia, and engaged to work in a barren field. Here poverty and ill health overtook him and rendered his circumstances all but intolerable. To earn livelihood he conducted for four men a private school, which, after having a promising beginning, proved inadequate to his support.

He then went to England, where he was well received as a preacher and given the opportunity to prosecute further his studies at Queen's College, Cambridge University, from which he obtained the degree of Bachelor of Arts in 1853. Crummell then began his career as a missionary and educator, working in Liberia and Sierra Leone for about twenty years. He returned to the United States in 1873 and entered upon his work as an Episcopal priest in Washington, where, as the rector of St. Mary's, and as the founder of the American Negro Academy, he experienced the culmination of his usefulness as a scholar, a clergyman, and a champion of the rights of his people.

Among these workers should be mentioned also James W. C. Pennington, another minister of the Presbyterian Church. Pennington was born a slave on a farm in Maryland and there became a blacksmith by trade. Upon reaching maturity he escaped to the North, where he early embraced the opportunities for learning. He developed into an unusually bright scholar in Greek, Latin, and German; and soon manifested an inclination for the study of theology, in which he showed much proficiency. Impressed with his worth as an educated man well trained for the ministry, the Presbyterians ordained him to preach and stationed him at Hartford, Connecticut, where he served some years. He later became the pastor of the Shiloh Church in New York City.

While Dr. Pennington did not drift so far from the ministry as many of his co-laborers, he was at once in demand for work in various other fields. He went to Europe three times in the capacity of a lecturer. His second visit was the occasion on which he remained for four years, preaching, lecturing and attending the Peace Congresses held at Paris, Brussels, and London. While at Paris in 1849 he was invited to conduct divine services at the Protestant Church, which on that occasion was visited by the American and English delegates. His sermon was an elegant production, left a marked impression upon his hearers, and above all made a more logical case for the Negro. While in Germany the degree of Doctor of Divinity was conferred upon him by the University of Heidelberg. Returning to this country, he labored zealously and successfully for the education and the moral, social, and religious elevation of the race, until he went to Jamaica, where he died.

Rev. E. Payson Rogers, another Presbyterian preacher stationed as pastor of a church at Newark, New Jersey, divided his time between writing and preaching. He was a man of education, research, and literary ability. Although not a fluent and easy speaker, he was logical and spoke with a degree of refinement seldom observed. Possessing the inclination to write verse to express the thought and feeling of a struggling people, he wrote a poem on the Missouri Compromise which he read in many of the New

England cities and towns in 1856. This poem contained brilliant thought and amusing suggestions. Anxious to benefit his race, he visited Africa in 1861, where he was attacked by a fever and died in a few days.

J. Theodore Holly was another minister of versatile genius. He acquired a good education through studious habits and contact with men of culture. Although he became a clergyman of the Protestant Episcopal Church and was for several years pastor at New Haven, where he sustained the reputation of being an interesting and eloquent preacher, he set about to establish what he called Negro nationality. He was not primarily interested in African colonization, but believed that the redemption of Africa could be affected through Haitian emigration. In the *Anglo-African*, a magazine published in 1859, he contributed a dissertation setting forth these facts. Impressed with the idea that Haiti might be used as an asylum for free persons of color, he raised a colony in keeping with the resolution passed by the Convention of Free Persons of Color in Rochester in 1853 and sailed for Haiti in 1861. As the location which he selected was infelicitous, most of those who went with him, including his own family, died, and he returned to the United States, where he finally rendered greater service and from which he was later commissioned as Bishop of the Protestant Episcopal Church in Haiti.

One of the most interesting men of this type was Leonard A. Grimes, a Baptist minister, born in Leesburg, Loudoun County, Virginia, in 1815. Although he was a man of free parentage he was subjected to all of the disabilities that his race had to endure in the South except that of an actual slave. He spent his youth working at the butcher's trade and at an apothecary's establishment in Washington but subsequently hired himself out to a slaveholder whose confidence he gained. In accompanying his employer in his travels in the remote parts of the South he had an opportunity to see slavery in its worst form and to reach a decision that he would make every effort possible to destroy the evil. Returning to Washington very soon thereafter, he began to express an interest in the operations of the Underground Railroad, in connection with which he rendered valuable service. Upon being appealed to by a free man of color with a slave wife and seven children, he aided them to escape to Canada. Suspicion, however, fell upon Grimes and he was soon thereafter apprehended, tried, found guilty, and sent to the State penitentiary at Richmond for two years.

Upon the expiration of his imprisonment Grimes returned to Washington and soon then went to New Bedford, Massachusetts, where he resided two years. He next went to Boston. Having early in his career been impressed with the thought that he was called to the ministry, he had spent much of his time in this work while engaged as an agent of the Underground Railroad. Finding a group of persons in Boston at that time in need of a pastor, he entered upon the task of serving them in that capacity.

This congregation was known as the Twelfth Baptist Church, of which he was the pastor for more than twenty-five years, ministering to some of the best persons of color in that city in such a way as to make his work a monument to which Bostonians still point with pride. As a preacher he was a man of power, though not an easy speaker. He manifested great amiability of character and always had a pleasant word for those with whom be came into contact. Although primarily engaged in the work of the ministry during the great crisis in this country, he never abandoned entirely the anti-slavery cause, in spite of the fact that many of his denomination were trying to defend that institution. He passed away in 1873, after having experienced some of the freedom for which he struggled.

Among the prominent Negro ministers who lived through this critical period no one exhibited more versatility than Samuel R. Ward. Impressed with the superior gifts with which he was endowed, Gerrit Smith enabled him to secure a liberal education. Ward then entered upon the ministry in the Presbyterian Church. For several years he was settled over a white church at South Butler, New York, where, according to William Wells Brown, Ward "preached with great acceptance and was highly respected." Coming to the aid of his race during the trying days of the abolition agitation, Ward took the platform and from 1840 to the passage of the Fugitive Slave Law of 1850 preached or lectured in every church, hall, or schoolhouse in Western and Central New York. "Standing about six feet in height, possessing a strong voice, and energetic in his gestures, Ward," says his biographer, "always impressed his highly finished and logical speeches upon his hearers."

Ward became more of a platform orator than a preacher. His aim seemed to be not so much to preach the gospel of heaven as to preach the gospel of this world that men calling themselves Christians might learn to respect the natural and political rights of their fellows. In the interest of this cause he traveled through much of this country, visited England in 1852, and then went to Jamaica, where he finally resided until he died at an early age. Referring to the death of R. B. Elliot, Frederick Douglass, Ward's most famous contemporary, remarked: "I have known but one other black man to be compared with Elliot, and that was Samuel R. Ward, who, like Elliot, died in the midst of his years. The thought of both men makes me sad. We are not over rich with such men, and we may well mourn when one such has fallen."

No better example of the varying interests of the Negro can be mentioned than that of Hiram R. Revells, who after the Civil War became one of the two Negroes who have served in the United States Senate. Revells was born a free man at Fayetteville, North Carolina, in 1822. There he passed his boyhood and then went to Indiana, because the laws of North Carolina in 1835 forbade the establishment of schools for persons of color.

He had experienced some educational development by private instruction and was prepared to profit by the advanced training received in a Quaker school in Indiana. He then moved to Darke County, Ohio, where he remained for some time. He was subsequently graduated at Knox College, Galesburg, Illinois. Revells then entered the ministry as a preacher of the African Methodist Church at the age of twenty-five, holding his first charge in Indiana. He filled important posts in Missouri, Maryland, Kentucky, and Kansas, but did not succeed so well in St. Louis, where the church developed into a turmoil, resulting in the resignation of the pastor.

Upon the outbreak of the war, Revells directed his attention to other matters. He assisted in raising the first Negro regiment in Maryland and the first one in Missouri. He then returned to Mississippi in 1864, settling at Vicksburg and later at Jackson, where he had charge of congregations. He also assisted in the extension of the work of the African Methodist Episcopal Church in other parts and in establishing a school system. His health having failed, however, he returned to the North after the close of hostilities and remained there eighteen months, at the expiration of which he again came to Natchez, Mississippi, where he preached regularly to large audiences. Entering politics, he was appointed alderman by General Ames, who was then military governor there. In 1869 he was elected to the State Senate and the following year to the United States Senate.

CHAPTER IX
THE CIVIL WAR AND THE CHURCH

THE OUTBREAK OF the Civil War was also an outbreak in the church. The versatile minister then proclaimed war and sometimes donned the uniform. One half of the nation had preached that God hath made of one blood all nations that dwell upon the face of the earth; the other half insisted that the plan of the Creator was a caste system by which one element of the population should be made hewers of wood and drawers of water for the other. The ordeal of battle was then on, and it was believed that the exhibition of the greater force on one of the two sides would determine the will of God. Men of both sections fought for what they believed to be right. Sermons resounded with the ring of freedom, the Bible was quoted to strengthen the belief in a just war, and songs of a militant tone made the welkin ring with that enthusiasm with which the Christian boy was inspired to give his life as a sacrifice, fighting for freedom or defending his section from the invasion of the ruthless foe. God was here; God was there; in fact, he was, as the participants would have it, fighting the battles of all.

Negroes realized that the Christianity of America was being subjected to a test. They had entered the church themselves but only with the belief that this liberal doctrine of the power of God to free a man's soul from sin meant also that such power would eventually be adequate to free the body. They had borne the burden in the heat of the day, even walked through the flames of that fiery ordeal of death; but they had never lost faith in God. Here and there an old hero in the midst of his martyrdom had prophesied upon his dying bed that God would deliver his people from the hands of the oppressors; a heroine of vision had dreamed that her Maker had poured healing oils upon her lacerated back, assuaged her excruciating pain, and made her free. Patience had been the watchword of the Negro. God was moving in a mysterious way to perform wonders which in the near future would make all things plain. Stand still, therefore, and see the salvation of the Lord.

Would these dreams come true? Evidently they would, the Negroes thought, when they heard of churchmen denouncing slavery in no uncertain terms, memorializing the State legislatures and Congress for its abolition, and assuring the nation of their heartiest support in the suppression of the rebellion occasioned by the effort to save the tottering institution. The Negroes could not fail to see the hand of God in the declaration of these churchmen that our national sorrows and calamities had resulted from our forgetfulness of God and the oppression of our fellowmen. Chastened by the affliction of the Civil War, many like the Methodists hoped that the nation might humbly repent of its sins, lay aside its haughty pride, honor God in all her future legislation, and render justice to all who had been wronged. They honored Lincoln for his proclamation of freedom and rejoiced in the enactment of the measures designed to reach this end. And so impressed with this militant service of the church, Lincoln had to say in reply to this denomination: "The Methodist Episcopal Church, not less devoted than the best, is, by its greater numbers the most important of all. It is no fault in others that the Methodist Church sends more soldiers to the field, more nurses to the hospitals, more prayers to Heaven, than any. God bless the Methodist Church! Bless all the Churches! And blessed be God, who, in this our great trial, giveth us the churches!"

Because of this militant attitude of the church, the Negroes thought more of fighting for freedom than they did of saving souls. The slaves breathed the spirit of the song:

> *Oh, freedom! Freedom over me!*
> *Before I'd be a slave,*
> *I'd be buried in my grave*
> *And go home to my Lord and be free!*

Negroes known to be pious gladly donned the uniform and some ministers of the gospel abandoned their charges to recruit men to fight for the cause. The friends of the Negroes, moreover, were militantly arrayed against their former brethren in the South. The abolition churches of the North received the anathemas of the churches of the South and vice versa. The war was religious as well as political, causing wounds which having not yet been healed even unto this day seriously affect church work among Negroes in the South.

The Civil War as a social and political upheaval made necessary some readjustments in the church. The Negroes in the South were no longer bondmen to be circumscribed in keeping with the regulations of a slave commonwealth and the Negroes in the North might then exercise more liberty without the fear of incurring the displeasure of those having the impression that the Negroes should in religious as well as in other matters be subject to men who enjoy a superior social position. It was then, moreover, a different question from what it was before. Prior to the Civil War one had inquired as to what should be done for the Negro. It was then a question as to what the Negro would do for himself. Things for which he had long asked theretofore were thereafter readily given or taken.

For example, during the period intervening between the separation of the northern and southern wings of the church in 1844 and the Civil War, the Negro members of the Methodist Episcopal Church in the North asked for separate conferences, a more general recognition of their local preachers, and a larger participation in the affairs of the church. The reason given was that the African Methodists, holding up to these Negro communicants the contempt with which they had been treated by their white superiors, caused large numbers of Negro Methodists to join the independent African churches. The policy of the Methodist Church was not to grant such recognition, deciding, as it did in 1848, that such separate conferences were inexpedient. Some encouragement was given the employment of Negro local preachers. In 1852, in reply to an urgent request of this sort from the Negro Methodists of the Philadelphia and New Jersey conferences, where they were losing many to the African Methodists, a sort of annual meeting of the Negro Methodist pastors was allowed, if the bishop of the diocese concerned found it practicable. The Methodist Church held this position, however, despite the fact that on this account it lost not less than one-fourth of the membership of its churches from the year 1844 to the time when the annual conference of the Negro pastors was provided for in 1866. These white Methodists, however, consecrated Francis Burns for the service as Bishop of Africa in 1858 and in 1866 thus elevated to the episcopacy John W. Roberts, another man of color. As the appeal for the Negro conference was still more urgent this time not only from the Negroes of the Philadelphia and New Jersey conferences but from that of Baltimore, the General Conference had to take more definite action than merely to say that such a step was inexpedient.

The reasons for this action were many and complicated. In the first place, even after the secession of those in the South, there were in the Methodist Episcopal Church a number of members who, wishing to get rid of the Negroes, thought that a refusal to grant this request would alienate their affections to the extent that they would secede as the other African Methodists had done. Some of these communicants actually encouraged the Negroes in saying that, should the blacks go out and establish themselves independently of the whites, the latter would have more respect for them because of this exhibition of their self-reliance. To impress this on the Negro, some white Methodists went so far as to invite to their pulpits the ministers of the African Methodist Churches, whereas the Negro ministers in the Methodist Church itself were ignored. When this method of trying to convince the Negro that he was an intruder failed, the busy-bodies would often say that the white management of the Methodist Church was merely using the Negro members as tools.

Some then thought that, because of love for the Negroes, the Methodist Church did not want to see them go. Others believed that a majority felt that the Negroes should have their own choice whether for separate organization or to unite with one of the African Methodist Churches but that, should such action be taken, the public would get the impression that the Methodists had organized another Negro church to break the other two down. It was thought wise, moreover, to defer action of such far-reaching effects until the Negro question then so intensely agitated should approach nearer a definite settlement. A Negro national church, furthermore, could not minister to the wants of all Negroes inasmuch as the one proposed, like the other two already in the field, could not have prior to emancipation operated among the Negro Methodists in the South. The Methodist Church was neutral, if anything, during the Civil War period. It did not try to get rid of its Negro membership and it made no particular effort to increase it. Wherever one of the two African Methodist Churches was in a position to minister to the spiritual needs of the Negroes, the Methodists made no effort to proselyte such Negroes, although Negroes desiring admission to the Methodist churches were not refused.

This question was further agitated and had to be given serious consideration in 1864. The conference after discussing the memorials from the Negro membership took the position that it must retain oversight of the Negroes to give them efficient supervision. The conference, however, encouraged *colored pastorates for colored people* wherever practicable. It authorized the organization of mission conferences. These separate conferences, however, were not to impair the existing rights of the colored members nor yet to forbid the transfer of white ministers to such conferences where it might be deemed practicable and necessary. The Negroes in the Methodist Church had at last received some right to share in the management of their own pastorates, which, however, were still subject to the supervision of the white bishops. The African Methodists still made inroads on the Negro membership, therefore, because they could point with pride to men in authority in their church and the Negro members of the white connection usually conceded their point as well taken in that they received the bishops of the African Methodists in their homes and churches and gave them every possible consideration.

Some less numerous Negro communicants of white denominations were at this time severing their connection with their former coworkers. In 1865 the Negro members of the white Primitive Baptist Churches of the South organized at Columbia, Tennessee, the Colored Primitive Baptists in America. In 1866 the African Union First Colored Methodist Protestant Church of America and elsewhere was established by merging the African Union Church with the First Colored Methodist Protestant Church. In 1869 the General Assembly of the Cumberland Presbyterian Church organized its Negro membership as the Colored Cumberland Presbyterian Church.

The Methodist Episcopal Church, South, with a much larger number of Negro members than all of these denominations easily solved the problem of Negro membership, as the Cumberland Presbyterians had done. While the Methodists in the North reluctantly loosed their hold on the Negro membership by granting the people of color active participation in their affairs through an annual conference, the Methodist Church, South, almost voluntarily agreed to organize its Negro constituency as a separate organization known as the Colored Methodist Episcopal Church. Whether the southern Methodists did this to eliminate the Negroes or because they thought that the Negroes in their new status as freemen could do their own work better than white men, is a much mooted question. It is clear that many of the slaveholding type of Christians would want to get rid of the Negro members since they could no longer determine their faith and how it should be exercised. The only reason there was for the Negro to belong to the same church as that of his master was to control the exercise of his religious belief. As this was no longer necessary, the Negroes, so far as one element was concerned, could then easily go.

Desiring to attach to this branch of the Methodist Church the stigma of their having been once connected with their oppressors, some Negroes themselves have referred to these Colored Methodists as "seceders" and "a Democratic Rebel concern" intended to lead the Negroes back into slavery. Such statements are most uncharitable and they not only do the Negroes concerned an injustice but question the good motives of a number of benevolent southern men who took this step, feeling that it was the best way for the Negroes to develop their religious life after emancipation. There were many masters who believed that, since the Negroes had finally become free, they should have every encouragement to learn how to take care of themselves.

It would be most uncharitable, moreover, to suffer any stigma to attach to the Colored Methodists on this account. The Negroes who constituted this church went with the southern wing of that denomination at the time of its secession because they were compelled so to do. The independent African Methodists were by law and public opinion prohibited from extensive proselyting in the South and prior to the Civil War they had with the exception of their establishments in the liberal border States hardly touched the large body of the black population south of the Mason and Dixon line. The free Negroes in the South were, as in the case of Morris Brown and his followers in 1822, cut off from their brethren in the North and the slaves were compelled to worship according to the rigid regulations set forth above and in the same churches to which their masters belonged.

The separation of the Negro membership from the Methodist Episcopal Church, South, came after the Civil War. In 1866 the conference meeting that year in New Orleans made provision for the organization of the Negro members in separate congregations and for district and annual conferences, if the Negroes so desired. It was further provided on this occasion that if it were acceptable to the Negroes and it met the approval of the bishops of the church, the freedmen might have a general conference like that of the Methodist Episcopal Church, South, according to the regulations of which the Negro deacons, elders, and bishops, if necessary, should be ordained to conduct this work among their own people. It was further determined that should the time arrive when the Negro members should be so set apart, all the property intended for the use of such members, held by the trustees of the Methodist Episcopal Church, South, should be transferred to duly qualified trustees of the new organization.

At the next conference of the Methodist Episcopal Church, South, meeting in Memphis in 1870, it was reported that the Negro membership had organized five annual conferences and unanimously desired to be organized as a distinct body. The Memphis Conference thereupon agreed to comply with this request. Delegates were then elected to the first general conference which assembled in Jackson, Tennessee, December 15, 1870. From the Methodist Episcopal Church, South, there were sent as representatives Bishops Robert Paine and H. N. McTyeire; and as ministers, A. L. P. Green, Samuel Watson, Thomas Taylor, Edmund W. Sehon, Thomas Whitehead, and B. J. Morgan. The prominent delegates from the five annual conferences of the Negro members were Richard Samuels, Solon Graham, Anderson Jackson, R. T. Thiergood, L. H. Holsey, I. H. Anderson, R. H. Vanderhorst, W. H. Miles, W. P. Churchill, Isaac Lane, John W. Lane, Job Grouch, F. Ambrose, and William Jones.

After having had read to this body the action of the conference it was suggested that a committee be appointed to find a new name for this proposed body. The name proposed was the Colored Methodist Episcopal Church in America, which was unanimously accepted. The body then proceeded to elect bishops. W. H. Miles was elected on the first ballot. Afterward R. H. Vanderhorst was also chosen. Bishops Paine and McTyeire then consecrated them the first two bishops of the Colored Methodist Episcopal Church in America. Three additional bishops, L. H. Holsey, J. A. Beebe, and Isaac Lane, were elected and ordained in March, 1873.

The large body of Negroes, however, were attracted after the war not by the Methodist Church but by the Baptist. The freedom, which even prior to emancipation meant so much in the growth of the Baptists, was thereafter a still greater cause for their expansion. It was easier than ever for a man to become a prominent figure in the Baptist Church. While the Methodists were hesitating as to what recognition should be allowed the Negroes or whether they should be set apart as a separate body, the Negro Baptists were realizing upon their new freedom which made possible the enjoyment of greater democracy in the church. Every man was to be equal to every other man and no power without had authority to interfere.

This situation in the Baptist Church appealed very strongly to the then recently enfranchised Negro in the reconstructed States. As the white man of the South had over emphasized politics and the professions to the extent that these avenues in that section were overmanned, the Negro in his undeveloped state accordingly made the same mistake in trying to escape drudgery. A rather hard row to hoe, or an unusually heavy burden was too often abandoned on hearing a call to the ministry, and the devotee thus impressed had practically no difficulty in securing a hearing in this locally democratic Baptist Church. The grade of intellect possessed by the novice in this ministerial service had little to do with his acceptability; for there were all sorts of degrees of mental development among the freedmen and every man preferred to follow the one who saw the spiritual world from his own particular angle and explained its mysteries in the dialect and in the manner in which he could understand it. If in delivering the gospel message the verb might not every time agree with the subject, that had little to do with the power to start a soul on the way to glory.

Operating on this basis, local churches sprang up here and there as Baptist preachers, a law unto themselves, went abroad seeking a following. Out of some of these efforts came several good results. Many of the churches thus established have in our day developed into beacon lights. And so was it true of some of those churches which branched off from or drew out of the old Baptist Churches of long standing established years before the Civil War. There were not so many such African Baptist churches in the South during that period. Because of fear of servile insurrection the whites would not permit many Negro churches to have an independent existence. The pressure once removed, however, groups of Negroes long waiting for religious freedom found adequate opportunity for exercising it in the organization of numerous Baptist churches. This was not in all cases abruptly effected, for the Negroes had no church buildings of their own and could not easily purchase them; but in their poverty they made unusual sacrifices to meet this emergency and whites liberally inclined assisted them in the rapid promotion of this work. Yet this movement did not reach its climax until some years later; for the lure of politics presented another field of so much interest to the Negroes that even the preachers of long standing too often abandoned their posts altogether. After the Reconstruction, moreover, when the Negro in the South had been removed from politics, a much larger number of bankrupt leaders entered the ministry or devised schemes to make use of the various churches.

An impetus toward improvement came from mutual associations. The Baptist churches were not obligated to unite to form associations and when formed did not necessarily have to be bound by the action of these annual meetings; but immediately after the war Negro Baptist churches, which in the South had formerly been coolly received by white bodies and were not permitted to form associations of their own, readily united for mutual benefit in the exercise of their new freedom. In those meetings the uninformed heard of the urgent need to educate the masses, the duty of the ministry to elevate the laity, and the call upon all to Christianize the heathen. The periodical visits of white churchmen, interested either in the

Negro or in exploiting them, brought new light as to what was going on in the other bodies conducted by men of higher attainments.

As the Negro Baptists, however, did not soon effect more potential organizations than the district Baptist Associations then composed of a few churches, they never had a national policy; and their local democracy would have furnished no machinery to carry out such a policy, if they had adopted one. To the State groups, then, must the reader look for the signs of progress and thanks to the genius of the Negro, such evidence was not long wanting.

The Negro Baptists of North Carolina organized the first State Convention in 1866. Alabama and Virginia followed in 1867, and very soon thereafter came Arkansas, Kentucky, and finally all of the States in the South. Immediately thereafter they began to affiliate with larger national bodies. The first of these larger groups was the Northwestern and Southern Baptist Convention, organized in 1864. In 1866 there was held an important convention in Richmond, when it was determined to consolidate all of the general interests of the Negro Baptists, the Missionary, the Northwestern and Southern conventions as one large body, to be called the Consolidated American Baptist Missionary Convention.[41]

This convention operated largely in the South and tended to decline. In 1873 the West revived its organization under the name of the Baptist Association of the Western States and Territories, while the northern churches adhered to another organization called the New England Missionary Convention, organized in 1875. In the course of time these two bodies so expanded as to embrace the whole country, yet in 1880 certain Baptists here and there formed a national body to do work in foreign lands, designating it the Baptist Foreign Mission Convention of the United States. The feeling, however, that there should be a concentration of the efforts of all Baptists directed through one national body to a particular point of attack led to a more significant national meeting of the Negro Baptists held in St. Louis in 1886. The work of the Baptist Foreign Mission Convention was later so modified that all of the national and international church work of the denomination was unified through the organization of the National Baptist Convention.

That these Baptists despite their excess of liberty succeeded as well as they did, was due in a measure to the fact that they exercised the good judgment in not immediately getting too far from their friends. The Negroes used the same polity, the same literature, and sometimes the same national agencies as the white Baptists. The southern Baptists were then less interested in these communicants whom, some say, they gladly got rid of when they could no longer dictate their spiritual development as the master did that of the slave; but the northern Baptists felt obligated to send their missionaries among the freedmen. These apostles to the lowly brought words of good cheer, expounded the gospel, established new churches, and distributed books for the enlightenment of the masses. Among some of these lowly people these men were received as apostles of old, welcomed to a new harvest which had long been waiting, for the laborers among the lowly were few.

CHAPTER X
RELIGIOUS EDUCATION AS A PREPARATION

THE SEPARATION OF the Negro churchmen from the white organizations, however, was not necessarily a declaration of war. Most Negroes regarded this as the right step toward doing for themselves what others had hitherto done for them and some whites so considered it. As a matter of fact, the ties which have bound the Negro church organization to the whites were not such as could be severed by a more change in the management of church affairs. The Negroes had already been divided from the whites by an unwritten law. The upheaval of the Civil War merely furnished the occasion for the separation. There still remained among the northern whites numerous philanthropists who desired to help them in the promotion of religion and morality. From this group, therefore, came numerous Christian workers supported by funds freely contributed to deliver the captive and proclaim the year of jubilee.

These Christian workers, however, cared not so much about proselyting as they did about education, the greatest need of the freedmen. The Baptists, Methodists, and Presbyterians, who had considerable communicants among the Negroes prior to the Civil War, took the lead in this movement, establishing at strategic points schools which they believed would become centers of culture for the whole race. The Baptists established Shaw University at Raleigh in 1865; Roger Williams at Nashville and Morehouse at Atlanta in 1867; Leland at New Orleans and Benedict at Columbia in 1871. The Free-Will Baptists founded Storer College at Harpers Ferry in 1867. The Methodists, who were no less active, established Walden at Nashville in 1865, Rust at Holly Springs in 1866, Morgan at Baltimore in 1867, Haven Academy in Waynesboro in 1868, Claflin at Orangeburg in 1869, and Clark at Atlanta in 1870. The Presbyterians, who could not compete with the Baptist and Methodists in proselyting Negroes, largely restricted their efforts to the establishment of Biddle at Charlotte in 1867 and to the promotion of the work begun at Lincoln University in Pennsylvania, established as Ashmun Institute in 1854. The Episcopal Church showing the tender mercy of the wicked, established St. Augustine at Raleigh in 1867. The American Missionary Association, an agency of the Congregational Church, established Avery Institute at Charleston, Ballard Normal School at Macon, and Washburn at Beaufort, North Carolina, in 1865; Trinity at Athens, Alabama, Gregory at Wilmington, North Carolina, and Fisk at Nashville in 1866; Talladega in Alabama, Emerson at Mobile, Storrs at Atlanta, and Beach at Savannah in 1867; Hampton Institute in Virginia, Knox at Athens, Burwell at Selma, now at Florence; Ely Normal in Louisville in 1868; Straight University at New Orleans, Tougaloo in Mississippi, Le Moyne at Memphis, and Lincoln at Marion, Alabama, in 1869; Dorchester Academy at McIntosh, and the Albany Normal in Georgia in 1870. The Congregationalists, moreover, figured in the establishment of Howard University, which was chartered by the United States Government in 1867 with provision for the education of all persons regardless of race.

Some other less effective forces were at work during this period accomplishing here and there results seemingly unimportant but in the end productive of much good. In 1862 Miss Towne and Miss Murray, members of the Society of Friends, established the Penn School on St. Helena Island. Cornelia Hancock, a Philadelphia woman of the same sect, founded the Laing School at Mount Pleasant, near Charleston, South Carolina. Martha Schofield, another Friend of Pennsylvania, opened at Aiken in 1865 the Schofield Industrial School. In 1864 Alida Clark, supported by Friends in Indiana, engaged in relief work among Negro orphans in Helena, Arkansas, and in 1869 established near that city what is now known as Southland College. The Reformed Presbyterians maintained a school at Natchez between 1864 and 1866, and in 1874 established Knox Academy at Selma, Alabama. The United Presbyterians opened a sort of clandestine school in Nashville in 1863, and in 1875 established Knoxville College as a center for a group of schools for Negroes in Eastern Tennessee, Virginia, North Carolina, and Northern Alabama. Franklinton Christian College, maintained by the American Christian Convention, was opened in 1878 and chartered in 1890. Stillman Institute was established by the southern Presbyterians at Tuscaloosa in 1876. Paine College was founded at Augusta in 1884.

With these striking examples of sacrifice in behalf of the education of their race, the Negro churches themselves began to participate in the extension of education as a means to spread the gospel through an intelligent ministry and to enable the laity to appreciate it as the great leverage in the uplift of the man far down. The African Methodists had through the efforts of Bishop Payne already undertaken the establishment of Union Seminary near Columbus, which was finally merged with Wilberforce, established by the Methodists in 1858 near Xenia, Ohio. The African Methodists also established Western University in Kansas. To extend their educational work in the South, however, this same denomination established Allen University at Columbia in 1881; Morris Brown at Atlanta in 1885; and later other schools at Waco, Texas; Jackson, Mississippi; and Selma, Alabama. The Zion Methodist Church too was planning the establishment of Livingstone College in 1879 and removed to the present site of Salisbury in 1882, was popularized extensively by the eloquent J. C. Price. Early emphasizing education, the Colored Methodist Church opened Lane College at Jackson, Tennessee, in 1882 and later established other schools at Birmingham, Alabama, Holly Springs, Mississippi, and Tyler, Texas. With the support of the American Baptist Home Mission Society the Negro Baptists have done likewise and, moreover, have established independently of the whites other such schools as the Virginia Theological Seminary and College at Lynchburg, largely developed by the talented Gregory W. Hayes; the William J. Simmons University of Louisville; the Arkansas Baptist College, now under the direction of the efficient J. A. Booker; and the National Training School for Girls in Washington, D. C., an institution so well managed by the noted orator and indefatigable worker, Nannie H. Burroughs.

To make proper use of the schools various organizations cooperating under the name of Freedmen's Aid Societies sent workers into the South to meet every need of the Negro. These efforts were not altogether those of the church, but so many churchmen were connected therewith that the story of the Negro church would be incomplete without it. Cooperating with these agencies, the American Missionary Association had in 1868 as many as 532 missionaries and teachers working among the Negroes, spending as much as $400,000 a year.

Then there came the National Freedmen's Relief Association of New York with 14 teachers and funds amounting to $400,000 and $250,000 in supplies; the Pennsylvania Freedmen's Relief Association or Philadelphia Society with a force of 60 teachers and a fund of $250,000 in 1865; the Western Freedmen's Aid Commission with receipts aggregating $227,000 to support teachers in the South in 1865; the Northwestern Freedmen's Aid Commission sending to the South in 1865 as many as 50 teachers. In the District of Columbia, among the Negroes themselves, there were organized and operated the National Freedmen's Relief Association and the National Association for the Relief of Destitute Colored women and children, the latter being supported by funds appropriated by Congress.

The Friends, a distinctly religious body, early participated in the same work through various local agencies. Among the first was the Friends Association of Philadelphia and its vicinity for the Relief of Colored Freedmen, which between 1863 and 1867 expended $210,500 among the freedmen in Virginia and North Carolina. More interested in education and religion, the Friends' Association for the Aid and Elevation of the Freedmen worked among the Negroes of Virginia and South Carolina, where between 1862 and 1869 they maintained 14 schools with 732 students and expended for schools, seeds, supplies, donations to asylums, and 50,000 copies of the New Testament, $57,500.

The New England Friends began work among the freedmen in 1864 in Washington, D. C., operating there a store at cost prices and conducting day, evening, and Sunday schools. Finally there cooperated with the New England Friends those of Maryland organized in 1864 as the Baltimore Association for the Moral and Educational Improvement of the Colored People. This society was fortunate in receiving annually for some time a subsidy from the city of Baltimore to the amount of $20,000.

Foreign friends of the race were equally active in promoting education and religion among the freedmen. In 1863, members of the Society of Friends in England contributed to this relief work £3,000. The following year £5,000 came from this source in England and £1,500 from Ireland. That same year there came through the New England Society $2,100 from the London Freedmen's Aid Society, smaller sums from France and Ireland, and $1,313 from five Parsee firms in London. Similar contributions were secured from abroad by other relief societies organized in the United States. According to facts obtained by the Freedman's Bureau the English aid societies contributed to the relief of the Negroes between 1865 and 1869 at least $500,000. Dr. J. L. M. Curry believed that the total receipts in money and supplies reached $1,000,000.

The facts set forth above well represent the activities of the Friends and of the Congregationalists, Free Will Baptists, Wesleyans, Methodists, and Reformed Dutch, for whom the American Missionary Association served as an agent; but there were in the field several churches working independently. Among these were the Methodists, Baptists and Presbyterians. To systematize its efforts the Methodists organized in 1866 "The Freedmen Aid Society of the Methodist Church." The first efforts of this society were directed toward primary, normal, and higher education. In 1868 the Methodists had then established through this agency 29 schools with 51 teachers and 5,000 students in Virginia, Kentucky, Tennessee, Mississippi, Louisiana, Alabama, and Georgia. By the end of the sixth year of its existence the receipts of the society amounted to $315,100.

During these years the American Baptist Home Missionary Association supported by Presbyterians and United Brethren in Christ, was sending workers right in the wake of the Union armies invading the Mississippi Valley. The Baptists had opened a school for Negroes in Alexandria in 1862, and by 1864 had sent missionaries into the District of Columbia, Virginia, the Carolinas, Tennessee, and Louisiana. Because of the freedom exercised by the Baptists locally, there was among them much duplication of effort which resulted in confusion; but the American Baptist Home Missionary Association finally emerged as a unifying factor among these workers. This society had made such rapid strides by 1867 that it had in the field 50 ordained ministers and a large number of Negro students in training for the work. The Free-Will Baptists while cooperating with the American Home Missionary Association made some efforts by themselves. They carried on some work in the Shenandoah Valley and in the West with 40 missionaries and teachers and 3,467 students.

The Presbyterians also took this work seriously. The General Assembly in session at Pittsburg in 1865 appointed a special committee on freedmen, with 18 members, two of whom were designated as secretary and treasurer. As there were already in the field 36 teachers as missionaries supported by local societies, this general bureau took over their work. The following year there were in the field 55 missionaries, reporting 3,256 day pupils, 2,043 Sunday School scholars, and six churches with 526 members, in Tennessee, Alabama, North Carolina, and Kansas. The income for this work was $25,350 in 1865, together with 30 or 40 boxes of clothing; but between 1865 and 1870 this denomination expended $244,700 to maintain their workers, who in 1820 had increased to 157, of whom 105 were Negroes. The Old School and United Presbyterians did not accomplish so much but they had a few missions here and there. In 1864, there were in Washington five schools with 174 students supported by the Reformed Presbyterian Board of Missions with an expenditure of $3,000 a year.

Some other sporadic efforts in behalf of the freedmen deserve at least casual mention. The Protestant Episcopal Freedmen's Commission was organized in 1865 to engage in this work, but with the exception of some physical relief extended the unfortunate it accomplished very little. From The Massachusetts Episcopal Association for the Promotion of Christian Knowledge among the Freedmen and other Colored Persons of the South and Southwest, organized that same year, still less assistance came. The American Bible Society up to 1868, however, distributed a million copies of scriptural and religious works among the freedmen. The American Tract Society also sent out such works, opened some schools, and conducted church services in Washington.

The Negroes, although poor in the goods of this world, soon made sufficient sacrifice materially to give impetus to the relief work among themselves. The Negroes in Maryland gave $23,371 to aid the relief work promoted by the Baltimore Association for the Moral and Educational Improvement of the Colored People. They organized bodies of their own, moreover, to participate directly in this uplift work. In 1864 there was established in Brooklyn "The African Civilization Society," which gradually extended its work through churches and schools into the District of Columbia, the Carolinas, Maryland, Virginia, Georgia, Mississippi, and Louisiana. The reports of this organization show that in 1868 it employed 129 teachers instructing 8,000 students at an expense of $53,700. For some years the society operated in Brooklyn an orphan asylum with the aid of the Freedmen's Bureau, but in 1869 the management found itself embarrassed for lack of funds. From 1864 to 1868 the African Methodists so extended its mission and school work as to have 40,000 Sunday school pupils and 39,000 volumes in school libraries.

It will be interesting to mention some of the men in the North, who constituted the management of the home offices of these aid societies and who used their time and influence in raising the necessary funds. Among the officers of the American Freedmen's Aid Commission, a sort of general agency in New York for several relief societies, were William Lloyd Garrison, the famous abolitionist, as vice-president; Frederick Law Olmsted, the noted traveler through the South prior to the war, serving as general secretary; and, as directors, John G. Whittier, the antislavery poet, Francis G. Shaw, another abolitionist, and Henry Ward Beecher, the true and tried friend of the Negro. Lyman Abbott became general secretary of the combined organizations. The American Freedmen's Aid Commission and The American Union Commission added to their staff William Cullen Bryant, Phillip Brooks, Bellamy Storer, and Edward L. Pierce, who had done so much for the contrabands in South Carolina prior to the close of the war. When most of these societies in a convention in Cleveland united under the name of the American Freedmen's Union Commission, they had for president Chief Justice Chase, who not only by word but by actual sacrifice of his means did much to promote the Christian education of the freedmen.

Among the supporters of the New England Society there appeared many workers known before as friends of the Negro. The Rev. Edward Everett Hale and J. M. Manning were most active in Boston in raising funds and finding teachers and missionaries to work in Negro schools. Gov. John A. Andrew served as the first president of the New England Freedmen's Aid Society, Edward Atkinson as secretary, and James Freeman Clarke as vice-president. And from New England came scores of workers, following up the work commenced by those gallant soldiers, Thomas Wentworth Higginson, and Robert Gould Shaw.

Southern people were not exactly neutral on the enlightenment of the Negro. They did not, as a whole, seriously object to it and in the course of time there appeared among them men of their own group fearlessly advocating Negro education. Dr. A. G. Haygood, a distinguished churchman among the Methodists, deserves here some mention. He represented in a large measure the best thought in the South concerning the Negro. He came forward to impress upon the South the claims of the Negro on the "sympathy and helpfulness of all who were more fortunate, especially those who called themselves the followers of Jesus Christ." This sentiment he set forth in a book, entitled *Our Brother in Black*, which struck the North with agreeable surprise and led the South to think more seriously of another solution of the so-called Negro problem. Invited to be the Director of the John F. Slater Fund established soon thereafter, Dr. Haygood had an opportunity to spend nine years translating into action the theory set forth in his book.

Less interested in Christian education but nevertheless effective in promoting generally the cause which made the situation of the Negro church so much better in the South was Dr. J. L. M. Curry, a lawyer and congressman, representative of the Southern Confederacy. His work as Director of the Peabody Fund, easily connected with the systematic efforts of

Dr. Amory Dwight Mayo, a northern man, who investigated the Negro schools in the South, set forth methods for their improvement and kept the North and the South well informed as to the forces at work among Negroes for the good of all. The southern churches as a whole during this period, however, did not so quickly forget their prejudices as to do anything of consequence for the good of the Negroes. The Negro had been begrudgingly granted his freedom and the northern teacher and missionary seemed like interlopers to be tolerated but not worthy of cooperation. The South, moreover, could not have done very much for Negro missions for the reason that immediately after the war it was decidedly impoverished; for many of the aid societies which assisted the Negroes ministered also to the whites in the desolated areas.

These missionary teachers came with a determination to do something like that of Francis Xavier, Henry Martyn, and Adoniram Judson, who bore the religious message to the Orient. They came to change the character of the freedmen through an intelligent religion based upon actual knowledge of God as revealed in the Bible. Among these workers one should mention Rev. D. L. Johnson, a teacher of refugees in Washington; Solomon Peck, a volunteer teacher of the contrabands at Beaufort, South Carolina, in 1862; Horace Bumstead, afterward President of Atlanta University; and Gen. O. O. Howard, President of Howard University.

The sort of education promoted by these workers will further explain the significance of the movement. All of the church aid societies and many of those beyond the control of churchmen had for their purpose the industrial, social, intellectual, and religious improvement of the freedmen. The capstone of the structure they would build then had its foundation in moral and religious instruction. Most workers, therefore, were chosen with regard to their fitness to function in these positions as missionaries in the school room. Few persons volunteering to do such work at that time could be devoid of a sympathetic nature, but more than this was required to build in these new citizens that Christian character which would make them helpful to their fellows and useful in the work of the Master. While education was necessary for the Negroes as for all other persons, the chief need of the Negro, as most of these workers observed it, was religion.

Acting upon this idea, therefore, almost every Negro school provided in some way for religious instruction. If the course of study were not sufficiently broad to base thereupon a more advanced course, there was usually provided some instruction in the English Bible. In case the course of study became so pretentious as to style itself a college curriculum, there was usually added the regular course in theology, which, in spite of the fact that it was the only professional work in which such institutions engaged, was sufficient for them to take over the title of university. Although lacking adequate understanding sometimes, however, these institutions had so much of the right spirit that they accomplished all but wonders. While they did not always hold the students long enough to impart all that a college graduate or a professional man should know, they so inspired the youth with the love of study that the habit once formed led them into fields of research and endeavor which men much better trained often failed to reach.

The emphasis of the northern churches upon instruction rather than upon mere proselyting immediately after the war, therefore, was not misplaced. They no doubt wrought more wisely than they thought. The Negro already had his predilections toward the Methodists and the Baptists and the mere contest for the increase of church membership to be recruited among a people, the masses of whom could not then serve God intelligently would have been love's labor lost. Northern denominations wisely cooperated with one another regardless of sectarian lines to do whatever was needful whether or not the largest contributor to the success of the enterprise received credit for it. Negroes who went from these schools had, of course, the impress of the respective denominations to which they owed their education, but very often, as it was in the case of the Presbyterians, the denomination lost to the others of a more popular appeal most of the men which it trained. Lincoln and Biddle Universities have by their training of men who, on leaving school joined the Methodists or Baptists, contributed to the success of these denominations. When one thinks of Walter H. Brooks, the popular Baptist minister in Washington, and of Joseph C. Price, the idol of the Zion Church, as graduates of Lincoln University, this contention becomes convincing.

With all of these workers in the field promoting religious education without regard to creed, the Negro churches soon had a much larger number of men equipped to extend their work. The minister who could neither read nor write became an exception to the rule and when still ambitious in spite of such shortcomings he sometimes ceased to have a following. Preaching became more of an appeal to the intellect than an effort to stir one's emotions. Sermons were made as an effort to minister to a need observed by careful consideration of the circumstances of the persons served, hymns in keeping with the thought of the discourse harmonized therewith, and prayers became the occasion of thanksgiving for blessings, which the intelligent pastor could lead his congregation to appreciate and of a petition for God's help to live more righteously. In fact, the tone of worship in the Negro church had been as a result of the post bellum efforts in education very much changed as early as 1875 and decidedly so by 1885.

Given such an impetus the work of the Christian church among Negroes was rapidly carried forward. Within a few years the neglected masses of the freedmen unto whom the gospel had never been successfully preached were generally evangelized and provided with some sort of facilities for religious instruction. Publication societies sold through colporters and missionaries religious literature adapted to the special needs of the freedmen and religious workers organized in churches circles devoted to the study of Christian doctrine and the Bible. As the church thus liberalized offered the Negroes a much better opportunity for development than the other institutions, many of which for years after emancipation were regarded as spheres which the Negro should not enter, the freedmen specialized in the study of this one concern thrown open to them, mastering in a few years the principles of the Christian religion and the story of the Bible to the extent that their friends and enemies were all but startled. As a result, therefore, Negroes of today have a much more thorough knowledge of these fundamentals than most white men.

CHAPTER XI
THE CALL OF POLITICS

THIS FAVORABLE BEGINNING, however, was not indicative of a straight-forward attack on the tents of wickedness. Many Negroes who were trained for the ministry never entered thereupon because of the lure of politics during the days of Reconstruction. Some who had engaged in this Christian work found out that in spite of the most thorough training by pious men, they were not fitted for such a calling and abandoned it for the political arena. Others who were seemingly successful in the ministry divided their time between their profession and politics, either because of the exigencies of the situation or the desire to attain positions of prominence in keeping with the traditions of the white people of the South, who have emphasized unduly the status of the professional class.

There were during the Reconstruction period, moreover, so many other necessities with which the Negroes had to be supplied that the Negro preacher, often the only one in a community usually sufficiently well developed to lead the people, had to devote his time not only to church work but to every matter of concern to the race. In some respects, the Negroes after the war were not far removed from the conditions obtaining in the North before the war. Many of their former problems still confronted them. The chief difference was that after the war the Negroes had fighting ground on which to stand to wage a battle for those things which, having been begrudgingly granted, were being gradually taken away.

That the Negro preacher should continue a man of so many interests was but a natural consequence of the trend in the development of the race in this country. Up to this time the Negroes had established and maintained only one institution of their own. That was their church. When the time came for them to exercise other functions in society this one institution had to be overworked to supply the needs of others. Inasmuch as the church then became the center of so many activities the minister in charge often had to take the lead in shaping the policy of his people that they might advance in the right way. Ministers who abandoned their pulpits for the political world may be condemned as deserting their post of duty; but when one considers the call of their race in the situation in which it was and the valuable services some of them rendered, he cannot hastily conclude that the race thereby lost more than it gained. History should be studied sympathetically. The devotee to the faith should not denounce these men as recreant to Christianity and the student of politics must not dub them as interlopers in a forbidden field. Never before had a race been liberated under such circumstances. Never before had a group in such an undeveloped state been called upon to do so many things in such a short time. That the procedure of the race in this infinitely complex situation differed somewhat from that of others who had centuries to do what the Negroes were required to accomplish in a day, should be no cause of surprise.

In this respect, moreover, the Negroes did not differ widely from the whites. It is true that there has not been any period in the history of the whites when such a large percentage of the ministry freely participated in matters of the world, but the Negro minister found in the record of the whites precedents for all of his deviation from the customary course of the preacher of the Word. In their frontier condition the pioneering whites had often been reduced to the necessity of following the leadership of the versatile minister just as the Negroes were during the Reconstruction period. Among them the minister was sometimes the man of all work. He had a farm or business from which he obtained most of his means of subsistence; he of necessity often studied law and practiced in the local courts; he not infrequently aspired to office and, if successful, sometimes forgot his beginnings. And even within the memory of the living, examples are not wanting. Ex-Governor Atkinson of West Virginia was a minister in the Methodist Church and, like the Negro during these trying days, answered the call of his constituents. James A. Garfield, who attained the presidency of the United States, abandoned this exalted profession for the more interesting role of politics.

The salient facts of the careers of some of these ministers thus allured are more than interesting. Dr. William J. Simmons after being educated and engaged in the Baptist ministry for some time entered politics in Florida about 1874. Well received by his neighbors, he soon became county clerk and then county commissioner. He served as chairman of the county campaign committee and a member of the district congressional committee. In the campaign of Hayes and Tilden, Simmons was a conspicuous figure. He stumped the State for the Republican candidates with such success as materially to aid the cause in that he helped to raise the Republican majority of his county from 525 to 986 when the whole State gave Hayes a majority of only 147. Dr. Simmons later settled in Louisville, where he distinguished himself as a minister and as the founder of what is now known as the William J. Simmons University.

Dr. James Poindexter's career shows how difficult it was for the Negro ministers to avoid politics. Coming from Virginia, as a pioneer among those who sought better opportunities in the Northwest, he was at once a serious leader. He became a minister in the Baptist Church even before the Civil War and never actually sought an official position, hoping rather to maintain himself as a fearless speaker and writer in behalf of his oppressed people. Yet he too was to some extent attracted to politics in self-defense. He was the first man of color in Ohio nominated for the House of Delegates, but was defeated. We find him some years later serving as the foreman of a grand jury. He was appointed a trustee of the Ohio University at Athens but the Democratic Senate of the State would not confirm him. He was for four years a member of the City Council of Columbus, serving that body as vice-president. Later he was appointed to fill a vacancy on the School Board of Columbus, was elected to the position at the expiration of the term, and reelected against great odds over a Democratic opponent in 1887.

Poindexter's position in this case, like that of so many others, may be stated in his own words. Addressing an audience on the "Pulpit and Politics," he said: "Nor can a preacher more than any other citizen plead his religious work or the sacredness of that work as an exemption from duty. Going to the Bible to learn the relation of the pulpit to politics, and accepting the prophets, Christ, and apostles, and the pulpit of their times, and their precepts and examples as the guide of the pulpit today, I think that their conclusion will be that wherever there is a sin to be rebuked, no matter by whom committed, and ill to be averted or good to be achieved by our country or mankind, there is a place for the pulpit to make itself felt and heard. The truth is, all the help the preachers and all other good and worthy citizens can give by taking hold of politics is needed in order to keep the government out of bad hands and secure the ends for which governments are formed."

Dr. J. T. White, another preacher of the Reconstruction period, attained much distinction in this field. Fortunate in having acquired a fundamental education in Indianapolis prior to the war, he easily made an impression at the Consolidated Baptist Convention in St. Louis in 1865 when he received a call to a small Baptist Church of Helena, Arkansas. Among these communicants he toiled successfully without concern as to other affairs until 1868, when the reconstruction of the State was begun. He was induced to present himself as a candidate for delegate to the constitutional convention and was elected. He figured conspicuously in framing the constitution and canvassed the State to secure its ratification. He then became a part of the restored State government, serving his fellow citizens as a member of the House of Delegates, to which he was twice re-elected. He was chosen to serve one term in the State Senate, after which he was appointed by the Governor, Commissioner of Public Works and Internal Improvements. During this same period, however, he was doing his best work in building and edifying churches at Helena and Little Rock, and extending Baptist influence throughout the State and nation.

G. W. Gayles, a Mississippian of this type, acquired before his emancipation enough education to read intelligently. Having an inclination to study the Bible, he aspired to the ministry, for which he was set apart by a council of reputable Baptist ministers of Greenville in 1867. Going to Bolivar County to find a more inviting field, he became the pastor of the

Kindling Altar Church in which he made an honorable record. He soon became involved in public affairs, however, as is evidenced by his appointment as member of the Board of Police for a district in Bolivar County by Governor A. Ames. The following year he was appointed Justice of the Peace in that county by Governor J. L. Alcorn, but later in that same mouth he was made a supervisor of another district in that county. He was then elected a member of the Mississippi Legislature, serving a term of two years in the lower house and then as State Senator from the 28th district, beginning 1877 and continuing into the eighties, when there had been no other Negro in that body since 1875.

In spite of his political activities, however, Gayles did not abandon religious work. Beginning in 1872, he served for many years as missionary for the counties of Bolivar and Sunflower and then in that capacity for Coahoma. Appreciating his worth, the Baptist State Missionary Convention made him its corresponding secretary in 1874 and president in 1876, with the power to edit a denominational organ known as *The Baptist Signal*, by which he showed himself a national as well as a State character.

Jesse Freeman Boulden was forced into politics against his will. In Philadelphia he acquired an elementary education. He later embraced religion in Maryland, and in 1853 connected himself with the Union Baptist Church in Philadelphia. He then became pastor of the Zion Baptist Church in Chicago, where he was succeeded by Richard DeBaptiste as pastor of the combined Olivet Baptist Church in 1863. As the war was then turning out favorable to the Union forces, Boulden called together at Brooklyn, Illinois, in 1864, a group of Illinois Baptist churches known as the Wood River Association to consider the importance of following the army and looking after the interests of the denomination in the South. This work then engaged the attention of Mr. Boulden to the extent that he gave up his church in 1865 and settled at Natchez, Mississippi. This was in many respects the turning point of his career. He immediately plunged into political matters as a leader to the manner born. He presented to Congress the first petition of that State praying that Negroes be granted the right of franchise. Boulden held the first emancipation celebration in 1866, and began to lecture to Negroes on the duty of the hour. Thus interested, he was made a factor in the organization of the Republican party in the north-eastern part of the State. He made the first Republican speech in the court house at Columbus and was a member of the first Mississippi Republican State Convention in 1867.

In all of this, however, he was not seeking personal gain; for brought out against his will as a candidate for the lower house of the legislature, he once thought of declining, but finally yielded, thinking that he might be able to do some good. In this position he took the lead in piloting through the legislature the election of Hiram Revells as United States Senator, and, after helping B. K. Bruce to become Sergeant-at-Arms of the Senate, used his influence to make him also a member of the upper national body. He, like many others of his time, however, never deserted the ministry altogether for politics. After serving various churches and editing *The Baptist Reflector* of Columbus, Mississippi, he rendered his most valuable service as general agent of the American Baptist Home Mission Society for the State of New York.

P. H. A. Braxton, pastor of the Calvary Baptist Church in Baltimore, and the Rev. D. F. Rivers, once a member of the Tennessee Legislature, seemed to have had their day in politics and then entered upon the ministry in contradistinction to most men of their time. Leaving the farm on which he was born a slave in Virginia, Braxton went into the stave business. Entering politics in King William county soon thereafter, however, he became constable in 1872, acquitting himself with honor. In the meantime he studied law with some degree of success. He then went to Washington, D. C., where he received an appointment in the custom house service in which he was converted in 1875. It seems that he lost the desire for politics thereafter. He was commissioned to preach in 1875, and appointed general agent of the consolidated American Baptist Missionary Convention in 1878. He took charge of the Calvary Baptist Church in Baltimore in 1879 and there made a record for himself and his denomination as a forceful preacher, successful organizer, and radical reformer. Rev. Mr. Rivers, after toiling in the West, came to Washington where he is still an active pastor.

Allen Allensworth prepared for the ministry at the Ely Normal School and at Roger Williams University. He rose rapidly in the denomination, serving the Kentucky Baptists as their financial agent, the pastor of churches at Elizabethtown, Franklin, Louisville, Bowling Green, and Cincinnati, and as a missionary in the employ of the American Baptist Publication Society. During these years, however, he was equally active as a leader in politics. The Republicans of Kentucky made much use of him as a campaigner, as he was a speaker of well-known power. By this party he was chosen to serve as an elector for the State-at-large on the Garfield-Arthur ticket in 1880 and was sent as delegate from that State to the National Republican Convention which met in Chicago in 1884. No one knows how far his political activity would have gone, had he not entered the army as chaplain before the Negro political organization in the South had collapsed.

Christopher H. Payne, who with the possible exception of Mordecai W. Johnson, has been the most intelligent preacher of color to toil in West Virginia, shows in his career how the political world finally absorbed some Negro ministers altogether. He began as a teacher In West Virginia, where by dint of energy he mastered the fundamentals of education. He then became converted and on realizing a call to the ministry, entered the Richmond Institute where he distinguished himself as a promising scholar. After serving the American Baptist Publication Society as a Sunday school missionary and as pastor of churches in Virginia and West Virginia, he became interested in politics in which he participated not only as a speaker but as an editor. He spent some time reading law, secured admission to the bar, and practiced in the local courts. In the course of time, he became more widely known as a figure in politics than as a churchman, although he was at the same time serving as pastor of some church and presiding over Baptist Associations and for years the Baptist State Convention of West Virginia. In 1896, he was elected a Member of the West Virginia Legislature, the first Negro to be so honored in that State. He was later appointed a deputy Collector of Internal Revenue under Nathan B. Scott, and in 1903 was appointed Consul to the Virgin Islands, where he served fourteen years. Since the recent purchase of these possessions by the United States he has remained there to practice law.

Bishop W. B. Derrick of the African Methodist Episcopal Church also had a political career. From a brief career on the high seas he enlisted in the United States Navy during the Civil War and upon being converted entered the ministry of the African Methodist Church, serving with distinction in the Virginia Conference. Having by the end of the seventies attained this position of influence, he was induced to take an active part in the politics of that State at the time when one of the local parties desired to readjust the State debt. He allied himself with the "Funders," the party in favor of paying the debt as it was contracted, since he believed that his attitude was in harmony with the principles of the National Republican Party. Thinking that his people were about to be made tools in the hands of ambitious and unscrupulous men, Dr. Derrick fearlessly denounced the "Readjusters" as a clique seeking to repudiate the payment of an honest debt. As this contest developed into a vindictive political battle engendering much local strife out of which the "Readjusters" emerged victors, Dr. Derrick, deeming it best to leave Virginia, resigned his charge and spent some time visiting his relatives in the West Indies. He returned to this country to resume his ministry in which he so rapidly developed that he became a popular bishop of his church.

Bishop H. M. Turner, one of the outstanding men of the Negro race, had his day also in politics. He equipped himself for the ministry by private instruction obtained under adverse circumstances, joined the Methodist Church in 1848, and transferred to the African Methodists in 1867, rising rapidly in this last-mentioned connection from the position of an itinerant preacher in St. Louis to an eldership in Washington, and a chaplaincy in the United States Army. During these years, however, he was most active in politics. In 1867 he was appointed by the National Republican Committee to superintend the organization of the Negroes in Georgia. In this capacity he stumped the State and wrote many articles which he spread broadcast to direct his people in his way. That year he was elected a member of the State Constitutional Convention. He was next chosen a member of the legislature the following year and re-elected in 1870, when he was expelled on account of his color. President Grant appointed him postmaster of Macon in 1869; but he had to resign on account of persecution. He was afterward appointed Coast Inspector of Customs and United States Government Detective, but after holding the position a few years he resigned it to meet the demands of the church whose cause, in spite of his political activities, he had never abandoned, and whose good judgment made him the influential bishop of the denomination.

Speaking of his career himself, he said on an occasion: "And my labors have not stopped in the religious sphere, but it is well known to everyone that I have done more work in the political field than any five men in the State, if you will take out Colonel Bryant. I first organized the Republican party in this State, and have worked for its maintenance and perpetuity as no other man in the State has. I have put more men in the field, made more speeches, organized more union leagues, political associations, clubs, and have written more campaign documents, that received larger circulation, than any other man in the State. Why, one campaign document I wrote alone was so acceptable that it took four million copies to satisfy the public. And as you are well aware, these labors have not been performed amid sunshine and prosperity. I have been the constant target of Democratic abuse and venom, and white Republican jealousy. The newspapers have teemed with all kind of slander, accusing me of every crime in the catalogue of villainy; I have been arrested and tried on some of the wildest charges and most groundless accusations ever distilled from the laboratory of hell. Witnesses have been paid as high as four thousand dollars to swear me into the penitentiary; white preachers have sworn that I tried to get up insurrections, etc., a crime punishable with death; and all such deviltry has been resorted to for the purpose of breaking me down, and with all they have not hurt a hair of my head, nor even bothered my brain longer than they were going through the farce of adjudication. . . . I invariably let them say their say and do their do; while they were studying against me, I was studying for the interest of the church, and working for the success of my party."

Richard Harvey Cain, converted in 1841 and installed as a preacher in the African Methodist Episcopal Church in 1844, saw himself rising to a position of usefulness after his training at Wilberforce, followed by his pastoral work in the New York and South Carolina Conferences. Although he had unusually extended his field of labor by successful efforts at Summerville, Lincolnville, Georgetown, Marion, and Sumter, he had too much energy to be confined altogether to the church. Interesting himself in whatever touched the life of his people, he edited a Republican newspaper in 1868.

He secured his election as a member of the Reconstruction constitutional convention in South Carolina and played an important role in rebuilding the government of that State along liberal lines. He served two years as State Senator from the Charleston District. In 1879 he was given a much more honorable recognition in being elected a member of the Forty-third Congress. He was again thus honored in being elected to the Forty-fifth Congress in 1881 and "served with distinction and marked ability," making most eloquent speeches in the advocacy of civil rights for the Negro.

His close connection with the church, however, was still maintained, for he was elected bishop in 1880 and assigned to the Louisiana and Texas district. Speaking of him as a man remarkable for uniting these two fields, Bishop Derrick said: "He surely could be considered a captain of the hosts, one of the kindliest and pleasantest of Christian statesmen and a man of clear good judgment blended with a strong resolution and firmness, which made him the master of many difficult situations in the active and political career which marked his statesmanship with brilliant success.

Bishop B. W. Arnett, one of the most popular men who have hitherto risen in the African Methodist Church, served his people also in these two ways. When political opportunities were first offered the Negroes in the South he had already served as a teacher and had passed through the gradations of the ministry to a position of influence in his denomination in Ohio. The need was too urgent and the call too imperative for him not to participate in the affairs of his State and nation. Once in politics, he easily became a commanding figure even in Ohio, where because of the small black population a Negro could not secure the following easily obtained at that time in the Southern States. In 1885 he was elected to the Ohio Legislature from Greene County, thus securing the opportunity to fight for the repeal of the nefarious "Black Laws" which disgraced the statute books of Ohio prior to the Civil War. Arnett piloted through the lower house the bill to this effect and with Senator Ely supporting it in the Senate, the feat was triumphantly accomplished. Never did a Negro serve his people to better advantage. At the same time he was using his influence to correct national abuses and was earnestly laboring for the extension of his church, which he honorably served as financial secretary, statistician, and finally as bishop.

Bishop James W. Hood, of the African Methodist Episcopal Zion Church, in his day one of the most influential men of color in the United States, found himself also in the political world. He began as a preacher in Nova Scotia in 1860, served later at Bridgeport, Connecticut, and then went to North Carolina, where his successful work exalted him to the bishopric in 1872. His very going to North Carolina, however, had a political setting. He went to Newbern as a missionary under General Butler's invitation to the churches to send missionaries, even while the place was under the fire of the Confederate forces. When the war in that area was cleared up and Reconstruction was undertaken Bishop Hood was among the first to participate therein. He was elected president of the convention of Negroes assembled at Raleigh in October, 1865, one of the first, if not the first, political convocation of this sort ever assembled in the South. On this occasion he so fearlessly advocated equal rights for the Negro that he was warned by the people around that his life would be in danger, if he did not desist therefrom In 1867 he was elected as delegate to the constitutional convention of North Carolina, in which he took such an active part in framing the fundamental law, incorporating into it such liberal provisions for homesteads and public schools that it was spoken of by the reactionaries as Hood's constitution until it was amended in 1875. He served as a magistrate under the provisional government in North Carolina and later became a deputy Collector of Internal Revenue for the United States.

In 1868 he was appointed an agent of the State Board of Education and Assistant Superintendent of Public Instruction, receiving a salary of $1,500 a year; but he did not abandon his church work, having built up a large congregation at Charlotte during the three years he served in these positions. He traveled also in the interest of the Freedmen's Bureau in the capacity of an Assistant Superintendent. Thus in a position to help his people, Bishop Hood had in 1870 as many as 49,000 Negro children in school. He had established for Negroes a department for the deaf, dumb, and blind and had about sixty inmates under care and instruction at the expense of the State. He hoped to establish a State university, but the undoing of Reconstruction prevented him from reaching that end. He was named in 1872 by the Republican caucus as their candidate for Secretary of State, but he declined the honor. He served that year as delegate at large to the National Republican Convention, which nominated Grant the second time. In 1876 he was chosen temporary chairman of the Republican State Convention, which he served with much satisfaction.

This account of the Negro in politics, however, does not establish the fact that either the majority or even the best prepared of the Negro ministry devoted all of their time to politics. There were many striking examples to the contrary. Bishop Daniel Payne lived long after the Civil War to promote education and religion, and when he died was regarded by many as the most useful man of the race. Bishop Lee, as President of Wilberforce University and a functionary of the African Methodist Episcopal Church, rendered his race constructive service. Dr. Alexander Crummell took no active part in politics, although he fearlessly spoke out for the political and civil rights of his race. Dr. J. Sella Martin, prominent in the ministry before and after the Civil War, attained the distinction of one of the most eloquent men of his race without permitting politics to consume much of his time. Bishop Grant, one of the most useful men of his denomination, did not find it necessary to seek honors beyond the limits of the church. John Jasper, known to fame as the Baptist preacher of the Sun-Moving theory, established for himself throughout Virginia and adjacent States a reputation for piety and sincerity, which, without political influence, made him a power in the country.

Among these consecrated churchmen, moreover, none can be considered a better example than Bishop B. T. Tanner, a well-educated man, who became distinguished in the services of his church years before the emancipation. His addresses exhibited learning and mature thought and the several works which he published entitled him to the distinction of being one of the most scholarly Negroes of his time. Among these works may be mentioned his *Apology for African Methodism, The Negro's Origin, An Outline of Our History and Government; the Negro, African and American.* In 1884 he was made editor of the *African Biblical Review,* which he so popularized that he was soon chosen bishop by his denomination.

Bishop L. H. Holsey of the C. M. E. Church distinguished himself by a career equally as honorable. After rendering faithful service as a minister in the church he was elevated to the episcopacy at a time when the church needed the guidance of a master hand. The manner in which he addressed himself to his task and the good results which he obtained soon convinced his communicants that the selection was not a mistake. That during his day the Colored Methodists did their task so well was due in a measure, of course, to the numerous sacrifices made by other faithful churchmen of his denomination. Among these should be mentioned Bishops Elias Cottrell, Isaac Lane, R. S. Williams, N. C. Cleaves, R. A. Carter and C. H. Phillips, who still stand as the respectable and trustworthy leaders of their denomination.

Deserving of honorable mention in this connection are many distinguished Negroes who impressed the world as preachers of power. They not only built imposing edifices and pastored large congregations, but went from place to place in the State and country impressing the world with the power of God unto salvation. So generally did they ingratiate themselves into the favor of the public that they passed among the people as seers and prophets of a former period. Among these should be mentioned Dr. W. Bishop Johnson and Dr. C. M. Tanner of the District of Columbia; Dr. Harvey Johnson of Baltimore; E. K. Love and W. J. White of Georgia; Daniel Stratton, Nelson Barnett, and R. J. Perkins of West Virginia; and J. J. Worlds and L. W. Boone of North Carolina. There were also James Holmes, for years the pastor of the First Baptist Church of Richmond, Virginia; Dr. Richard Wells, the pastor of the Ebenezer Baptist Church in the same city; Anthony Binga, a churchman of scholarly bearing, who wrote important dissertations of a theological nature while pastoring the leading Baptist Church in Manchester, Virginia; and Dr. William H. Stokes, a worker of much influence in Richmond, still speaking fearlessly in behalf of his people.

Identified with this serious group was Richard DeBaptiste, who migrated with his free parents of color from Fredericksburg, Virginia, to the Northwest after the restrictions placed upon the Negroes of this class in Virginia became intolerable. His first important work was that of teaching a public school for colored youth in the Springfield township at Mt. Pleasant, Ohio, where he later organized and pastored a Baptist Church from 1860 to 1863. He then became pastor of the Olivet Baptist Church in Chicago, a charge which he held until 1882. Serving in this capacity, he purchased two building sites at a cost of $16,000 and built two brick church edifices costing respectively $15,000 and $18,000.

His work as a minister, however, was in no sense local. He was elected corresponding secretary of the Wood River Association in 1864, was a prominent figure and officer in the Northwestern and Southern Baptist Convention organized in 1865, and was chosen president of the American Baptist Missionary Convention in Nashville, Tennessee, serving it consecutively for four years. He was thereafter elected president at intervals and remained a commanding figure in the convention because of his power and influence in the church. Manifesting further interest in the work of the denomination, he contributed to the church literature through the *Chicago Conservator*, the *Western Herald*, and the *National Monitor*. In fact, in his day he was not only the outstanding minister of his denomination in the West, but one of the most influential men of his race.

One of the most prominent ministers of the Reconstruction period who were not deterred from their course by politics was Rufus L. Perry. Born a slave in Nashville, Tennessee, where because of the liberal attitude of the whites toward the Negroes, he, in spite of his condition, was permitted to attend a free school for Negroes, Perry had, even before the Civil War, laid a foundation upon which he well built thereafter. He escaped from slavery in 1852 and entered upon the study of theology at the Kalamazoo (Michigan) Seminary, graduating with the class of 1861, when he was ordained as pastor of the Baptist Church at Ann Arbor, Michigan. He later served as a pastor at St. Catherine's, Ontario, and at Buffalo and Brooklyn, New York. He had then convinced the world that he was "very logical, a clear reasoner, close and active debater, deep thinker, and excellent writer," "a man of splendid natural abilities," who "goes at once to the bottom of any subject that he undertakes."

Upon the dawn of freedom he entered upon the larger duties in the service of the Negroes, doing at first missionary and educational work among the freedmen, endeavoring to evangelize and elevate the race through the system of religious education. Seeing the need for an organ through which his people and his denomination could speak to the world, he edited *The*

Sunbeam, served as coeditor of the *American Baptist*, and later edited *The People's Journal* and *The National Monitor*. His articles always showed his interest in his denomination, his knowledge of general literature, and his grasp of men and things. For ten years he served as corresponding secretary of the Consolidated American Baptist Missionary Convention and was later made corresponding secretary of the American Educational Association and of the American Baptist Free Mission Society.

Having given much attention to the study of ethnology and the classics, he doubtless impressed the world most by writing a book entitled *The Cushites; or the Children of Ham as seen by the Ancient Historians and Poets*. In this work he showed remarkable ability for research and extensive knowledge of the social sciences. He undertook to refute the statement that the Ethiopians and the Egyptians were not black persons, endeavored to disabuse the public mind of the impropriety of a contemptuous attitude to the Negroes because of their bondage, inasmuch as all races have at times been enslaved, and eloquently produced historical facts to convince thinking men as to the important achievements of the Negroes in their more fortunate ages in the past. He certainly made the impression of being one of the ablest men in the United States, and will long be remembered as a scholar making for the race a defense which many of his contemporaries were not prepared to appreciate.

The ministry was sufficiently attractive also to Dr. George W. Lee, who began his career in North Carolina. After having distinguished himself by efficient service in that State, he was, in 1885, called to the pastorate of the Vermont Avenue Baptist Church to succeed the Rev. J. H. Brooks, its founder, who passed away the previous year. Dr. Lee was noted especially for three significant elements of character. He was a promoter of African missions, was always disposed to help the under-man in a struggle, and made himself a patron of the youth aspiring to leadership. His pastorate was characterized by important achievements bearing on the progress of not only his congregation but that of his denomination. Noted for his originality and ability to master a situation, he soon attracted a large following and increased the membership of his church almost to 4,000. He easily became a man of national reputation, and in his travels abroad so impressed the people wherever he went that he passed as an international character.

With the possible exception of Dr. C. A. Tindley, the talented Methodist minister of Philadelphia, probably the greatest preacher of power developed during the last generation has been Dr. C. T. Walker. Coming under the influence of Christian missionaries and of the Atlanta Baptist College, he had his beginnings determined in an atmosphere of religious education. For forty years, excepting five years when he had charge of the Mt. Olivet Baptist Church, New York City, he was pastor of the Tabernacle Baptist

Church of Augusta, Georgia. His church in Augusta was attended not only by thousands of his own race, but by hundreds of winter tourists, who heard him with unusual satisfaction. Among these were former President Taft, John D. Rockefeller, Gen. Rush C. Hawkins, Dr. David Gregg and Lyman B. Goff. With the support of such a large number this church undertook to supply the needs of the community, developing into an institutional enterprise with all of the activities of a social welfare agency. This expansion necessitated a new building, which he erected at a cost of $185,000.

Dr. Walker was interested in all things promoting the uplift of the race. He was the founder of the now spacious 135th Street Branch, Young Men's Christian Association, New York City, and figured largely in the establishment of a similar branch for his people in Augusta, Georgia. He was one of the prominent figures of the National Baptist Convention of the United States, being vice-president of the organization when he died, as well as vice-president of the Georgia Baptist State Convention and moderator of the Walker Association. He traveled extensively in Europe and the Holy Land and was the author of a number of books of travel and also of sermons. His main work at home and abroad, however, was that of an evangelist whose fame as such so rapidly extended that he was one of the most popular speakers in the country, attracting larger crowds than any other Negro of his time.

CHAPTER XII
THE CONSERVATIVE AND PROGRESSIVE

IT IS CLEAR from the account set forth above that the Negro church as such had some difficulty in finding itself. There was still a question as to what its functions and ideals should be, and this very question all but divided the church into conservative and progressive groups. The conservative element in control became so dogmatic in its treatment of the rising progressive minority that the institution for a number of years lost ground among the talented tenth. For this reason the ministry once became decidedly uninviting to young men. Young people so rapidly lost interest in the church that the Sunday sermon denouncing the waywardness of the wicked generation was generally expected; and, if a special discourse of this vitriolic nature did not periodically follow, pastors availed themselves of the opportunity to digress from the discussion of the hardships of slavery, hell, and the grave to express their deep regret that the intellectual youth were disinclined to walk in the footsteps of their fathers. Such sermons frightened some into repentance, but drove as many away from contact with the Christian element of the community.

The waywardness of the youth, however, was not so much a wickedness as it was a divergence in the Negro social mind. The ex-slaves had remained conservative. The old-time religion was good enough for them. They rejoiced to be able to sing in freedom the songs of their fathers, and deemed it a privilege to testify in "their experience or class meetings" and to offer at their Sunday services long drawn out invocations which afforded them the once forbidden exercise of the outpouring of a pent-up soul. Preachers who came down from that well-fought age appreciated, of course, the unique position which they then occupied. For all a new world had been created, so to speak, and what they needed then was only to enjoy the new boon vouchsafed to the lowly. The Negroes should thank God for their freedom, and the only way to express that gratitude was through vociferous praise and stentorian thanksgiving within the courts of the Lord. God had brought the Negro up out of Egypt through Sodom and Gomorrah, and to show his gratitude the chief concern of the Negro should then be "to be ready to walk into Jerusalem just like John."

The Negroes then under the instruction of well-enlightened missionaries from the North could not long remain in this backward state. Although not taught radical doctrines but, on the contrary, influenced by conservative religious teachers, the educational process itself had to work some changes in the young Negro's point of view, inasmuch as he was taught not what to think but how to think. The young Negroes, therefore, had not attended school very long or moved very much among persons mentally developed before they found themselves far removed from the members of their race less favorably circumstanced. They developed an inquiring disposition which leveled shafts at the strongholds of churchmen whose chief protection lay in their unfortunate plight of being embalmed in their ignorance along with a majority constituency hopelessly lost to the "eternal truths" coming into the mind of the Negro youth by "natural light."

During the last quarter of the nineteenth century, therefore, the conservative and progressive elements in the church unconsciously drifted far apart. In the course of time it was no longer a struggle between the old and young. The difference in age ceased to be the line of cleavage. It was rather a difference of ideas. These groups were widely differing in their interpretation of religion, in their ideas as to the importance of the church in the life of the community, in their attitudes as to the relation of the church to the individual, and in their standards of public conduct. On the whole, there was an effort to stand together; but in spite of themselves the line of cleavage had to be recognized and dealt with as a fact. As poverty is jealous of opulence, so is ignorance jealous of intelligence; and in this case the jealousy all but developed into caste hate.

The progressive element commonly dubbed by the conservatives as the educated Negroes could not accept the crude notions of Biblical interpretation nor the grotesque vision of the hereafter as portrayed by the illiterate ministers of the church. This developed mind found itself unwillingly at war with such extravagant claims and seeking a hearing for a new idea. Religion to the progressives became a Christian experience rather than the wild notions of revelation, which among some of the uninformed too often bordered on superstition and so-called voodooism of the middle age, after the restraint of slavery had been removed and the Negroes as groups exercising religious freedom could indulge their fancy at will.

The educated Negro, moreover, no longer thought of religion as the panacea for all the ills of the race. Along with religion he would insist that education should go as its handmaiden, inasmuch as there can be little revelation of God where there is arrested mental development. The very example of Christ himself, as understood by the progressive Negro, furnished no evidence as to the virtue of unrestrained emotion resulting from a lack of understanding and from an unwillingness to search the Scriptures for the real revelation of God.

Being weak on the intellectual side, the conservative Negro churchman could not fail to decry the educated communicants as a growing menace to the church. The church militant was ordered forward to attack the strongholds of this unbelief lest the institution might be shaken from its very foundation. The toleration of such views might bring upon this generation the wrath of God, who would visit the race with condign affliction. The educated class had information, not judgment; and the principles of religion, moreover, must be accepted as they are without question. The effort here was to crush the scion because it was producing a more vigorous species than the root from which it sprang, to destroy life because in the new generation it meant living too abundantly.

The churchmen of the conservative order observed with regret, moreover, that the talented Negro had a differing conception as to the relation of the church to the individual. Among the conservatives, the church, the only institution in which they could participate in the days of slavery, engaged their undivided attention with the exception of politics in self-defense during the Reconstruction period. The conservatives believed that the individual should sacrifice all for the church. On Sunday, they would come from afar to swell the chorus of the faithful, and there they would remain during the day, leaving their net earnings in the hands of the management, given at the cost of a sacrifice placed on a common altar. The educated Negro, on the other hand, thought of the church as existing for the good of the individual. It was to him a means for making the bad good, and if the institution were defective it might be so reshaped and reorganized as to serve the useful purposes of man.

The church, moreover, as the progressive Negro saw it, was not necessarily Christ-like unless the persons composing it were of such character themselves. As there were too often found here and there impostors serving as important functionaries in churches in which they masqueraded as Christians, the educated Negro insisted upon a new interpretation of Christian doctrine, boldly asserting new principles as to the relation of man to his fellowman and man to God. Religion, the progressive element insisted, is a social virtue not an individual boon. Man cannot by his professed periodical baring of his soul to God set himself aright when his conduct has not been in conformity with the teachings of Jesus. Since an individual is what he does, an institution composed of individuals, too often shamed with ignorance and vice, could not be the ideal Christian organization to which Christ looked as his representative following here on earth.

The Negro in freedom, moreover, when given an opportunity for mental development, gradually became assimilated to the white man's standard of conduct. The educated Negro began to see little harm in dancing and card playing when representative white churches abrogated such prohibitions or suffered them to fall into desuetude. Taunted as to the evil desire for the ways of the world, the talented man usually retorted that while his conduct was questioned by his own people it was in keeping with the ethics of the most enlightened of the land, whereas the conservatives tended to follow the policy of practicing almost any sort of vice clandestinely and to masquerade as Christians until exposed.

This argument was of little worth; for many of the so-called vices of the Negro members of the church could be reduced largely to unconfirmed reports and indulgences of the imagination of persons having foul minds. While the writer offers no brief for the religious workers of long ago, he must insist that we have no evidence to justify the sweeping generalization that the Negro Christians of the conservative order were, as a rule, morally corrupt or that they generally harbored unclean persons in their group. Their record rather shows a most healthy attitude toward maintaining a high standard of morality. The adulterer, the gambler, the thief, and the like, were usually summarily expelled from the church as undesirables, who should not sit in the congregation of the righteous. In fact, had it not been for the hold of Christianity on these freedmen, their standards of morality would have been so much lower; for they saw for emulation little of the righteous in the white people with whom they came into contact when these generally imposed upon the blacks by lying and stealing and openly sought Negro women with whom the flower of southern families lived in open adultery. The conservatives stood for the right, although they were often too narrow to overlook the so-called vices which supplied to those of talent the harmless pleasures of this world.

The progressive element seriously objected to church management. Negro ministers and the governing bodies of the churches often manifested more zeal than tact in the conduct of church affairs. They too frequently built rather costly edifices, paid their pastors disproportionately large salaries, and lavished unduly upon them and their families gifts which the poor of their congregations could ill afford. The Negroes wanted a well-groomed leader in a heaven on earth to lead them to the heaven beyond. The management then incurred debts of such magnitude that the church too often developed into a money raising machine dominated from without by white speculators who profited by this folly. The progressive element militantly arrayed itself against this outlay made at the expense of the moral and religious life of the community. In their zeal they too often denounced the conservatives in control as tricksters and grafters, when, as a matter of fact, the management lost more by inefficient administration than it acquired by so-called corruption.

The progressive Negroes boldly advocated a change in the worship. From the more advanced white churches they had learned to appreciate the value of serious and classical music, of intelligent sermonizing, and of collecting offerings in the pews. The old-time plaintive plantation hymns, they insisted, should give place to music of a refined order, supported by the piano, organ, or other instruments; the tiresome minister, covering all things in creation in his discourse, should yield to a man prepared to preach to the point at issue; and instead of the dress-parade lifting of collections the raising of funds to support the church should be reduced to a business transaction conducted without ostentation. The conservatives, however, would not have in their churches the musical instruments used in theaters and dance halls, would not even listen to an attack on their backward ministry, and scoffed at the proposal to supplant time-honored customs by innovations taken from the practices of their former cruel oppressors.

The general result was that in many communities a much larger number of intelligent people were driven from the church or rendered inefficient therein than were saved to it. There was little chance for cooperation so long as the conservatives were unyielding; and the progressives, unable to treat the conservatives diplomatically, failed to put aside complaint to begin with the masses where they were that they might carry them where they should be. Some of the progressive element left their names on the church books only to forfeit membership by non-attendance or the failure to pay required dues. Others saw themselves excluded for violation of the sacred rules of the congregation proscribing participation in the worldly joys. A few who felt compunction of conscience on realizing how disgraceful in the eyes of the community it seemed to put one's hand to the plow and then turn back, had their backsliding healed and returned to the fold.

Those who left the conservative churches were often received by the Congregationalists, the Presbyterians, the Episcopalians, and the Catholics, who, having a more flexible attitude toward the pleasures of the world, offered asylum to the outcasts driven from the former sanctuaries. This separation included not only laymen but in some cases ministers, who, on connecting themselves with some other denominations, served their people in churches differing widely from those which were so handicapped by unprogressive elements that they had no hope to toil upward therein. The large majority of the members of these smaller denominations were once members of Baptist or Methodist churches or were the children of persons who were once thus connected.

It was not necessary, however, for a large number of Baptists thus to be lost to that denomination. Unlike the Methodists, who are restrained by Episcopal government, the Baptists needed only to exercise the privileges of democracy guaranteed in that church. A dissatisfied group of the "upper crust" in a Baptist Church could at any time organize another Baptist Church without any restraint except that of the fear of the failure of the enterprise from the economic point of view. Schismatic churches or exclusively aristocratic congregations, therefore, followed in large cities where a sufficient number of the malcontents in the various denominations could unite for this common purpose.

This schismatic movement was followed by both good and bad results. The separation of the progressive and the conservative elements in the church made it impossible for the unprogressive to learn by example from those with whom they came into contact. Each remained happier in the new state so long as the results of this divergence were not strikingly apparent. The conservatives could better remain what they were and the progressives could more easily become what they wanted to be. The cessation of hostilities, however, did not always follow; for both churches representing different points of view made their appeals to the same community, endeavoring to secure financial and moral support. In small communities what was done for the one could not be done for the other for the reason that the community had so much and no more to spare. The success or failure of the one or the other, therefore, too often meant grudge or ill will.

This contest between the progressive and conservative, however, has been more than local. There have arisen serious situations, some of which have been handled so diplomatically as to avoid outbreaks in the ranks, and others which have led to radical changes. For example, the progressive Negro in the Methodist Episcopal Church for a number of years bore it grievously that, although the members of the race constituted an important element in this denomination, they were not allowed freely to participate in its management. The objective was to make a Negro one of the regular bishops, but conservative whites insisted that the time had not come for such a radical step.

During this long struggle in the Methodist Church the progressive group became very impatient. It was in favor of separation from the white connection either to establish an independent church or to join one of the African Methodist churches already in the making. The conservative element frowned down upon any such proposal as a suicidal scheme, believing that in cooperating with the whites the Negroes had much more to gain than to lose. The advocacy of continued union with the whites under the prevailing circumstances, however, was dubbed by the progressive Negroes a manifestation of the spirit of servility resulting from a slavish attachment to their former masters. The counsel of the conservative prevailed, however, and although the Negro membership does not enjoy exactly the same privileges as the white, it has steadily gained ground.

The best example of a situation which could not be thus handled is that of the repudiation of the white Baptists by the progressive Negro element of this church. The white Baptists, of course, had no actual control of the Negro communicants, but had some very strong moral claims on them. White missionaries of this denomination had distributed literature, organized churches, constructed edifices, and established schools among Negroes; and the boards supporting the missionaries had supplied some of the funds by which most of these institutions were maintained. To say anything derogatory to the policies of the management directing this beneficent work, therefore, seemed to the conservative Negroes all but blasphemous.

The progressive Baptist element, however, had a different attitude. Thousands of Negro teachers and preachers whom these Baptist schools had trained had entered upon their life's work with the hope that they would figure conspicuously in the life of their people. When they faced the stern realities of the situation they too often found their way was blocked. White men, to be sure, did not aspire to the pastorate of Negro churches; but they undertook to dictate the policy of associations and conventions to retain their hold on the Negro Baptists. The conflict came when Negroes after being refused the privilege of participating in the management of the American Baptist Home Mission Society began to question the motives of its official staff. More fuel was furnished for the flames when, after having all but agreed to accept contributions of Negroes to its Sunday school literature, the American Baptist Publication Society, upon protest from Southern churchmen, receded from that position. The issue was then joined. The National Baptist Convention, a union of the Negro Baptists, was effected in 1886, and as the struggle grew more intense every effort was made so to extend it as to destroy the influence of white national bodies among Negroes.

The Negroes had a just cause for complaint. If under the leadership of the white Baptists their way to promotion would be blocked and their literary aspirations crushed, what hope was there for the race to rise and of what benefit would education be to the Negro, if it did not equip him to do for himself what the white man at first had to do for him? How could the motives of the white Baptists be lofty, moreover, if they did not believe that Negroes should rise in the church and school? To this the whites replied that they looked forward with the most pleasant anticipation to the day when the Negroes would be prepared to enjoy the good things for which they clamored, but that the time for the Negroes to dispense with the leadership of the whites had not then come. Many years of education and social uplift were still necessary before the Negroes could successfully set out to do for themselves.

This argument had little weight with the progressive Negroes and they were not wanting in logical speakers to place their case before the world. There was that courageous leader, Dr. Harvey Johnson, of Baltimore, who belabored his former friends as enemies of the race. Equally effective, too, was the eloquent Dr. Walter H. Brooks of Washington, who fearlessly took up the cudgel and dealt the white Baptists many a blow from which they never recovered. With the National Baptist Convention emerging as a common concern of Negroes under the organizing hand of Dr. E. C. Morris, and the National Baptist Publishing House extending the circulation of elementary literature throughout the country under the direction of the efficient Dr. R. H. Boyd, this self-assertion of the Negro Baptists became a factor to be reckoned with.

All problems, however, were not immediately solved. The progressive Negroes had the right spirit, but did not every time have adequate understanding. They had had no experience in editing literature and practically none in raising sums of money necessary for the maintenance of educational establishments and missionary enterprise. The majority of the Negro Baptist ministry trained in the schools of the American Baptist Home Mission Society at first adhered to this organization and persisted in using the Sunday school literature of the American Baptist Publication Society, deriding the publication efforts of the Negro Baptists as the greatest travesty on Biblical literature. This criticism was most uncharitable, but nevertheless effective, for the reason that some who at first wished the movement well made the mistake of despising the day of small things.

The struggle was most intense in the Southeast. The influence of Shaw University in North Carolina and Virginia Union University in Richmond had given the white Baptists an all but firm hold on the Negroes in these and adjacent States. The presidents of these institutions and the white agents of the denomination attended the Negro associations and conventions, hoping to dictate their policies; but this interference only widened the breach. Under the leadership of that forceful orator and successful leader, Gregory W. Hayes, a large number at first and finally a majority of the Baptists of Virginia disclaimed connection with these white friends and concentrated their efforts on supporting the Virginia Theological Seminary and College through the Baptist State Convention of that commonwealth. The leading Baptists of North Carolina, however, still adhered in large numbers to the American Baptist Home Mission Society, cooperating therewith through the local associations, their State conventions, and the conservative national body known as the Lott Cary Convention, which had also many adherents in Virginia and scattered followers throughout adjacent States. In other parts, the factions about equally divided, except in the southwestern section of the country, where the Negroes have tended to break away from the white Baptists.

As to which faction was right, history alone will tell. Even at the present, however, one can see a decided advantage in the independent Negro movement. Everyone will admit that the Negro must eventually rely solely upon himself, and that not until he emerges from a state of dependency can he hope to secure the recognition of the other groups. The white man is rapidly tiring of carrying the so-called burdens of the Negro. The Negro home, church, and school must, as fast as possible, become sufficient unto themselves. The sooner they attain this stage in their development, the better will it be for the race. The Negro institutions which during the turbulent period have, in separating from the whites, learned to supply their own needs, have made a step far in advance of those dependent on the whites. In this day, when the northern philanthropists are either withholding their donations to Negro schools or restricting them to Hampton and Tuskegee, it is difficult for some of these establishments to eke out a subsistence, while the independent Negro schools, having had years of experience in developing a following, find their prospects growing brighter from year to year.

The National Training School for Girls, founded and successfully directed by the noted Nannie H. Burroughs, obtains practically all of its funds from Negroes. The Virginia Theological Seminary and College, under the direction of the efficient Dr. R. C. Woods, depends for its support altogether upon Negroes, who contribute to it annually about $60,000.00. There is not in this country a Negro institution dominated by whites that can raise half of this sum in this way. A few years ago when Wilberforce University was heavily indebted and it seemed that it needed someone to rescue it, the State of Ohio proposed to buy the church portion of the institution; but the trustees, with the spirit of the progressive Negro, emphatically replied that the whole State of Ohio did not have enough money to buy Wilberforce. Rallying under the leadership of Bishop Joshua H. Jones, the African Methodists raised $50,000 in one year and cleared the institution of debt.

In this changing order, moreover, when the white administrators of Negro schools find themselves deprived of the former financial support received from the North, they veer around to the position of southern white people, accepting and sometimes enforcing in Negro institutions themselves the unwritten laws of caste that the white management may curry favor with the prejudiced community. As these administrators must under such circumstances lose the support of the Negroes and experience has not yet shown that many southern white men will make sacrifices for Negro education, the institutions in the hands of such misguided white friends of the Negro will probably suffer.

CHAPTER XIII
THE NEGRO CHURCH SOCIALIZED

THE NEGRO CHURCH as a social force in the life of the race is nothing new. Prior to emancipation the church was the only institution which the Negro, in a few places in the South and throughout the North, was permitted to maintain for his own peculiar needs. Offering the only avenue for the expressional activities of the race, the church answered many a social purpose for which this institution among other groups differently circumstanced had never before been required to serve. It was, in the first place, a center at which friend looked forward to meeting friend, contact with whom was denied by the rigorous demands of slavery. It was then a place of enlightenment through the information disseminating from the better informed or by actual teaching in the Sunday school. It served often as an outlet for expression of the Negro social mind, now for a renewed determination to break their chains through prayer, then to resort to concerted action on the basis that he who would be free must himself first strike the blow.

After the emancipation, moreover, the Negro church developed a social atmosphere which somewhat strengthened its hold on the youth about to go astray. Not only education found its basis in the church, but fraternal associations developed therefrom. Business enterprises accepted the church as an ally, and professional men to some extent often became dependent thereupon. Most movements among the Negroes, moreover, have owed their success to the leadership of Negroes prominent in the church. No better examples can be mentioned than W. W. Browne, a minister who organized the True Reformers fraternity; W. R. Pettiford, another preacher, who became one of the pioneer Negro bankers; John R. Hawkins, the Financial Secretary of the African Methodist Episcopal Church, who in applying efficiency to the business of his office secured for his denomination an unusually large income, and Dr. W. F. Graham, who in addition to his significant achievements in the church, has well invaded various businesses, in which he has exhibited evidence of unusual ability.

Since the Civil War, the Negro church as a factor in general uplift has become what the oppressed Negro longed to make it prior to that conflict. In the first place, Negroes regularly attend church whether Christians or sinners. They have not yet accumulated wealth adequate to the construction of clubhouses, amusement parks, and theaters, although dance halls have attracted many. Whether they derive any particular joy therefrom or not, the Negroes must go to church, to see their friends, as they are barred from social centers open to whites. They must attend church, moreover, to find out what is going on; for the race has not sufficient interests to maintain in every locality a newspaper of its own, and the white dailies generally mention Negroes only when they happen to commit crimes against white persons. The young Negro must go to church to meet his sweetheart, to impress her with his worth and woo her in marriage, the Negro farmer to find out the developments in the business world, the Negro mechanic to learn the needs of his community and how he may supply them.

Attached to the church is the Sunday school. Many a Negro had in attending it learned clandestinely to read and write before the war. Now they without fear of punishment eagerly studied in the churches on Sunday, learned the alphabet, the spelling of words with one, two and three syllables, and finally to read the Bible, that they might know for themselves the truths hitherto kept from their fathers but now revealed to their children in freedom. Education here was decidedly easy, the motive actuating the student being the immediate results in the form of a better knowledge of one's Christian duty and the reward awaiting the faithful. Many of these Negroes often learned more on a single Sunday than the average student acquired in a day school during a week. In these Sunday schools, not a few Negroes laid the foundation for the more liberal education which they thereafter obtained in the schools established by the religious and philanthropic friends of the Negroes working in the South immediately after the Civil War.

The church not only promoted education through the pulpit and Sunday school, but through its emphasis on the Bible unconsciously stimulated the efforts toward self-education. Whether a Negro attended Sunday school or not, he heard read to him from the Bible two or three times a week dramatic history, philosophical essays, charming poetry, and beautiful oratory. Hearing these repeated again and again and under circumstances securing undivided attention, he had many of these precious passages sink into his heart like seed planted in fertile ground to bring forth fruit fourfold. Under the continuous instruction of the Negro preacher, who in expounding the Bible drew such striking figures and portrayed life, death, and the beyond in a dramatic fashion, the youth not only experienced the emotion so characteristic of the Negro communicant but had his intellectual appetite whetted with the desire to seek after the mysteries.

The majority of Negroes, therefore, became Bible readers. Reading the Bible, they not only found what a minister of limited education could point out, but facts drawn from the best thought of the ancient world. And it was not mere reading; for many of them committed to memory choice passages of the Scriptures. Hundreds of them could recite accurately chapter after chapter of the treasures of Holy Writ; almost as many could give a crude but logical exposition of these literary treasures. From the study of the Bible the Negro developed, moreover, a desire for Biblical literature. He heard the moral appeal and gladly accepted the message to those in quest of the higher life in Christ.

This influence of the Bible, moreover, did more than lead to the reading of literature of a kindred nature. Some read books on ancient and medieval history, and finally works on the history of modern Europe. Others more seriously concerned were by this mere exposition of the Scriptures led to study collaterally commentaries on the Bible and to take up theology. In this they exhibited the power of self-education which with a strong spirituality combined with unusual imagination made so many Negroes preach with success. They had no more formal education than to read, and that was often picked up in the Sunday school; but they had the experience of a seeker, the light of the Bible, and the guidance of men who eloquently expounded it to the waiting multitude. These they freely drew on and from them they obtained help abundantly. Crude sometimes as the language might be, the thought of this self-made philosopher was original and few heard one preach without wondering how men of limited opportunities could speak so fluently and wisely.

Equally helpful was the socialized church as a forum for the Negro. The older members developed an unusually valuable and sometimes a troublesome knowledge of parliamentary practice by participating in the debates on the business centering around communications received, resolutions voicing the sentiment of the body, and policies shaping the destinies of the local church. Here, then, was a constructive field which to the Negro seemed like an invitation to enter the creative world. He entered it and freely participated. True enough the formal procedure too often overshadowed the actual program to the extent that no plan at all could sometimes be carried out, because of unnecessary debate and contention; but the training thereafter served many a Negro in good stead in preventing his race from being imposed upon or in doing something constructive in politics, in the school, and in the church.

The church through the literary societies attached thereto supplied a similar need of the younger Negro. Having more formal education than the older Negroes, the youth were more easily interested in the live questions of the day, the desire to discuss which usually resulted in the organization of a literary society. The declamations and recitations were not always highly literary and sometimes the questions discussed could not be thus dignified when we observe such debates as whether the dog is more useful than the gun, or whether water is more destructive than fire; but the scale ascends a little in the discussion as to whether the pen is mightier than the sword. It matters little, however, whether or not the procedure was in keeping with that of the best literary circles, these Negroes were thereby undergoing training which resulted in valuable discipline. Not any of them knew very much, but one learned from the other. They developed the power to think and to think on their feet, to express that thought and to express it so eloquently as to make a lasting impression. The church, then, has been a training school for the Negro orators who have impressed the world as the inspired spokesmen of a persecuted people.

The Negro church, in short, has served as a clearing house for the community. It has not only afforded opportunities for the evangelical minister coming with an inspiring message to revive the lukewarm, but every public man has had to reach the Negro through his church. The lecturer on "men, women, children and things in general" asks for a hearing there; the phrenologist holds his séances in this sanctuary; the spurious "foreigner" in quest of a collection seeks there the opportunity to tell a credulous people about wonders of other lands; and the race leader demands this rostrum from which he, like a watchman on the wall, sounds the alarm for an advance against the bold enemy who, if not checked, will fix upon the race disabilities and burdens until all the hopes of liberty will be lost.

The latest development in the socialized church is its service as a welfare agency. The Negro in his religious development has not yet gone so far as the white man in divesting Christian duty of spiritual ministration and reducing it to a mere service for social uplift; but he has gradually realized the necessity for connecting the church more closely with the things of this world to make it a decent place to live in. In other words, if man is his brother's keeper, the church, the important institution in the community, must be the keeper of other institutions. If it would build in men Christian character, it must influence the more or less direct control of the forces in the community which prevent the attainment of such an end. If men are to be saved, they must be saved for service, not merely for their refuge at the last hour. The church, then, must not let a man destroy himself and accept him when he is no longer useful because of the loss of physical and mental power through depravity, but it must by preaching the gospel or prevention save a man from himself.

The coming of the church to this position, however, has not been affected without much difficulty. The conservative element for many years looked upon the participation of churches in certain sorts of social welfare work as compromising with the devil. The more conservative idea was that man should be meditative and seclusive, that he should withdraw himself altogether from the pleasures of this world and work out his salvation with his eye "single to the honor and glory of God." The Young Men's Christian Association and the Young Women's Christian Association with a different point of view were, therefore, for a number of years unwelcome among some Negro churches.

During the last generation, however, the Negro church has decidedly changed in its attitude toward this work, as is evidenced by the fact that wherever these social welfare agencies have succeeded in carrying out their program they have done so largely with the aid of Negro churchmen. In the midst of the health crusades and the community service organizations favorably impressing the public, the Negro church in many urban centers where it might have continued conservative, found itself facing the alternative of either responding to these social needs of the membership or seeing its constituency gradually drawn away by agencies which would. In case some social uplift agency failed to attract the youth, they too often drifted to the dance halls or places where their needs were supplied in the midst of vices. Many churches have, therefore, modified their program. Seeing that the young Negro is decidedly social and hoping to save him, they have done what many formerly questioned. The Negro church, moreover, has become in many respects a social welfare agency itself, doing in several communities so much of this work that it has been unnecessary for the national agencies to invade some of their parishes with an intensive program.

The form this social work of the church takes in our day varies from that of a mere church club or so with a precarious existence to that of an organization almost like that of the Young Men's Christian Association. The beginnings of this work appear first in such as the men's forum, the women's league, the girls' club, or the boys' athletic association. When these clubs tend to endure they finally work toward the natural end of constituting themselves branches of an organization directed by one trusted worker assisted by those in charge of the various activities.

A church on this order takes the name of the institutional church. At the head of this body, of course, is the pastor of the church; but in charge of this work sometimes is a director well trained in the social sciences and with the modern method of attacking the problems of today. The work scheduled is more than the mere supervision of clubs voluntarily organized. The director has a program which that particular community needs, and he is there to show the people how to work out their social salvation. If he is wise in presenting the case, he usually secures the cooperation necessary to organize the community for the purpose of self-education. The community is given an introduction to itself. Every talent lying dormant is here given an opportunity to be helpful in some way. What the individual from afar may bring for the good of a few through this well-organized community service becomes the heritage of all. No club can be large enough to accommodate the large membership in a city, but what the clubs of one church acquire is communicated to similar groups in another through such friendly rivalry as athletic contests, debates, periodical reports, and conferences. Many of the persons participating in this work are not in the beginning spiritually inclined, but the experience of the church in working with such groups has shown that the church has a better chance for success in making its evangelical appeal to persons under its control than in the case of delivering its message to those who have not been to any great extent influenced by Christian contact.

Churches which have undertaken this work have had varied experiences.

The Institutional Church in Chicago under Dr. R. C. Ransom helped to blaze the way in this new field of endeavor. Under Dr. J. Milton Waldron and later under Dr. J. E. Ford, the Baptist Church of Jacksonville, Florida, made itself, through its clubs and Bible Institute, an effective community center. Dr. H. H. Proctor, a Congregational minister of Atlanta, practically converted his church into an organization of such groups as the day nursery, kindergarten, gymnasium, school of music, employment bureau, and Bible school.

Dr. W. N. DeBerry, the pastor of a Congregational church in Springfield, Massachusetts, has probably solved the problem about as well as any of these workers. In the first place, the church has a well-equipped modern plant so beautifully located and managed as to attract large numbers. It has, moreover, a parish home for working girls and a branch church at Amherst, Massachusetts. In the main plant are maintained a free employment bureau, a women's welfare league, a night school of domestic training, a girls' and a boys' club emphasizing the handicrafts, music, and athletics. This church has solved the problem of supplying the needs of the people during the week as well as their spiritual needs on Sunday, by emphasizing some life activity for every day in the week.

Other ministers of the gospel, who have not seen fit to carry out in their parishes in such detail the establishment of social welfare work, have nevertheless done much along special lines to socialize their churches. One hears of that indefatigable worker, the Rev. Mr. Bradby, of Detroit; R. W. Bagnall, the rector of the Episcopal Church of the same city; the fearless George Frazier Miller, an Episcopal rector of Brooklyn; the talented leader, Dr. W. H. Brooks of New York City; the popular western worker, Dr. S. W. Bacote of Kansas City; Dr. J. M. Riddle of Pasadena, California; and Dr. W. H. Jernagin, of Washington, D. C. Others of this group are Dr. Richard Carroll of Greenville, South Carolina; Bishop Sampson Brooks, as pastor of the Bethel Methodist Episcopal Church in Baltimore; Dr. W. D. Johnson of Plains, Georgia, now a bishop of his denomination; the picturesque pulpit orator and beautiful word painter, Dr. Peter James Bryant, of Atlanta, Georgia; and that popular preacher of the social gospel, Dr. W. W. Browne, of the Metropolitan Baptist Church in New York City.

Dr. L. K. Williams, pastor of the Olivet Baptist Church in Chicago, has doubtless surpassed all in this group. Under his direction the church conducts forty-two departments and auxiliaries with 512 officers, among whom are twenty-four paid workers. The membership of both church and Sunday School enormously increased through these agencies, that of the former being 8,743 and of the latter 3,100. This church has two edifices and five assistant pastors. During 1919 it collected $56,209 and disbursed $54,959. In an eighty-day rally it raised $29,235 in cash. In fact, so effective has been the socializing influence of this church that the community, in consideration of its inestimable value, gladly responds to any call it makes.

The Negro ambitious to rule, moreover, finds in the church about the only institution in which he may freely exercise authority. Fortunately here the Church and State are no longer connected. In the extension of the boon of toleration, the Negroes in countries in which they have been found in large numbers, have been permitted to conduct their spiritual affairs as they like. There are in the South today, however, white men who regret that immediately after the Civil War they permitted the Negroes to establish their separate churches. As these bodies are today being used to promote truths and foster movements which are prejudicial to the interest of the Southern restriction program for the Negro, the heirs of the former master class now rue the day when their fathers permitted these Negro churchmen to get from under their control. They complain that, whereas formerly they could learn from their Negro servants exactly what was going on in their group, the development the Negro church has in our day produced a reticent Negro loathe to disclose the forces operating in their churches.

No one understands this better than the Negro himself. The law of the South otherwise interpreted to the detriment of the Negro vouchsafes to him a little protection in the exercise of religion and in most parts public opinion has not become so unhealthy as to warrant action to the contrary. The Negro preacher, therefore, is granted more freedom of speech and permitted to exercise more influence than any other Negro in his community. Some fearless Negro ministers, like Bishop Lampton, have been driven out of the South because of utterances which enraged the whites, who have considered the exercise of free speech among Negroes an attack on their social laws; but, as a rule, the Negro minister may in criticism of the white race and in the defense of his people say things which other Negroes of good standing in the South would not dare to utter. Although the State may chide an outspoken minister here and there, it will hardly be so unwise so to restrict the Negro church as to interfere materially with its development as the South has done in the case of the Negro school in making Negro education altogether industrial. The church serves as a moral force, a power acting as a restraint upon the bad and stimulating the good to further moral achievement. Among the Negroes its valuable service is readily apparent when one considers the fact that this race, oppressed as it has been by the government of the State and nation, is at heart rebellious, while the church, as outspoken as it may seem, is not radical. Coming under the influence of the church, the safety valve in the South, the race has been dissuaded from any rash action by the patient and long suffering ministry reiterating the admonition that "vengeance is mine, I will repay."

Yet some men, like the sanguine and prophetic Kelly Miller, see in the Negro church of today the opportunity to become the unbridled servant of the people. The support of the Negro preacher comes from the people and he can fearlessly speak for them within the limits of public opinion. The Negro teacher or politician must be careful as to what he says; for, inasmuch as his support comes through the white race, he must proceed cautiously lest he be deprived of his position. As a rule, their lips are forever sealed on the rights of the Negro. As social proscription has retarded the development of the Negro lawyer, the impetus toward the uplift of the race must come from its ministry, and with the entrance of a larger number of intelligent men upon this work the masses of the Negro race will be willing to have them lead the way.

The ministry too is more attractive among Negroes than among whites. The white minister has only one important function to perform in his group, that of spiritual leadership. To the Negro community the preacher is this and besides the walking encyclopedia, the counselor of the unwise, the friend of the unfortunate, the social welfare organizer, and the interpreter of the signs of the times. No man is properly introduced to the Negro community unless he comes through the minister, and no movement can expect success there unless it has his cooperation or endorsement. The rise of the Negro physician has during recent years comparatively diminished the influence of the Negro preacher, but the latter is still the greater force in the community and will remain so unless the Negro learns to imitate the white people in substituting in their faith the doing of the will of their race for that of doing the revealed will of God.

The importance of the position of the Negro minister is apparent when one considers the large following which some of these churches have. Here the minister controls not only hundreds but thousands, as in the cases of Rev. J. E. Willis of the Vermont Avenue Baptist Church in Washington, of the Rev. Mr. Adams of the Concord Baptist Church in Brooklyn, Dr. M. W. Reddick in the leadership of thousands of Baptists in Georgia, and the eloquent Dr. M. W. D. Norman, who after years of service as a minister in North Carolina and Virginia and as Dean of the Theological Department of Shaw University, succeeded the lamented Rev. Robert Johnson at the Metropolitan Baptist Church in Washington, where thousands wait upon Dr. Norman's words. Some of these ministers are drawing very large numbers, because, instead of merely building large edifices and buying fine clothes and gifts for themselves, they are putting efficiency in the management of the churches, as in the cases of R. H. Bowling in Norfolk, Mordecai W. Johnson in Charleston, and Dr. A. Clayton Powell in New York City. In the Negro churches, moreover, as with Dr. J. C. Austin in Pittsburgh, there are being organized banks, housing corporations, insurance companies, and even steamship projects in keeping with the ideas of Dr. L. G. Jordan. Yet despite this change in point of view, the Negro church has not become a corrupt machine. Its affairs are still in the hands of men who, as a majority, are interested in their race rather than in themselves. The opportunity here sought is not that of leadership but that of service.

One service of which the race is in need, as the Negro minister is beginning to understand it, is the prevention of poverty. The poor you have with you always, and the poor will sometimes steal before they will starve. The masses must be elevated above dependence on another race for what they shall eat or drink or the wherewithal they shall be clothed. The saving of young men and women of the race from those pursuits in which they are unduly exposed to the temptations of the low and the contemptible of both races, is becoming a most important concern of many Negro churches. The Negro minister is now beginning to realize that every time he saves a youth from such undesirable conditions he himself becomes like unto Christ, a savior of man. If to do this it will be necessary to establish a business enterprise or make the church a fraternal insurance company, the new Negro minister will act accordingly. This is the way the race should go. The minister is the shepherd of the flock. The sheep know the voice of the shepherd and a stranger they will not follow.

Out of the exercise of these many privileges in the Negro church, moreover, has come unusually important results. Although the Negro learned in this way much that he had to forget, received many impressions which led to improper expression, the experiences in the end redounded to the good of the race. Misinformation when detected served but to emphasize the need of information; imposition accentuated the necessity for honest leadership; and the results of too much credulity led to conservatism in the masses. It was the school of experience for the Negro community. The church furnished the opportunity for this experience and the people learned their lesson well. They learned how to discriminate, how to think for themselves, how to take care of themselves in a critical situation, in short, how to be self-sufficient.

The most important of all lessons the Negro has learned through his church has been that of perseverance in cooperative effort. This is the most striking result of this social work. Negroes have not readily responded to the call of men in other fields, but the fact that these church groups, large and small, have held together for decades, and even generations, in the sacrificing effort to purchase houses of worship for which some of them have well paid two or three times because of thieves within and thieves without—that fact alone is evidence of the development of the power of consolidation among Negroes, an asset which in our day is being drawn upon for organization in education and in business and bids fair to have tremendous results when properly exploited by honest leaders enjoying the confidence of the masses.

THE STUDENT OF this phase of history will naturally inquire as to the actual results from all of these efforts to promote the progress of Christianity among these people. Here we are at a loss for facts as to the early period; but after 1890, when the first census of Negro churches was taken, we have some very informing statistics: and although the general census of 1900 took no account of such statistics, the United States Bureau of the Census took a special census of religious institutions in 1906, basing its report upon returns received from the local organizations themselves. The items of this report covered the membership, places of worship, seating capacity of the edifices, the value of church property, and the number of ministers. There were reported also the number and value of parsonages, the debt on church property, and later the statistics of Sunday schools.

Summarizing the details, the census showed that in 1906 there were 36,770 Negro church organizations with a membership of 3,685,097. They had 35,160 church edifices and 1,261 halls used as places of worship, affording a seating capacity of 10,481,738. There were 4,779 parsonages worth $3,727,884, whereas the church edifices were worth $56,636,159. The debt on such church property, however, was $5,005,905. These churches had 34,681 Sunday schools administered by 210,148 officers and teachers in charge of 1,740,009 scholars.

Comparing these statistics of 1906 with those of 1890, one sees the rapid growth of the Negro church. Although the Negro population increased only 26.1 percent during these sixteen years, the number of church organizations increased 56.7 percent; the number of communicants, 37.8 percent; the number of edifices, 47.9; the seating capacity, 54.1 percent; and the value of church property, 112.7 percent. The proportionately smaller increase in the membership is accounted for by the discovery of an overstatement of this item through error by the African Methodist Episcopal Zion Church in 1890, which in 1906 was corrected. It is worthy of note here that the number of halls decreased, showing that they gave place to permanent buildings for those who had been housed in temporary quarters.

The distribution of these churches is of value to determine the extent of this progress. Over 90 percent of the organizations were in the South, where the large majority of the Negroes are. Because of the social and economic conditions in that section, however, the proportion of the total value of church property was smaller, being only 73.5 percent, and the proportionate amount of debt on church property accordingly smaller, being 53.1 percent. Considering State by State, one finds that the southern group, of course, took the lead, whereas Idaho, Nevada, New Hampshire, North and South Dakota, and Vermont reported no Negro churches at all in 1890; but South Dakota and New Hampshire carried such an item in their returns in 1906. Georgia held first rank in the number of Negro communicants in 1890 and 1906, while Alabama advanced from third to second place in 1906, and Mississippi from the sixth in 1890 to fourth in 1906. Oklahoma did the unusual thing of advancing from the thirty-third place in 1890 to the twentieth in 1906. Most of these changes, however, followed corresponding changes in the Negro population of these States, resulting not every time as a natural increase but from migration.

A smaller number of Negro communicants were distributed among 18 white organizations in 1906. Between 1890 and 1906, however, the Southern Baptist Conventions and the Evangelical Lutheran churches lost their Negro members; but for the first time the following reported Negro churches in 1906: The Advent Christian Church, the Seventh Day Adventists, the General Council of the Evangelical Lutheran Church in North America, the General Eldership of the Churches of God in North America, the Wesleyan Methodist Connection, the Moravian Church, the Reformed Church in America, and the Church of the United Brethren in Christ. Other difficulties arise in making the comparison here; for the Colored Primitive Baptists were not reported as a separate denomination in 1890, but in 1906 they, with the exception of four churches of this faith, constituted a body of their own. The white denomination reporting the largest number of Negro members was the Methodist Episcopal Church.

The sectarian would be interested in learning, moreover, the progress reported for the various denominations. The greater achievements were accredited to the 11 exclusively Negro organizations reporting in 1890 and the 17 of this same composition making returns in 1906. These were Baptists, Methodists, and Presbyterians, with a sprinkling of such smaller groups as the Church of God and Saints of Christ, organized in 1896; Churches of the Living God, organized in 1899; the Voluntary Missionary Society in America, organized in 1900; the Free Christian Zion Church of Christ, organized by Schismatic Methodists of all sects in 1905; the Union American Methodist Episcopal Church, the African Union Methodist Protestant Church, organized in 1866; the Reformed Union Apostolic Church, organized in 1882; and the Reformed Methodist Union Episcopal Church, organized in 1896. While these smaller bodies were developing between 1890 and 1906 there disappeared other small Negro national church organizations known as the Congregational Methodist Church and the Evangelical Missionary Church. Of the distinctly Negro denominations, the one reporting the largest number of communicants was the National Baptist Convention. Following thus in the order of their numerical rank came next the African Methodist Episcopal Church, the African Methodist Episcopal Zion Church, and the Colored Methodist Episcopal Church.

Further statistics show more definitely the progress along sectarian lines. In 1906 the six Baptist bodies reported 19,891 organizations with 2,354,789 communicants and church property valued at $26,562,845. The ten Methodist bodies combined came second with 15,317 organizations, 1,182,131 communicants and church property valued at $25,771,262. Taken together, the Methodists and Baptists had 35,208 or 95.8 percent of the total number of Negro organizations; 3,536,920 or 96 percent of the total number of Negro communicants and $52,334,107 or 92.4 percent of the total value of church property.

Other statistics show further tendencies of little importance. The marked increase in the number of Free Baptists between 1890 and 1906 is accounted for by better returns the latter year. The falling off of the Disciples of Christ was said to be due to the change resulting from separation of the Disciples and the churches of Christ. There were, moreover, during the same period significant changes in the membership of the Negroes in such white organizations as the Roman Catholic, the Congregational, the Presbyterian, and the Episcopal churches.

The progress of the Negro church, however, has been made, as shown above, in the denominations organized and controlled exclusively by Negroes. In 1906 they had 85.4 percent of the organizations, 87 percent of the membership, 83.2 percent of the scholars in the Sunday School; 78.9 percent of the value of the church property, 74.5 percent of the total amount of the debt on church property, and 67 percent of the value of parsonages. The statistician accounts for the relatively larger proportion of the value of property and debt among the partly Negro denominations by the fact that these organizations are largely in Northern States where church buildings are of better type and parsonages more common. These figures show that the Negro denominations are growing more rapidly than the others. The statistician says: "While in 1890 they had 81.7 percent of the organizations against 18.3 percent for the other class, in 1906, they reported 85.4 percent, while in the past Negro bodies had dropped 14.6 percent." The variations, instead of refuting this statement, tend to confirm it. The National Baptist Convention, for example, dropped from 53.4 percent to 50.4 percent in organizations but advanced from 50.4 percent to 61.4 percent in membership and from 33.9 percent to 43.1 percent in value of church property. The Northern Convention showed a decrease in every item as to its report on the Negro membership. The African Methodists apparently fell behind but the difference was due not to any actual decrease in membership but to more accurate returns as is confirmed by more recent reports in their histories and their year books. The Presbyterians and Congregational churches show a slightly increased percentage in membership but a decreased percentage in value of property. The Protestant Episcopal Church reported a general increase, especially in the value of church property. The percentages of increase in the case of Catholic Churches are not striking except in the case of membership. These last mentioned denominations, moreover, still have a comparatively small following among the Negroes.

The Bureau of the United States Census has fortunately compiled statistics to show even the sex of these communicants. These tend to confirm the oft repeated declaration that the women largely support Negro churches. "Of the total number of organizations reported," says the statistician, "34,648, or 94.2 percent, made returns showing the sex of communicants or members, and the number thus reported, 3,527,660 was 95.7 percent of the total membership. Of this number 1,324,123, or 37.5 percent, were males, and 2,203,537, or 62.5 percent, were females. As compared with the figures for all religious bodies, white and Negro, which show 43.1 percent males and 56.9 percent females, they indicate a greater preponderance of females in Negro bodies." The census reports account for this difference in contending that the Roman Catholic bodies, among which the proportion of males is relatively large (49.3 percent), constituted over 36 percent of the total church membership reported by the census of 1906, but only one percent of the Negro church membership. In the total Protestant church membership the percentage of females is 60.3, or only slightly lower than that of the membership of the Negro churches alone.

The few denominations which show the larger proportion of males are the Catholics with 47.5 percent, the colored Cumberland Presbyterian, 46.5 percent, and the United American Free-Will Baptist Church, 43.9 percent. Those showing the smallest proportion of males are the Protestant Episcopal Church, with 35.2 percent; the Colored Primitive Baptists in America, 35.7 percent, and the Northern Baptist Convention, 35.9 percent.

Statistics of the Sunday schools exhibit direct evidence as to how largely this institution functions in the religious life of the Negroes. The Bureau of the Census believes that the most significant fact regarding the Sunday schools reported by Negro churches is the exceptionally large proportion of organizations reporting them. "Whereas the percentage of all church organizations in the United States reporting Sunday schools," says the census, "was only 79 percent, 91.2 percent of the entire number of Negro organizations made such a report." The two classes of denominations are nearly even, the rate for the exclusively Negro bodies being a little lower than that for Negro organizations in other bodies. Among the single denominations, those showing the highest percentage of Sunday schools, as compared with the total number of organizations, are the Colored Cumberland Presbyterian Church, with 98 percent, and the Presbyterian Church in the United States of America, with 97.1 percent. The denominations showing the lowest percentage, as compared with the total number of organizations, are the Colored Primitive Baptists in America, with 20.8 percent, and the United American Free-Will Baptists, with 39.9 percent. Of all the Sunday schools given, the National Baptist Convention reported 17,910, or 51.6 percent, a little more than one-half; the African Methodist Episcopal Church, 18.1 percent; the Methodist Episcopal Church, 10.8 percent; the Colored Methodist Episcopal Church, 6.7 percent, and the African Methodist Episcopal Zion Church, 6 percent. These five bodies reported 32,360 Sunday schools, or 93.3 percent of the total number reported by Negro organizations. The statistics as to officers, teachers, and scholars show about the same proportions.

The report on Negro ministers shows a very rapid increase, in fact, a much larger number than in the case of other professional men among Negroes. The results show that although when brought into comparison with the white race the professions among Negroes are generally undermanned, the Negro ministry, so far as numbers are concerned, is well supplied. In 1906 there were 31,624 Negro ministers. The Baptists then had 17,117, the African Methodist Church 6,200, the African Methodist Episcopal Zion Church 3,082, the Colored Methodist Episcopal Church 2,671, the Colored Primitive Baptists in America 1,480, the Colored Cumberland Presbyterian Church 375, and the United Free-Will Baptists 136. The remaining number of ministers were distributed among the smaller denominations.

Another essential in the estimate of the religious progress of the Negro is the work done by the churches for their expansion into neglected parts. It has been said that the Negroes of the United States annually contribute more than $125,000 to home missions, supporting about 250 home missionaries and aiding more than 400 churches in backward districts. Owing to the recent migration resulting in all but the depletion of many churches in the South, and the necessity for others in the North, there has been much stimulus from without in some centers where churches have had little support from those migrants primarily interested in economic gain. Ever alive to the situation, however, the various Negro denominations have raised large sums to organize and maintain new churches wherever these migrants of color have settled in large numbers.

In foreign missions the Negro denominations have done almost as well. They annually contribute to this work more than $150,000. While some of this sum has been expended in promoting this cause in various foreign fields, the larger portion of it, by special designation, has been used in countries having a preponderance of Negro population, especially in Africa. The Negro Baptists, through the Foreign Mission Board of the National Baptist Convention, the work of which is directed by that untiring apostle to the lowly, Dr. L. G. Jordan, carries on missionary work in five foreign countries. This body has established 61 stations, 83 out-stations, and 43 churches, having altogether 14,700 communicants, among whom are 43 native workers and 451 assistants. The African Methodist Episcopal Church, having organized their mission work earlier than the Baptists—

that is, in 1844, whereas the Baptists did not organize theirs until 1880—have been more successful abroad. This denomination has invaded as many as eight foreign countries. Most of its efforts, however, have been restricted to Africa, where this denomination has two bishops reaching 17,178 members through 118 ordained ministers and 479 local preachers and teachers. This work in Africa was promoted largely through Bishops Levi J. Coppin and J. Albert Johnson, who, transferred to districts in this country, are still rendering their denomination valuable service. The African Methodist Episcopal Zion Church, which did not organize its foreign mission work until 1892, has established three foreign mission stations, five out-stations, and eleven churches. Other denominations have also done much to support missionary effort in foreign parts.

To promote Christian education both at home and in foreign fields these denominations have well supported publishing houses. The Colored Methodists have for a number of years had a successful plant for this work, which reached a stage of progress under its efficient agent, Dr. J. C. Martin. The African Methodist Episcopal Zion Church was earlier in the field and saw the work recently expanded under the well-known Dr. J. W. Crockett. The African Methodist Episcopal Church, a pioneer in this enterprise, has easily taken the lead in this work among the Negro churches, especially under such efficient managers as Dr. R. R. Wright, in charge of the Publishing House and editor of *The Christian Recorder* in Philadelphia, under Dr. R. C. Ransom, the brilliant editor of the *African Methodist Episcopal Church Review*, and under the progressive Ira T. Bryant, the director of the publications of the Sunday School Union in Nashville, founded by Bishop C. S. Smith. The Negro Baptists, having become enraged at the refusal of the white Baptists to recognize them as constituents of an all comprehending denomination, organized the National Baptist Convention, which accepted as one of its most important concerns the establishment of The National Baptist Publishing House. After attaining a high degree of success under the efficient Dr. R. H. Boyd, however, this establishment became the business of only that portion of the Baptists who supported Dr. Boyd in his efforts to direct the work on what his opponents called a private basis. The other Baptist faction has established another publishing house in Nashville.

Still another idea of the growth of the Negro church may be obtained from the statistics as to their administrative officers. The work of the Negro denominations has grown to the extent that the African Methodist Episcopal Church has fifteen bishops and nine other administrative officers, the Colored Methodists seven bishops and eleven other administrative officers, and the African Methodist Episcopal Zion Church ten bishops and fifteen other administrative officers. The affairs of the National Baptist Convention, incorporated, are administered by thirteen officers, and the National Baptist Convention, unincorporated, by an equal number of functionaries.

These, however, are not all regularly engaged in administrative work as in most of the Methodist denominations. The smaller groups of Baptists and Methodists show here and there top-heavy administrative staffs, whereas very large groups of Negro members in white churches have fewer supervisors.

The Methodist Episcopal Church, however, has for some years maintained for the Negroes abroad a missionary bishop, in the capacity of whom Bishops Alexander P. Camphor and Isaiah B. Scott have served. The noble fight as indicated by favorable ballots taken in various conferences, moreover, all but resulted in the election of the eloquent Dr. J. W. E. Bowen as a regular bishop. Becoming sufficiently liberal, however, to override race prejudice, the Conference of 1920 not only chose as bishop for Africa that pleasing preacher and successful pastor, Dr. M. W. Clair, but at the same time set apart for the New Orleans diocese the scholarly and brilliant editor of the *Southwestern Christian Advocate*, Dr. R. E. Jones.

CHAPTER XV
THE NEGRO CHURCH OF TODAY

THESE NEW DEVELOPMENTS have kept the Negro ministry still attractive, but because of many undesirable situations here and there in the church comparatively few young men have, during the last decade or so, aspired to this work. Some young Negroes have learned to look upon the calling as a necessary nuisance. Except in church schools where the preparation for the ministry is an objective, it has often been unusual to find one Negro student out of a hundred aspiring to the ministry, and too often those who have such aspirations represent the inferior intellect of the group, as it happened in the church during the middle ages. So rapidly did the ministry fall into discredit in many quarters a few years ago that most women of promise would not dare to engage themselves to men who thought of becoming clergymen; and, if the marital connection happened to be effected before the lot of the bride was known, it was in many cases considered a calamity. Because Negroes now realize how limited the opportunity for the race is in politics and some of the professions, however, the ministry will doubtless continue, as it has since the Reconstruction, a sort of avenue through which the ambitious youth must pass to secure a hearing and become a man of influence among his people. This does not mean that irreligious men will masquerade as spiritual advisers but that, inasmuch as the church as an institution is considered a welfare agency as well as a spiritual body to edify souls, some Negroes, interested in the social uplift of the race, are learning to accomplish this task by accepting leadership in the church.

Negroes see in the ministry, moreover, a new mission. The world, having now gone mad after the trifles of this life, is sadly in need of a redeemer to save men from themselves. In the contest between selfishness and godliness the former has been victor in the soul of the American and European. There are those like Bishop John Hurst believing that the Negro church must play the role of keeping the fire burning on the altar until the day when men again become reverent, and that the Negro's liberal interpretation of the Christian religion, based upon the brotherhood of man and the fatherhood of God, must gain ascendancy and be accepted by a regenerated world of tomorrow.

As a preparation to this end the afflictions of the Negro have adequately developed self-control in the race. The watchword of the Negro church has been patience while waiting on the Lord. The Negro has learned not to avenge his own wrongs, believing that God will adjust matters in the end. The Negro agrees with Professor Joseph A. Booker, that he that taken up the sword shall perish by the sword. Even during these days, when we learn much about the lawless, the behavior of the Negroes is no exception to the rule. An investigation shows that the Negroes never do any more than to defend themselves in keeping with the first law of nature. White persons who once found it possible to intimidate the whole group by shooting or lynching one or two now face persons of color bent upon defending their homes. At heart, however, the Negro is conservatively Christian and looks forward to that favorable turn in the affairs of man when the wrongs of the oppressed shall be righted without the shedding of blood.

The Negro church is criticized by a few radical members of the race as a hindrance to the immediate achievement of the aims of the race, in that the white race in the exercise of foresight encourages and even subsidizes the Negro ministry in carrying out this conservative program. This will tend, it is said, to keep the Negro down, whereas the white people themselves do not actually believe in such doctrine; for their own actions show that they use it as a means to an end. This, however, is hardly a fair criticism of the Negro church of today. No force from without can claim control of this institution, and certainly no one can bridle its fearless speakers who stand for the Negro of today. The Negro churchmen, moreover, are not any more conservative than other leaders of the people. They may be more generally effective because of their greater influence. That the Negro church is conservative is due to teaching and to tradition, and it is fortunate that Providence has had it so. Acting as a conservative force among the Negroes, the church has been a sort of balance wheel. It has not been unprogressive but rather wise in its generation in not rushing forward to a radical position in advance of public opinion. In other words, the Negro church has known how far it can safely instruct its people to go in righting their own wrongs, and this conservatism has no doubt saved the Negro from the fate of other oppressed groups who have suffered extermination because of the failure to handle their case more diplomatically.

This does not mean, however, that the Negro church of today is not alive to the sufferings of the race and is not critical of the attitude of the so-called Christian elements in this country. Some Negro ministers like Dr. F. J. Grimké are decidedly outspoken, even to the extent of being classed with the militant Reds now being deported. Dr. Pezavia O'Connell, a gentleman of scholarship and character, has all but suffered professional martyrdom because he has always fearlessly championed the cause of the Negro. Inasmuch as such an advanced position does not always harmonize with the faith of his communicants, he has been proscribed in certain circles. R. W. Bagnall, George Frazier Miller, and Byron Gunner have actually preached the use of force and encouraged resistance to the mobs to the extent that some Negroes have probably addressed themselves vindictively to the task of retribution. Through the Negro churches, and these alone, have the Negroes been able to effect anything like a cooperative movement to counteract the evil influences of such combinations against the race as the revived Ku Klux Klan.

The church then is no longer the voice of one man crying in the wilderness, but a spiritual organization at last becoming alive to the needs of a people handicapped by social distinctions of which the race must gradually free itself to do here in this life that which will assure the larger life to come. To attain this, the earth must be made habitable for civilized people. Funds are daily raised in Negro churches to fight segregation, and an innocent Negro in danger of suffering injustice at the hands of the local oppressor may appeal with success to the communicants with whom he has frequented a common altar. The National Association for the Advancement of Colored People would be unable to carry out its program without the aid of the Negro church.

Although Negroes are not now attracted to the church as much as formerly, the census reports still show that there are more Negroes in the ministry than in any other profession. The only really close competitor of the Negro in this profession is the southern white man. While the educated white men of the North are taking up scientific pursuits and business, the southern whites are carrying out their designs on the ministry, in keeping with the well-laid plans by which they have succeeded in getting partial control of the northern press. During recent years so many southern white students have crowded northern schools of theology that, in keeping with the spirit of Beelzebub, some of these institutions now deny Negroes admission. The pulpits of the North are being gradually taken over by the apostles indoctrinated by the medieval agents of race hate.

Since the Negro ministry is still the largest factor in the life of this race, it naturally conflicts with the propaganda of the ministry preaching caste. These representatives of the master and slave classes must, in the capacity of spokesmen of widely differing groups, work out the solution of the problems of the church in the United States; for either the one or the other must dictate the religious program of the economically mad North. The North cares little about priest-craft. The struggle there for dollars and cents and for opportunities to spend them in riotous living is too keen to spare time for such matters as Christian living and the remote hereafter. The South, on the other hand, has never lost its bearing. In spite of riots here and there and lynchings almost anywhere, that section still considers itself a Christian land and, in its way, has lifted high the name of Christ without being influenced by his life. The North, then, if it ever awakes from its lethargy, will probably accept either the principles of Jesus of Nazareth as they have been preached and practiced by the Negroes, or the Anglo-Saxon-chosen-people-of-God faith for which many misguided white communicants have jeopardized their own lives and have taken those of Negroes unwilling to worship at the shrine of race prejudice.

The white people of this country are not interested in the real mission of Christ. In the North the church has surrendered to the materialistic system and developed into an agency seeking to assuage the pains of those suffering from the very economic evils which the institution has not the courage to attack. In the southern portion of the United States, the white churches have degenerated into perfunctory machines engaged in the service of deceiving the multitude with the doctrine that the Anglo-Saxon, being superior to other races by divine ordination, may justly oppress them to maintain its supremacy and that the principles of Jesus are exemplified in the lives of these newly chosen people of God when they permit their so-called inferiors to eat the crumbs let fall by those whom their idol god has carefully selected as the honor guests at the feast. If the humble Nazarene appeared there disturbing the present caste system, he would be speedily lynched as he was in Palestine.

In spite of the Negroes' logical preaching of the fatherhood of God and the brotherhood of man, however, the North now seems inclined to accept the faith of the South. Science has long since uprooted the theory that one race can be superior to another, but the northern churches are loath to act accordingly. The same churches, which prior to emancipation, championed the cause of the Negro, are today working indirectly to promote racial distinctions. The southern white man, wiser in his generation than most of his competitors, easily realized that he could not legally re-enslave the Negro, but early devised a scheme to convert the North to the doctrine of segregation, educational distinctions, and the elimination of the Negroes from the body politic, to make it improbable, if not impossible, for the Negroes to attain the status of white men. The Christian spirit of the North at first rebelled against the very idea; but, already pledged to the policy of the economic proscription of Negroes through trades unions, that section, once bristling with churches dominated by abolitionists, soon yielded to the temptation of sacrificing the principles of Jesus for dollars and cents. The Negro of today, therefore, is hated as much by the northern religious devotee as by the southern enthusiast at the shrine of race prejudice.

Evidence as to such conditions obtaining is not wanting. In the midst of the changing order involving all but the annihilation of the Negro, the race has repeatedly appealed to the "Christian" element of the North only to have a deaf ear turned to its petition. Inasmuch as the northern ministers are influenced by rich laymen whose businesses have so many ramifications in the South, they refrain from such criticism or interference in behalf of the Negro, since it might mean economic loss. Negroes at first secured from northern churches large sums of money to establish adequate private schools and colleges throughout the South, but before these institutions could be developed these funds were diverted to the support of industrial education which the South openly interpreted to signify that no Negro must be encouraged to become the equal of any white man, and that education for him must mean something entirely different from that training provided for the Caucasian. The northern white man, more interested in developing men to produce cotton and tobacco than in the training of a race to think for itself, again bowed to mammon. Churches which once annually raised sums for the maintenance of various Negro schools have now, as a majority, restricted their contributions to Hampton and Tuskegee, where, it is believed, the ultimate distinctions of the whites and blacks can, by the process of safeguarded education, be best effected. Practically all of the so-called Christian philanthropists have followed their example.

The Negro church, however, finds itself facing still another problem. During recent years Negroes have manifested more interest in the redemption of Africa, Negro churches have long since contributed to missions and the periodical return of the apostle to the lowly far away has been awaited with the anticipation of unwonted joy; but it is only recently that the church has begun to make sacrifices for the cause. Whereas a few years ago a congregation felt that it had done its duty in raising a missionary collection of ten or fifteen dollars, that same group is today supporting one or two missionaries in Africa. The raising of funds for this purpose and the administration of it have been of late so well extended as noted above, that the national church organizations have had to assign this work to boards, whose business is to supply the missionaries at the various posts and extend their operations by establishing schools where they have sufficiently well established the work to require systematic training.

In spite of their well-laid plans, however, the Negro church finds itself handicapped in reaching the Africans. Controlled as that continent is by the capitalistic powers of Europe, they have much apprehension as to the sort of gospel the Negro missionary may preach in Africa, lest the natives be stirred up to the point of self-assertion. They desire that missionaries to Africa, like race leaders in the United States, be "hand-picked." In other words, the missionary movement must bow to mammon. To the heathen, then, must go those who have served only as forerunners of foreign conquests involving the discomfiture, the oppression, and in many cases the annihilation of the very people whom they professed to be saving.

Following in their wake, a certain American "Christian" organization financed by "philanthropists" recently sent to Africa Thomas J. Jones who, in behalf of his race, sought to carry out this policy. The effect of this mission was soon apparent. After having nobly served in Africa and India, Max Yergan, in International Young Men's Christian Association Secretary, appointed to serve permanently in Africa, recently toured the United States for a mission fund which the Negroes freely contributed that through him some portion of Africa might be redeemed. This man in Africa having ingratiated himself into the favor of the capitalistic government there, however, according to Yergan's statement, influenced the administration to refuse him the permit to work among his own people. The same meddler, according to a complaint made by the colored branch of the Young Men's Christian Association, all but made himself the dictator of the appointments of that department and other Negro welfare agencies sent abroad during the World War. His business now seems to be that of furnishing the world with "hand-picked" Negro leaders to damn even the natives in Africa. The white church then, has not only failed to preach the social gospel of Jesus, but is preventing the Negroes from carrying that message to their own people. In other words, the principles of the humble Nazarene must be crushed out to make money and perpetuate caste.

This and other handicaps, however, have not prevented the progress of the church. Probably the most promising aspect is that Negro ministers of today measure up to a higher standard than formerly. They are not diverted from their course by politics and the like. Here and there, of course, are some of little promise, who in a poverty-stricken condition accept almost any bribe offered them by political bosses, but fortunately this number is known to be rapidly decreasing. During the last generation there has developed among Negroes the feeling that the political embroglio is an unclean sphere which the minister should not enter. The increasing duties of the Negro preachers, moreover, have recently so multiplied that they have no time for such service. Experience has shown that even in the case of those who have gone into politics in self-defense that they have accomplished little good or that some layman could have handled the matter more successfully.

We have recently had two striking cases in evidence. Bishop Alexander Walters, after having rendered valuable service to the cause as an educator and minister in Kentucky, California, and Tennessee, became the ranking bishop of the African Methodist Episcopal Zion Church. He then decided that his people had been so long duped by the grafters and tricksters masquerading as the successors of Lincoln and Grant, that he would use his influence to have the Negroes divide their vote by supporting Woodrow Wilson in 1912. Dr. J. Milton Waldron, an influential Baptist minister of Washington, feeling that it would mean a new day for the Negro to have this democratic college president of many promises elevated to the headship of the nation by the aid of the Negro vote, did likewise. Disappointed in the end, however, by the hypocrisy of Wilson, who, in his heart hated Negroes, these churchmen saw themselves painfully humiliated among their people, who, in return for the large number of votes which they gave Wilson, received nothing but segregation in the civil service, elimination from public office, and conscription to do forced labor in the World War, while he was promising that the Negroes should have justice and have it abundantly.

The Negro churchmen of today realize, as most leaders of the race do, that the hope of the blacks lies not in politics from without but in race uplift from within in the form of social amelioration and economic development. Neither Democrats nor Republicans are interested in the Negro except so far as the race may be used to enable them to [get] into office. Their platform promises have been not something to stand on but to get into office on. This does not in any sense, however, mean that the Negro minister has lost interest in public matters of concern to every citizen, but rather that he has learned the possibilities in the political world. He will in no sense withdraw from the contest in behalf of the rights of his people. His method of attack will be different. Carrying out this reconstructed policy for the rehabilitation of the race, the Negro minister, like a majority of the thinking members of this group today, will welcome the assistance and cooperation of the white man, but will not suffer himself to be used as a tool in connection with forces from without the circles of the race, pretending to be interested in the solution of its problems.

NOTES

1. Carter G. Woodson, *The History of the Negro Church* (Washington, 1921). A second revised edition was published in 1945 and reissued as a third edition in 1972. The most important overviews of black church history since Woodson are E. Franklin Frazier, *Negro Church in America* (New York, 1964); and Gayraud S. Wilmore, *Black Religion and Black Radicalism* (1972; reprint, Maryknoll, 1983). The former is a very brief and often unpersuasive sociological essay, while the latter focuses on the relationship of black religion to protest and political activities, so neither is an adequate replacement for Woodson.

2. No edition of Woodson, *History of the Negro Church*, contains footnotes or bibliography, so it is impossible to know clearly and precisely what sources its author used. For important scholarly work of the 1970s and 1980s, focusing wholly or significantly on the institutional history of Afro-American Christianity, see Carol V. R. George, *Segregated Sabbaths: Richard Allen and the Rise of the Independent Black Churches* (New York, 1973); Milton Sernett, *Black Religion and American Evangelicalism: White Protestantism, Plantation Missions, and the Flowering of Negro Christianity, 1787-1865* (Metuchen, 1975); Albert J. Raboteau, *Slave Religion: The "Invisible Institution" in the Antebellum South* (New York, 1978); Randall K. Burkett and Richard Newman, eds., *Black Apostles: Afro-American Clergy Confront the Twentieth Century* (Boston, 1978); Randall K. Burkett, *Garveyism as a Religious Movement: The Institutionalization of a Black Civil Religion* (Metuchen, 1978); Mechal Sobel, *Trabelin' On: The Slave Journey to an Afro-Baptist Faith* (Westport, 1979); William B. Gravely, "The Social, Political, and Religious Significance of the Foundation of the Colored Methodist Episcopal Church (1870)," *Methodist History*, 18 (Oct. 1979), 3-25; Jualynne Dodson, "Nineteenth Century AME Preaching Women: Cutting Edge of Women's Inclusion in Church Polity," in *Women in New Worlds*, ed. Hilah F. Thomas and Rosemary Skinner Keller (Nashville, 1981); David W. Wills and Richard Newman, *Black Apostles at Home and Abroad: Afro-Americans and the Christian Mission from the Revolution to Reconstruction* (Boston, 1982); Clarence E. Walker, *A Rock in a Weary Land: The African Methodist Episcopal Church during the Civil War and Reconstruction* (Baton Rouge, 1982); Walter E. Williams, *Black Americans and the Evangelization of Africa, 1877-1900* (Madison, 1982); Evelyn Brooks, "The Feminist Theology of the Black Baptist Church, 1880-1900," in *Class, Sex and Race: The Dynamics of Control*, ed. Amy Swerdlow and Hanna Lessinger (Boston, 1983); Will B. Gravely, "The Rise of African Churches in America (1786-1822): Re-Examining the Contexts," *Journal of Religious Thought*, 41 (Spring/Summer 1984), 58-73; Aldon D. Morris, *The Origins of the Civil Rights Movement: Black Communities Organizing for Change* (New York, 1984); Cheryl Townsend Gilkes, "'Together and in Harness': Women's Traditions in the Sanctified Church," *Signs*, 10 (Summer 1985), 678-99; James Melvin Washington, *Frustrated Fellowship: The Black Baptist Quest for Social Power* (Macon, 1986); special issue "The Black Catholic Experience," *U.S. Catholic Historian*, 5 (1986); Mechal Sobel, *The World They Made Together: Black and White Values in Eighteenth-Century Virginia* (Princeton, 1987); Margaret Washington Creel, *"A Peculiar People": Slave Religion and Community Culture among the*

Gullahs (New York, 1988); special issue "The Black Catholic Community, 1880-1987," *U.S. Catholic Historian, 1* (Spring/Summer 1988); Taylor Branch, *Parting the Waters: America in the King Years, 1954-63* (New York, 1988); David E. Swift, *Black Prophets of Justice: Activist Clergy before the Civil War* (Baton Rouge, 1989); David W. Wills, "An Enduring Distance: Black Americans and the Establishment," in *Between the Times: The Travail of the Protestant Establishment in America, 1900-1960,* ed. William R. Hutchison (New York, 1989), 168-92; and Albert J. Raboteau, "The Black Church: Continuity within Change," in *Altered Landscapes: Christianity in America, 1935-1985,* ed. David W. Lotz, Donald W. Shriver, Jr., and John F. Wilson (Grand Rapids, 1989), 77-91.

3. On the encounter of blacks and whites as a major religious theme in American history, see David W. Wills, "The Central Themes of American Religious History: Pluralism, Puritanism, and the Encounter of Black and White," *Religion and Intellectual Life,* 5 (Fall 1987), 30-41.

4. Nineteenth-century black denominational histories written from within include, for the African Methodist Episcopal (AME) church, Daniel A. Payne, *The Semi-Centenary and the Retrospection of the African Methodist Episcopal Church in the United States of America* (1866; reprint, Freeport, 1972); Daniel A. Payne, *History of the African Methodist Episcopal Church* (1891; reprint, New York, 1969); and N. C. W. Cannon, *History of the African Methodist Episcopal Church* (Rochester, 1842). For the AME Zion tradition, see Christopher Rush, *Short Account of the Rise and Progress of the African Methodist Episcopal [Zion] Church* (New York, 1843); John J. Moore, *History of the A.M.E. Zion Church* (York, 1884); and James W. Hood, *One Hundred Years of the African Methodist Episcopal Zion Church* (New York, 1895). For the Colored, later Christian, Methodist Episcopal (CME) church, see Fayette M. Hamilton, *Conversation on the Colored Methodist Episcopal Church* (Nashville, 1884); and Fayette M. Hamilton, *Plain Account of the Colored Methodist Episcopal Church* (Nashville, 1887). More comprehensive is Charles H. Phillips, *The History of the Colored Methodist Episcopal Church* (1898; reprint, New York, 1972). An expanded version of the same volume, called a second edition and bringing the story into the early twentieth century, was published in 1925. Important for their preservation of sources and of the story of blacks in biracial, but predominantly white, denominations are George F. Bragg, Jr., *History of the Afro-American Group of the Episcopal Church* (1922; reprint, New York, 1968); Matthew Anderson, *Presbyterianism. Its Relation to the Negro* (Philadelphia, 1897); L. Y. Cox, *Pioneer Foot Steps* (Cape May, 1917); and L. M. Hagood, *Colored Man in the Methodist Episcopal Church* (Cincinnati, 1890). Notable twentieth-century efforts in black denominational history include Charles S. Smith, *History of the African Methodist Episcopal Church* (Philadelphia, 1922); George A. Singleton, *Romance of African Methodism* (New York, 1952); Howard D. Gregg, *History of the African Methodist Episcopal Church: The Black Church in Action* (Nashville, 1980); David H. Bradley, *History of the A.M.E. Zion Church* (2 vols., Nashville, 1956-1970); William J. Walls, *African Methodist Episcopal Zion Church: Reality of the Black Church* (Charlotte, 1974); Othal H. Lakey, *History of the C.M.E. Church* (Memphis, 1985); Lewis G. Jordan, *Negro Baptist History, U.S.A., 1750-1930* (Nashville, 1930); Leroy Fitts, *History of Black Baptists*

(Nashville, 1985); and Andrew E. Murray, *Presbyterians and the Negro: A History* (Philadelphia, 1966). Interest within the black churches in documenting and writing their history has recently increased.

5. Walter Schatz, ed., *Directory of Afro-American Resources* (New York, 1970); Ethel L. Williams and Clifton Brown, comps., *Howard University Bibliography of African and Afro-American Religious Studies: With Locations in American Libraries* (Wilmington, 1977). For information on the *Newsletter*, address inquiries to the Editor, *Newsletter*, Du Bois Institute, Canaday Hall-B, Harvard University, Cambridge, MA 02138. Annual subscription is $5.00 (payable to the Afro-American Religious History Group). A reprint edition of previously published newsletters is planned.

6. Loretta L. Hefner, *The WPA Historical Records Survey: A Guide to the Unpublished Inventories, Indexes, and Transcripts* (Chicago, 1980). The Schomburg Center for Research in Black Culture, New York Public Library, is currently engaged in a nationwide effort, supported by the Lilly Endowment, to identify and gather documentary material on Afro-American religious history. One of its projects is to assemble in a single file copies of all Works Projects Administration (WPA) black church records surveys, which should greatly facilitate their use.

7. The Clipping File of the Schomburg Center is available from Chadwyck-Healey: *Schomburg Clipping File, Fart I, 1924-1975* (microfiche, 9500 cards, Alexandria, Va., 1988). For a guide, see *Index to the Schomburg Clipping File* (Teaneck, 1985). A second series of the Schomburg Clipping File, for 1975-1988, is being filmed. The Tuskegee Institute News Clipping File was organized by Monroe N. Work, who used it to provide data for *Negro Yearbooks* published at Tuskegee beginning in 1912. The comprehensive microfilm edition—*The Tuskegee Institute Clipping File, 1899-1966* (microfilm, 252 reels, Ann Arbor, 1978), available from University Microfilms International—includes the texts of all published volumes of the *Negro Yearbooks* (1912-1952). See John W. Kitchens, ed., *Guide to the Microfilm Edition of the Tuskegee Institute News Clipping File* (Tuskegee, 1978).

8. *The Hampton University Newspaper Clipping File* (microfiche, 826 cards, Teaneck, 1987) is available from Chadwyck-Healey. The Gumby Collection of American Negro Scrapbooks (Rare Book and Manuscript Library, Columbia University, New York, N.Y.) has been filmed and is available for interlibrary loan or purchase from Kenneth A. Lohf, Rare Book and Manuscript Library, Butler Library - 6th floor, 535 West 114th Street, Columbia University Libraries, New York, NY 10027.

9. On this document, see Payne, *History of the African Methodist Episcopal Church*, v. That lost or little-known manuscripts can still be recovered and given new life by researchers is evident from Jean McMahon Humez, ed., *Gifts of Power: The Writings of Rebecca Jackson: Black Visionary, Shaker Eldress* (Amherst, 1981). See also William L. Andrews, ed., *Sisters of the Spirit: Three Black Women's Autobiographies of the Nineteenth Century* (Bloomington, 1986).

10. This item is in the Carter G. Woodson Papers (Manuscript Division, Library of Congress), one of the most important multidenominational black church manuscript collections.

11. Historical Commission of the Southern Baptist Convention, 901 Commerce Street, Suite 400, Nashville, TN 37203.

12. For an index to *National Baptist Magazine*, see Lester B. Scherer, comp., *Newsletter of the Afro-American Religious History Group*, 6 (Spring 1982), 4-9. See also Lester B. Scherer, comp., *Afro-American Baptists: A Guide to Materials in the American Baptist Historical Society* (April 1985), a useful (though not definitive) guide to the Afro-American material of the American Baptist Historical Society, Rochester, N.Y.

13. The American Baptist Historical Society run, which covers the years 1898 to 1949 (with many breaks), is available on microfilm from the American Baptist Historical Society, 1106 S. Goodman Street, Rochester, NY 14620. The authors are indebted to Ralph E. Luker, associate editor, Martin Luther King, Jr., Papers, for information about the *Georgia Baptist* and other items cited in this article.

14. The Martin Luther King, Jr., Papers Project, which plans to publish a twelve-volume edition beginning in 1991, is drawing on these 2 major collections and 150 additional collections in dozens of archives and in private hands. Inquiries about this project should be directed to Professor Clayborne Carson, Editor, The Martin Luther King, Jr., Papers, Cyprus Hall-D, Stanford University, CA 94305-4146.

15. For the most important of the smaller black Methodist bodies, see Lewis V. Baldwin, *"Invisible" Strands* in African Methodism: A History of the African Union Methodist Protestant and Union American Methodist Episcopal Churches, 1805-1980 *(Metuchen, 1983)*. See also Will B. Gravely, "African Methodisms and the Rise of Black Denominationalism," in Rethinking Methodist History: A Bicentennial Historical Consultation, ed. *Russell E. Richey* and *Kenneth E. Rowe (Nashville, 1985)*, 111-24.

16. For information on the holdings of the AME Financial Department and on other points, the authors are indebted to Professor Dennis C. Dickerson of Williams College. Elected AME church historiographer in 1988, Dickerson is exploring the possibility of establishing a central denominational repository. He has produced a pamphlet guide to research in AME materials: Dennis C. Dickerson, *The Past Is in Your Hands: Writing Local AME Church History* (n.p., 1989), available from Dennis C. Dickerson, P.O. Box 301, Williamstown, MA 01267. *AME Church Review* (microfilm, 4 reels, Millwood, n.d.) is available from Kraus International Publications.

17. Inquiries concerning *Christian Recorder* (1854-1902) microfilm (12 reels) and *The Records of Mother Bethel AME Church, 1760-1972* (24 reels, Historical Commission, Mother Bethel AME Church, Philadelphia, Pa.) should be addressed to the Historical Society of Pennsylvania, 1300 Locust Street, Philadelphia, PA 19107 and Historical Commission, Mother Bethel AME Church, 419 South Sixth Street, Philadelphia, PA 19147. Inquiries concerning

Christian Recorder (1913-1936) microfilm may be addressed to Preservation Board, American Theological Library Association, 820 Church Street, 3rd floor, Evanston, IL 60201.

18. The William J. Walls Heritage Center, on the campus of Livingstone College and Hood Theological Seminary, Salisbury, N.C., was intended as the major denominational archive, but it is currently unstaffed and therefore not open to researchers.

19. For blacks in the Presbyterian churches, the researcher is advised to begin at the Presbyterian Historical Society, Philadelphia. For blacks in the Congregational tradition, an especially important collection is that of the Amistad Research Center, Tulane University, New Orleans. On the relevant holdings of the Disciples of Christ Historical Society in Nashville, Tennessee, see *Preliminary Guide to Black Materials in the Disciples of Christ Historical Society* (Nashville, 1971).

20. This detailed index was compiled over a lifetime by diocesan historiographer F. Garner Ranney.

21. Charles Edwin Jones, *Black Holiness: A Guide to the Study of Black Participation in Wesleyan Perfectionist and Glossolalic Pentecostal Movements* (Metuchen, 1987). For information concerning archival materials on the black Holiness and Pentecostal churches, the authors are indebted to Professor Hans Baer of the University of Arkansas at Little Rock; Professor David Daniels of McCormick Theological Seminary; Professor Robert Franklin of the Candler School of Theology, Emory University; Professor Cheryl Townsend Gilkes of Colby College; Albert Miller, doctoral student at Princeton University; and Richard Newman of the New York Public Library.

22. The American Home Missionary Society and American Missionary Association collections have been filmed and are available for purchase or interlibrary loan through the Amistad Research Center, Tilton Hall, Tulane University, New Orleans, LA 70118. Records of the Bureau of Refugees, Freedmen, and Abandoned Lands, RG 105 (National Archives) are available on microfilm from the National Archives Trust Fund Board, National Archives, Washington, DC 20408. *Black Studies: A Select Catalog of National Archives Microform Publications* (Washington, 1984), which includes a detailed description of this and other related microfilm collections, is available for $5.00 (including postage and handling) from the National Archives Trust Fund, P.O. Box 100793, Atlanta, GA 30384. For information on materials in the War Department records in the National Archives, we are indebted to the Military Reference Branch, National Archives and Records Administration, Washington. A more extensive description of these and related materials is forthcoming in the *Newsletter of the Afro-American Religious History Group.*

23. The Claude A. Barnett Papers (Chicago Historical Society, Chicago, Ill.) are available on microfilm from University Publications of America: *The Claude A. Barnett Papers: The Associated Negro Press* (microfilm, 198 reels, Frederick, Md., 1985-1986).

24. On this and related collections, see Deborah Gray White, "Mining the Forgotten: Manuscript Sources for Black Women's History," *Journal of American History*, 74 (June 1987),

237-42.

25. On the black church in American politics, see David W. Wills, "Beyond Commonality and Plurality: Persistent Racial Polarity in American Religion and Politics," in *Religion and American Politics: From the Colonial Period to the 1980s*, ed. Mark A. Noll (New York, 1990), 199-224. On the Black Abolitionist Papers, see George E. Carter and C. Peter Ripley, eds., *Black Abolitionist Papers, 1830-1865* (microfilm, 17 reels, Ann Arbor, 1981); and George E. Carter and C. Peter Ripley, eds., *Black Abolitionist Papers, 1830-1865: A Guide to the Microfilm Edition* (New York, 1981). The papers of Albion Tourgee are available on microfilm from University Microfilms International: *The Albion W. Tourgee Papers* (microfilm, 60 reels, Ann Arbor, 1965).

26. See Robert L. Zangrando, "Manuscript Sources for Twentieth-Century Civil Rights Research," *Journal of American History*, 74 (June 1987), 243-51.

27. Exhibitions can also supply important documentation. See, for example, Edward D. Smith, *Climbing Jacob's Ladder: The Rise of Black Churches in Eastern American Cities, 1740-1877* (Washington, 1988), published in connection with a major exhibition at the Anacostia Museum of the Smithsonian Institution. The exhibition "Climbing Jacobs Ladder" began a three-year tour of thirty-six American cities in the spring of 1990. In each locality, the exhibition will include manuscripts and artifacts newly gathered from congregations in that area; it will therefore augment, as well as display, the literary and material documentation of early black church history.

28. This collection is the work of one person, the Reverend L. O. Taylor. A documentary film on Taylor's life and work, "Sermons and Sacred Pictures," is available from the Center for Southern Folklore, 1216 Peabody Avenue, P.O. Box 40105, Memphis, TN 38104. The center has also published a two-volume catalog useful for locating films and videotapes relevant to the study of black churches (the catalog includes the addresses of distributors): *American Folklore Films and Videotapes: An Index* (Memphis, 1976), and *American Folklore Films and Videotapes: A Catalogue*, vol. II (New York, 1982). Three films deserve special mention. "Say Amen, Somebody," a commercially released film now on videotape, highlights the careers of gospel singer Willie Mae Ford Smith and gospel composer Thomas A. Dorsey. "Fannie Bell Chapman: Gospel Singer," a film depicting the ministry of a Mississippi gospel singer and faith healer, illustrates the importance of healing in Afro-American religious practice. "The Performed Word," a documentary film now on videotape, examines continuity and change in black preaching through a comparison of Bishop Elmer E. Cleveland, Ephesians Church of God in Christ, Berkeley, California, and his daughter, Ernestine Cleveland Reems, pastor of the Center of Hope, Oakland, California. The film is especially effective in presenting the sequential development and congregational response to the chanted sermon. Its producer has analyzed Bishop Cleveland's preaching—and that of other black preachers—in Gerald L. Davis, *I Got the Word in Me and I Can Sing It, You Know: A Study of the Performed African-American Sermon* (Philadelphia, 1985). See also Bruce A. Rosenberg, *Can These Bones Live? The Art of the American Folk Preacher* (Urbana, 1988); Albert J. Raboteau,

" A Fire in the Bones': The Afro-American Chanted Sermon," 1982 (in Albert J. Raboteau's possession); and Albert J. Raboteau, "The Afro-American Traditions" in *Caring and Curing: Health and Medicine in Western Religious Traditions*, ed. Ronald L. Numbers and Darrel W. Amundsen (New York, 1986), 539-62.

29. Inquiries concerning *Black Music Research Bulletin* may be addressed to Center for Black Music Research, Columbia College, Chicago, 600 S. Michigan Avenue, Chicago, IL 60605. The authors are indebted to Richard Newman for calling this periodical and related material to their attention. John Michael Spencer, *As the Black School Sings: Black Music Collections at Black Universities and Colleges, with a Union List of Book Holdings* (New York, 1987).

30. A collection of such "race records" is Paul Oliver, comp., *Songsters and Saints* (Matchbox Records MSEX 2001/2002 and MSEX 2003/2004, 2 vols., 4 disks).

31. C. L. Franklin's recorded sermons have largely gone out of print. Among the places where those still available can be ordered—and other hard-to-find recordings of black religious music and sermons obtained—is Down Home Records, 10341 San Pablo Avenue, El Cerrito, CA 94530. Information about a reissue of "classic recordings of C. L. Franklin" can be obtained from Stan Lewis, Jewel Records, P.O. Box 1125, Shreveport, LA 71163-1125. See also C. L. Franklin, *Give Me This Mountain: Life History and Selected Sermons*, ed. Jeff Todd Titon (Urbana, 1989), which contains texts of several of the recorded sermons.

32. At a love feast conducted by Bishop Asbury at the Virginia Conference in 1783, strong testimonials were borne in favor of African liberty. He said in 1785, speaking of the Virginia Conference: "I found the minds of the people greatly agitated with our rules against slavery and a proposed petition to the General Assembly for the emancipation of the blacks. A colonel and Dr. Coke disputed on the subject and the colonel used some threats; next day brother O'Kelly let fly at them, and they were made angry enough; we, however, came off with whole bones." Working in this field against slavery, these Methodists waited upon George Washington, who politely received them and gave his opinion against slavery. This conference, however, did not bring striking results. Saying that he was much pained in mind, Bishop Asbury asserted: "I am brought to conclude that slavery will exist in Virginia perhaps for ages. There is not a *sufficient sense of religion nor liberty to destroy it.*" In Georgia in 1741 he said, "Away with the false cant that the better you use the Negroes, the worse they will use you! Make them good; then, teach them the fear of God, and learn to fear him yourselves, ye masters. I understand not the doctrine of cruelty."

33. He published a pamphlet entitled *Involuntary, Unmerited, Perpetual, Absolute, Hereditary Slavery, examined on the principles of Nature, Reason, Justice, Policy, and Scripture.* The work is written in grave and manly style and with nice discriminations and candid reasons set forth the claims of the emancipating Baptists in a creditable manner.

In 1778, Mr. Barrow received an invitation to preach at the house of a gentleman who lived on Nansemond River, near the mouth of James River. A ministering brother accompanied him. They were informed on their arrival, that they might expect rough usage, and so it happened. A gang of well-dressed men came up to the stage, which had been erected under some trees, as soon as the hymn was given out, and sang one of their obscene songs. They then undertook to plunge both of the preachers. Mr. Barrow was plunged twice. They pressed him into the mud, held him long under the water, and came near drowning him. In the midst of their mocking, they asked him if he believed and throughout treated him with the most barbarous insolence and outrage. His companion they plunged but once. The whole assembly was shocked, the women shrieked, but no one durst interfere; for about twenty stout fellows were engaged in this horrid measure. They insulted and abused the gentleman who invited them to preach, and everyone who spoke a word in their favor. Before these persecuted men could change their clothes, they were dragged from the house, and driven off by these outrageous churchmen. But three or four of them died in a few weeks, in a distracted manner, and one of them wished himself in hell before he had joined the company, &c.

In Mr. Barrow's piece against slavery, we find the following note: "To see a man (a Christian) in the most serious period of all his life--making his last will and testament--and in the most solemn manner addressing the Judge of all the earth—*In the name of God, Amen.*— Hearken to him—he will very shortly appear before the Judge, where kings and slaves have equal thrones!—He proceeds:

"Item. I give and bequeath to my Son--a negro man named --, a negro woman named --[,] with five of her youngest children."

"Item. I give and bequeath to my daughter --, a negro man named --, also a negro woman named --, with her three children."

"Item. All my other slaves, whether men, women or children, with all my stock of horses, cattle, sheep, and hogs, I direct to be sold to the highest bidder, and the monies arising therefrom (after paying my just debts) to be equally divided between my two above-named children!!!"

"The above specimen is not exaggerated; the like of it often turns up. And what can a real lover of the rights of man say in vindication thereof?"

"Suppose for a moment, that the testator, or if the owner, dies intestate (which is often the case), was ever so humane a person, who can vouch for their heirs and successors? This consideration, if nothing else, ought to make all slaveholders take heed what they do, 'for they must give an account of themselves to God.'"

34. Departing under similar circumstances at the same time went Rev. Mr. Amos, a product of the same Christian environment, directing his course to New Providence, Bahama Islands, British West Indies, where he established a flourishing Baptist Church.

35. When he purchased the property for the Bethel Church on Lombard Street near Sixth and the majority of the committee refused to accept, Allen having given his word so to do,

kept it at a great personal loss.

36. A man of fair education, Willis was a power in that State as early as 1798. We hear of him in Louisiana in 1804. Mississippi sent two ministers to ordain him in Louisiana in 1812. He organized later the Louisiana Baptist Association and was chosen as its moderator in 1837.

37. "In all of his journeying," says a contributor to the *Baptist Magazine*, "he seemed to go among the people in the fullness of the blessings of the Gospel of Christ. He was not indeed an ordinary man, for without those advantages of good education in early life, he became distinguished as a preacher. His understanding was vigorous, his imagination was vivid, his personal appearance was interesting and his elocution was grateful. We have heard him preach to an audience of more than 1000 persons when he seemed to have the complete command of their feelings for an hour together. On baptismal occasions he was truly eloquent. His arguments were unanswerable, and his appeals to the heart were powerful. The slow and gentle manner in which he placed candidates under the water, and raised them up again, produced an indelible impression on the spectators, that they had indeed seen the burial with Christ in baptism. Near the close of his career in 1831 when he finally died of a painful illness, he bore striking testimony to his faith in Jesus. His mind being 'wonderfully sustained by the consolations of the Gospel,' he said on one occasion to a friend, 'Since I saw you last I have been happy in God—my sky has been without a cloud. I know that when the earthly house of my tabernacle is dissolved, I have a house not made with hands, eternal in the heavens.' When asked at another time if he had a good hope through grace, O, said he, I am altogether unworthy, but trust in him 'who of God is made unto me wisdom, righteousness, sanctification and redemption.' After a short pause, he observed, 'I know in whom I have believed, and that he is able to keep that which I have committed unto him until that day.' When his sufferings were great, and he felt as if he were dying, he would say in broken accents, 'Come—Lord—Jesus—come quickly.' But he would add, 'I pray for patience.' He frequently repeated, 'I know that my Redeemer liveth. Whom I shall see for myself, and mine eyes shall behold, and not another.' On his daughter's observing what a fine day it was, and how calm the water was, he said smiling, 'Just like my mind, my dear—not a wave—unruffled.' One morning being asked how he had rested the preceding night, he replied, 'The Lord has spared my life one night longer; but I never longed for anything so really, as to die and to be with my Saviour.' Towards the close of his last sickness, he exclaimed with emphasis and a voice stronger than usual—I am now ready to be offered up and the time of my departure is at hand. I have fought a good fight, I have finished my course, I have kept the faith; henceforth there is laid up for me a crown of righteousness, which the Lord the righteous Judge, shall give me at that day.'"

38. There appeared later between 1830 and 1840 others of much worth. These were Charles A. Boyd, Henry Johnson, William H. Bishop, Hosea Easton, James Simmons, Henry Drayton, David Blake, Adam Ford, Daniel Vandevier, Francis P. Graham, John W. Lewis, George Garnett, William Fuller, J. H. Williams, William Serrington, John A. King, John Tappen, John Dungy, Richard Noyee, Peter Ross, John Lyle, John P. Thompson, John Ches-

ter, Nathan Blunt, John N. Mars, J. B. Johnson, Thomas James, Edward Bishop, Thomas Jackson, Dempsey Kennedy, William Tilmon, George Washington, Benjamin Simms, W. L. Brown, John Wells, Samuel Serrington, George A. Spywood, Jesse Kemble, Leonard Collins, Basil McKall, William Jones, John Jackson, Abraham Cole, Samuel T. Gray, William McFarlan, Philip Lum, Shadrach Golden, and Abraham Miller.

39. The Assembly bore it grievously that slavery exhibits the persons of color as dependent on the will of others, "whether they shall know and worship the true God, whether they shall enjoy the ordinances of the gospel; whether they shall perform the duties and cherish the endearments of husbands and wives, parents and children, neighbors and friends; whether they shall preserve their chastity and purity, or regard the dictates of justice and humanity.... "The evils to which the slave is always exposed often take place in fact, and in their very worst degree and form; and where all of them do not take place, as we rejoice to say in many instances, through the influence of the principles of humanity and religion on the mind of masters, they do not—still the slave is deprived of his natural right, degraded as a human being, and exposed to the danger of passing into the hands of a master who may inflict upon him all the hardships and injuries which humanity and avarice may suggest."

"From this view of the consequences resulting from the practice into which Christian people have most inconsistently fallen, of enslaving a portion of their brethren of mankind—for 'God hath made of one blood all nations of men to dwell on the face of the earth'—it is manifestly the duty of all Christians who enjoy the light of the present day, when the inconsistency of slavery, both with the dictates of humanity and religion, has been demonstrated, and is generally seen and acknowledged, to use their honest, earnest, and unwearied endeavors, to correct the errors of former times, and as speedily as possible to efface this blot on our holy religion, and to obtain the complete abolition of slavery through Christendom, and if possible throughout the world."

40. The following is a specimen:

DEAR SIR:--My woman, Clarissa Hill, has expressed a wish to unite herself in Christian communion with the church of which you are the acting minister. She is a most faithful servant, and one, of whom it affords me pleasure to say, that I believe she endeavors to conform to the great principles of her faith, and I believe she will be an exemplary and honorable member of your church, should you think proper to receive her as such. She has belonged to me for sixteen years, during which time her conduct has been most unexceptionably moral, and therefore, I cheerfully consent to her being baptized and admitted to your communion.

Very respectfully, etc.,
C. S. M.

41. Some years later these Baptists sent six missionaries to Africa. These were J. H. Pressly, W. W. Colley together with their wives, J. J. Coles and H. McKinney. The National Convention was organized in 1880, out of a protest against the attitude of certain whites toward

the Negroes and they have since continued as a separate body having a publishing house of their own rather than patronize the American Baptist Publication Society.

INDEX

Shiloh Church in New York City 89-90

slave-holding South 4, 9, 15-16, 19, 56, 63, 65-7, 76, 79, 83, 91

slavery 3, 8-9, 15-19, 21, 38, 47, 49, 63-6, 75-6, 78, 87, 91, 99, 125, 129-31
  abolition of 14-15, 17, 19, 88
  churchmen denouncing 95

social welfare work 142-4, 147

society 3, 6-8, 15-16, 19-20, 34, 41-2, 46-7, 64, 70, 81, 107-10, 115
  literary 141
  relief 108-9

songs 72, 95-6, 129

South Carolina 4, 21-2, 24, 28, 40, 44, 51, 56, 59, 67, 73, 80, 82-3, 106-7, 110-11

Southern Baptist Convention 66, 150

Southern Christians 75, 81

Spain 1

St. George Methodist Episcopal Church 38

St. Paul's Church 89

St. Phillips Church 47-8

St. Thomas Church 38, 47, 86

State, slaveholding 65, 67, 86

statistics 72, 149, 151-4

Stevens, David 52-3

stigma 10, 63, 66, 82, 99

struggle 14, 18, 21-2, 71, 86, 126, 130, 135-6, 159

study 33-4, 71, 89, 111-13, 117, 126, 140-1

Sunday schools 39, 107, 135-6, 139-41, 149, 152-3

superintendents 53, 70

Synod 18-19

T

teachers 6-7, 83, 87, 107-11, 119, 122, 149, 153-4

Tennessee 60, 69, 77, 83, 98, 100, 106, 108-9, 125, 162

Texas 106

theology 34, 71, 88, 90, 111, 125, 141, 159

Third African Baptist Church 26, 58, 60

Thompson, Abraham 40-1, 52

trade 28, 57, 71, 90

U

Underground Railroad 85, 88, 91

Union American Methodist Episcopal Church 54, 150

Union Baptist Church in Philadelphia 118

Union Colored Church 60

Union Society 41

United American Free-Will Baptist Church 152

United States Senate 35, 92-3, 118

uplift 13, 49, 52, 71, 73, 106, 109, 127, 146

V

Varick, James 40, 42-3

Vermont 32, 150

Vermont Avenue Baptist Church 126, 146

Virginia 3, 9, 16-17, 22, 26-9, 34, 44, 56, 59, 68-9, 76-7, 105-9, 119-20, 124-5, 136

Virginia Theological Seminary 107, 136-7

vote 28, 39, 47, 49, 57, 162

W

Walker, William 30, 126-7

war 31, 59, 93, 95-6, 100, 105, 110-12, 115, 117-18, 123, 130, 140

Ward, Samuel R. 58, 92

Washington 49, 68, 89, 91, 107, 109, 111-12, 119-20, 135, 144

Wesleyan Church 43

Wesleyan Methodist Episcopal Church 54

West Indies (Caribbean) 2, 14, 120

West Virginia 116, 119-20, 124

white churches 22, 37, 42, 45, 55-6, 61, 63, 66, 80, 92, 131-2, 155, 160, 162

white communicants 47
  misguided 159

white denominations 98, 150

white missionaries. See also missionaries 134

Lightning Source UK Ltd.
Milton Keynes UK
UKHW021847060622
404005UK00011B/2567